Allah

Allah

God in the Qur'an

GABRIEL SAID REYNOLDS

Yale UNIVERSITY PRESS

New Haven and London

Published with assistance from the foundation established in memory of Amasa Stone Mather of the Class of 1907, Yale College.

Yale University Press books may be purchased in quantity for educational, business, or promotional use. For information, please e-mail sales.press@yale.edu (U.S. office) or sales@yaleup.co.uk (U.K. office).

Set in Minion type by Tseng Information Systems, Inc.
Printed in the United States of America.

Library of Congress Control Number: 2019947014
ISBN 978-0-300-24658-2 (hardcover : alk. paper)

A catalogue record for this book is available from the British Library.

This paper meets the requirements of ANSI/NISO z39.48–1992 (Permanence of Paper).

10 9 8 7 6 5 4 3 2 1

Contents

Part IV: A Personal God

Acknowledgments

Most of the work for this book was done during the academic year 2016–2017 when I was on academic leave at the Institute for Advanced Studies (Institut d'études avancées) of Nantes, France. I am deeply grateful to the institute for its support of my research and to all of the colleagues and friends who formed a welcoming community in Nantes. My research leave that year was also supported by a fellowship from the National Endowment for the Humanities, which was likewise instrumental in my ability to bring this project to completion.

I continued to edit and revise this work during the following two years as I taught in the Department of Theology at Notre Dame. The Department of Theology is an academic community that takes the study of God (and not only of religion) seriously and thereby nourished my thought on the God of the Qur'an. I have benefited greatly from the wisdom (and friendship) of all of my colleagues there. I owe a special debt of gratitude to John Cavadini, Timothy Matovina, and Mun'im Sirry. I am also grateful to the diverse group of colleagues from various faiths who have gathered together at the Scriptural Reasoning sessions run by Notre Dame's World Religions World Church (WRWC) program.

My thinking on the Qur'an has been shaped by a number of colleagues and friends through the years. These include (but are not limited to) Mohammad Ali Amir-Moezzi, Sean Anthony, Mehdi Azaiez, Emran El-Badawi, Anne-Sylvie Boisliveau, Martino Diez, Guillaume Dye, Asma Hilali, Mohammad Hassan Khalil, Daniel Madigan, Hythem Sidky, Nicolai Sinai, Mun'im Sirry, Devin Stewart, Shawkat Toorawa, and Holger Zellentin. I know many of these scholars through the International Qur'anic Studies Association (IQSA), a learned society dedicated to rigorous academic scholarship on the Qur'an.

I offer my thanks to the two anonymous readers of this manuscript, and to the excellent team at Yale University Press, notably Jennifer Banks. I also thank my copy editor, Jessie Dolch.

Finally, I am profoundly grateful to my entire family, and in a special way to my wife Lourdes and our children, for their love and for their patience with me.

Conventions

Qur'an passages in this work are cited, unless noted otherwise, from the revised translation of Ali Quli Qarai as it appears in *The Qur'an and the Bible* (New Haven: Yale University Press, 2018). Note that words italicized in quotations from this translation indicate a second person singular address. Bible passages are cited from the Revised Standard Version.

There is no perfect way to refer to the canonical hadith (collections of traditions recounting the sayings and deeds of the Prophet Muhammad), especially in a way that would allow a general readership to track down references. I give the number and Arabic name of the section (*kitab*) in which a hadith appears and the hadith number (#) that can be found on sunnah.com (which, for Bukhari, corresponds to the edition/translation of Muhsin Khan, based on the 1959 Cairo edition of *Fath al-Bari,* and, for Muslim, follows the Arabic edition of Muhammad Fu'ad 'Abd al-Baqi) in the hope that this will offer sufficient information for specialists and convenient information for nonspecialists.

I have used a simplified transliteration system for rendering Arabic terms in English letters (based on the *International Journal of Middle East Studies,* but without diacritical marks) and Anglicized versions of those Arabic terms that are commonly used in English.

I refer to the God of the Qur'an normally as "God," but when it is convenient to refer to the specifically qur'anic presentation of God, I use "Allah." This is merely a literary convention and is not meant to imply a position on whether the God of the Qur'an is distinct from the God of the Bible or from other conceptions of the divine.

Allah

Introduction
God of Mercy and Vengeance

You are the most merciful of the merciful.

— Moses, speaking to God, Qur'an 7:151

In early 2015 the militant group the "Islamic State" (ISIS) burned a Jordanian pilot named Muath al-Kasasbeh alive in a cage. They filmed the burning, and when the video was released, it provoked outrage around the world. Even some radical militant (or "jihadi") Muslims were outraged, for they held that burning is a form of punishment reserved for God alone. In what seems like an ironic twist, the video opens with a screen displaying the following words: "In the name of God the compassionate, the merciful." How could believers in a God of mercy do such a thing? How could a God of mercy be pleased with acts of such cruelty?

To Muslims across the globe, groups like ISIS twist Islam and falsify its fundamental message. The overwhelming majority of Muslims not only believe that God is merciful; they believe that God calls humans to be merciful, too.

One prominent American Muslim, Umar Faruq Abd-Allah, writes: "All that transpires—even temporal deprivation, harm, and evil—will, in due course, fall under the rubric of cosmic mercy."[1] Abd-Allah also insists that Islam calls on believers to show mercy to others. In fact, he suggests that those who fail to show mercy are likely to go to hell: "A heart that no longer has the capacity to feel mercy cannot be a receptacle of salvation or a container of true faith; to become ruthless and void of compassion is to carry the mark of divine wrath and bear the brand of damnation and is the sure sign of an evil end."[2]

The words in the ISIS video, "In the name of God the compassionate, the merciful," are an invocation, known as the *basmala*, which appears at the opening of every Sura, or chapter, in the Qur'an (except for Sura 9). In the Islamic world the *basmala* is also found frequently at the opening of books and even at the beginning of movies. When I was recently in the Middle East, I heard an Egyptian soccer announcer begin his commentary on a game by declaring the *basmala*.[3]

Yet references to God's mercy in the Qur'an, the scripture that Muslims hold to be the very word of God brought down from heaven to earth, are not limited to the *basmala*. The Qur'an frequently speaks of God as merciful, forgiving, gentle, and kind. Moreover, it not only speaks of God's mercy or compassion (*rahma*); it also quite simply names God "the Compassionate" (*al-rahman*).[4] Thus, for example, in Q 19:93 (that is, verse 93 of Sura 19 of the Qur'an), the Qur'an declares: "There is none in the heavens and the earth but he comes to the Compassionate (*al-rahman*) as a servant."[5]

Elsewhere the Qur'an encourages its audience to trust in God's mercy. For example, in Sura 5 the Qur'an asks in regard to Christians: "Will they not repent to God and plead to Him for forgiveness? Yet God is all-forgiving, all-merciful" (5:74). In Sura 2 the Qur'an turns to its own audience, the believers, and assures them that those who either emigrate or fight for the sake of God will receive divine mercy: "Indeed, those who are faithful and those who have migrated and waged *jihad* in the way of God—it is they who expect God's mercy, and God is all-forgiving, all-merciful" (Q 2:218).

One poignant passage of the Qur'an speaks of God's particular mercy for Zechariah (father of John the Baptist in the Bible), who was childless in his old age. There, God hears the "secret" prayer of Zechariah and has mercy (*rahma;* Q 19:2) on him, granting him a son.[6]

The centrality of mercy to Islam opens up the possibility of dialogue among Jews, Christians, and Muslims (and others). Believers in different faiths may differ about a number of issues regarding God and humanity, but they agree that God is merciful.

The authors of "A Common Word Between Us and You," a 2007 letter signed by a group of 138 Muslim scholars and addressed to the pope and other Christian leaders, argue that Muslims and Christians can agree on two fundamental principles: love of God and love of neighbor.[7] In describing God's love they note the references to divine mercy in *al-Fatihah,* the opening chapter of the Qur'an: "The *Fatihah,* recited at least seventeen times daily by Muslims in the canonical prayers, reminds us of the praise and gratitude due to God for His Attributes of Infinite Goodness and All-Mercifulness, not merely for His Goodness and Mercy to us in this life but ultimately, on the Day of Judgement when it matters the most and when we hope to be forgiven for our sins."[8]

These examples show that groups like ISIS do not rep-

resent mainstream Islamic opinion on the nature of divine
mercy. Yet even mainstream Muslims might disagree over
God's nature.

Indeed, to say that God is merciful raises a whole series
of questions: Is God's mercy unconditional, or does it extend
only to certain people? Is God merciful only to Muslims or
also to Jews and Christians? How about polytheists, atheists,
or apostates from Islam? Is God merciful only to the righteous
or also to sinners? Is sincere contrition, or an act of penitence,
a condition of gaining God's mercy? Are there other ways to
receive mercy, for example, by giving alms or fighting in a holy
war? Can mercy be earned? What does the Qur'an mean, in
other words, when it describes God as "the compassionate, the
merciful"?

Beyond Divine Mercy

In this book we will discover that understanding the God of
the Qur'an is more complicated than it may seem at first. In a
world greatly in need of religious dialogue, it has become common for scholars to emphasize the notion of Allah's mercy. In
2014 a German Muslim scholar named Mouhanad Khorchide
dedicated an entire work (titled, in English, "God Is Mercy") to
an Islamic "theology of mercy."[9] The American scholar Bruce
Lawrence, author of a book titled simply *Who Is Allah?*, argues
that whereas Christianity is about the love of God in Christ,
Islam is fundamentally about a merciful God: "Though the
Qur'an confirms all previous prophecies, it also supersedes
them and privileges Arabic as the language of that superses-
sion. One message, one messenger, one language prevail: the
message is Mercy, the messenger Muhammad, the language
Arabic."[10]

Fazlur Rahman, a Pakistani scholar who taught for years at the University of Chicago (and whose last name means "the compassionate"), goes still further. He speaks of the "infinite mercy" of God in the Qur'an, writing, "The immediate impression from a cursory reading of the Qur'an is that of the infinite majesty of God and His equally infinite mercy."[11]

But is Rahman right? Can Allah's mercy accurately be described as "infinite"? If this means that God will forgive everyone, then a close reading of the Qur'an suggests that Rahman is wrong. Allah will have mercy on some, but not on all.

This point is emphasized by a second Pakistani scholar, Daud Rahbar, who argues—in a book aptly titled *God of Justice*—that at the heart of the Qur'an is not God's mercy, but God's justice. God forgives those who deserve his forgiveness, and he condemns those who deserve his wrath.

In this book I argue that neither Rahman nor Rahbar paints a complete picture of Allah. The God of the Qur'an, I argue, is not simply a God of mercy or of justice. He is both. Allah does not merely observe humans and judge them. He intervenes in human affairs. He reacts to human decisions, sometimes with mercy, and sometimes with anger. He is merciful *and* wrathful.

Indeed, the prominence of the wrath of God in the Qur'an cannot be ignored. On twenty-eight occasions the Qur'an declares that God is "severe in punishment." Sixteen times the Qur'an says God is "quick to judge." On three occasions God declares that he will take vengeance on the unbelievers (Q 32: 22, 43:41, 44:16). On four occasions (Q 3:4, 5:95, 14:47, 39:37) the Qur'an simply describes God as "avenger" or "vengeful" (Arabic *dhu intiqam*).

Now just because the Qur'an says something does not mean that all Muslims agree with it or interpret it simplistically. For example, let's examine six different translations of the ending of Q 3:4 where the phrase *dhu intiqam* appears:

> Pickthall (1930): Allah is Mighty, Able to Requite
>   (the wrong).
> Yusuf Ali (1934): Allah is Exalted in Might, Lord
>   of Retribution.
> Arberry (1955): God is All-mighty, Vengeful.
> Asad (1980): God is almighty, an avenger of evil.
> Hilali and Khan (1996): Allah is All-Mighty, All-
>   Able of Retribution.
> Qarai (2011): God is all-mighty, avenger.[12]

For Muhammad Marmaduke Pickthall, an English convert to Islam, Allah is not "vengeful" but simply "Able to requite (the wrong)." Muhammad Asad, an Austrian convert to Islam from Judaism, has the same approach; he makes God "an avenger of evil." The translation of Taqi al-Din Hilali (a Moroccan) and Muhsin Khan (a Pakistani)—a Qur'an translation sponsored by Saudi Arabia—renders *dhu intiqam* "All-Able of Retribution." Abdullah Yusuf Ali ("Lord of Retribution") and Ali Quli Qarai ("avenger") render it in ways that emphasize God's paying humans back for their wrongdoing. Only Arthur Arberry (who is also the only non-Muslim in the group) renders this phrase in a way that describes God as "Vengeful."

Other passages in the Qur'an seem to juxtapose the mercy and vengefulness of God. In 6:133 the Qur'an speaks of God's mercy but then immediately threatens its audience:

> Your Lord is the All-sufficient dispenser of mercy. If
> He wishes, He will take you away, and make whom-

ever He wishes succeed you, just as He produced
you from the descendants of another people.[13]

Later in that same Sura the Qur'an makes it clear that God's
mercy does not extend to wrongdoers: "But if they impugn
you, say, 'Your Lord is dispenser of an all-embracing mercy,
but His punishment will not be averted from the guilty lot'"
(6:147).[14]

In his work *God and Man in the Koran,* the Japanese
scholar of Islam Toshihiko Izutsu identifies two aspects of God
in the Qur'an. Allah, he writes, is a "God of infinite goodness,
mercy, forgiveness, and benevolence on one hand, and, on the
other, God of wrath, and severe, strict and unrelenting justice."[15] In other words, Allah seems to have two personalities.

Decoding the Qur'an

So how can one arrive at a clear portrait of the God of the
Qur'an? One classical attempt at decoding the Qur'an is to read
the Islamic scripture according to a "chronology" or a "history" where individual passages are assigned to different moments during the prophetic career of the Prophet Muhammad.
Islamic traditions report that Muhammad proclaimed pieces
of the Qur'an (sometimes as small as a single verse, sometimes
as much as an entire Sura) between the time when the angel
Gabriel first visited him as he meditated on a mountain outside of Mecca (in modern-day Saudi Arabia) in AD 610 and
the time, twenty-two years later, when he died in his adopted
home city of Medina to the north.

Western scholars (even if they may dispense with the
story of the angel) generally accept this idea, holding that

Muhammad gradually proclaimed the Qur'an from AD 610 to 632. Through a painstaking process of "locating" one passage after another, a "history" of the Qur'an (to use an expression taken from a famous introduction to the Qur'an) can be written.[16] This approach seems to offer a possible solution to our problem: perhaps Muhammad emphasized divine mercy at certain moments and divine vengeance at others.

The traditional biographies of the Prophet relate that during the time when he was in Mecca, Muhammad held no worldly power. He preached his message of the oneness of God and the coming divine judgment, but he was not a political or military leader. This all changed during the Medinan period.

In Medina Muhammad assumed power and began to plan raids against unbelieving tribes (including his own tribe of the Quraysh in Mecca). In other words, whereas Muhammad once preached that God would punish unbelievers, he now took that punishment into his own hands.[17] The ex-Muslim Ayaan Hirsi Ali (author of a 2015 book titled *Heretic: Why Islam Needs a Reformation Now*) emphasizes the contrast between Muhammad's mission in Mecca and his mission in Medina:

> In the early days of Islam, when Mohammed was going from door to door in Mecca trying to persuade the polytheists to abandon their idols of worship, he was inviting them to accept that there was no god but Allah and that he was Allah's messenger.
>
> After 10 years of trying this kind of persuasion, however, he and his small band of believers went to Medina, and from that moment, Mohammed's mission took on a political dimension. Un-

> believers were still invited to submit to Allah, but
> after Medina, they were attacked if they refused.[18]

Hirsi Ali later proposes that even today we can divide the Islamic community into "Meccan" Muslims—those who favor only peaceful preaching—and "Medinan" Muslims—those who would like to see Islam dominate politically. If only Meccan Muslims were to prevail, she suggests, then many of the problems of human rights and jihadism in the Islamic world would disappear.

This may be an interesting way of addressing the problem of violence in the Qur'an, but it is less helpful when it comes to the portrait of God in the Qur'an. The two "personalities" of God—mercy and vengeance—are found throughout the scripture. Indeed, in some places these two personalities are found in the same verse.

In light of this I avoid a "chronological" approach to the Qur'an in this book.[19] Instead of asking "when" and "where" any particular passage of the Qur'an was originally proclaimed, I simply examine as a unity the entire text as it has been passed down to us (a method sometimes described as "narrative criticism"). This is how the majority of Muslim scholars, and believers, read their scripture.

Muslim Theology

In the course of this book I also examine closely how Muslim scholars, and believers generally, have seen God. Some Muslim scholars are so committed to the notion of God's justice that they interpret certain qur'anic passages in a metaphorical or symbolic manner (they will ask, for example: How could a just

God condemn sinners to hell if he compelled them to sin?).
Some of these same scholars are also committed to the notion
of divine transcendence or otherness and cannot imagine that
God would act in a human manner, for example, by mocking
unbelievers (Q 2:15) or by tricking them (Q 3:54, 7:99, 8:30,
10:21).

However, in this book I am principally interested in what
the Qur'an itself says about God, and not in later theological debates.[20] My thoughts in this regard can be compared
with those of Rahbar, who writes: "A scientific exposition of
Qur'anic doctrine must keep clear of all the theological or
philosophical interpretations that Muslim thought of ages
has put on Qur'anic words and phrases. After all between us
and the Prophet there lies a lapse of no less than thirteen centuries." (The only thing that needs to be changed for this statement to be relevant today is the amount of time that has passed
since the life of the Prophet Muhammad.) A few pages later
Rahbar uses more abrasive language when he warns scholars
against depending on the views of medieval Muslim authorities: "We must use our own judgement in deciding the *original*
signification of Qur'anic words and phrases instead of depending carelessly or blindly on commentaries that are full of ficti-
tious traditions."[21]

"God" or "Allah"?

So what does the Qur'an say about God? How distinctive is its
vision of God? Is the God of the Qur'an the same God we find
in the Bible?

One way to answer these questions is to consider the
sorts of names that the Qur'an gives to God. One long list of
these names is found in Sura 59:

[22]He is God—there is no god except Him—
Knower of the sensible and the Unseen, He is the
All-beneficent, the All-merciful.
[23]He is God—there is no god except Him—
the Sovereign, the All-holy, the All-benign, the Securer, the All-conserver, the All-mighty, the All-
compeller and the All-magnanimous. Clear is God
of any partners that they may ascribe [to Him]!

Such passages, and certain famous sayings (or "hadith") of the
Prophet, form the basis of an Islamic tradition that God has
ninety-nine "beautiful" or "best" names (a phrase in the following verse—Q 59:24—declares "To Him belong the Best
Names"). Muslim believers sometimes carry around "rosaries"
of thirty-three beads that allow them to count out these "beautiful" names. Such passages also paint a distinctive picture of
the qur'anic God.

This picture, intriguingly, does not line up in all respects
with other presentations of God. For example, a Christian who
reads this passage would likely agree with most of the characteristics that it assigns to God. Most Christians would agree
that God is "All-beneficent," "All-merciful," "Sovereign," "All-
holy," and "All-benign." However, there is at least one characteristic here—"All-compeller" (al-jabbar)—that a Christian
might not ascribe to God.

For believing Christians and believing Muslims, the de-
gree to which the Islamic and Christian concepts of God overlap becomes a theological problem. In recent decades Christian and Muslim theologians alike have debated whether
these two concepts overlap enough to justify the conclusion
that Muslims and Christians believe in the same God. In a
Vatican II document known as *Lumen gentium* the Catholic

Church, at least, answers that they do.[22] The authors of *Lumen gentium* underline what is common in the Muslim and Christian conception of God: like Christians, *Lumen gentium* declares, Muslims know God as (1) creator, (2) one, (3) merciful, and (4) judge.

Other Christian institutions, especially within the evangelical Protestant tradition, have been more hesitant. One case where these issues came to the forefront is that of Larycia Hawkins, the first female African American tenured professor at evangelical Wheaton College in Illinois. On December 10, 2015, Hawkins posted a picture of herself on Facebook wearing an Islamic headscarf and wrote: "I stand in religious solidarity with Muslims because they, like me, a Christian, are people of the book. And as Pope Francis stated last week, we worship the same God."[23] For this post (in which she not only reaches out to Muslims but summons Pope Francis to her side) and for a subsequent statement affirming her theological position, Hawkins was put on leave by Wheaton (the college made it clear that the issue was her affirmation of Muslims and Christians worshipping the same God, and not her wearing of a headscarf). Eventually, the two sides came to an agreement by which Hawkins was not fired but left Wheaton voluntarily.

For Wheaton, the problem with Hawkins's statements had to do with Jesus: the Qur'an explicitly denies the divinity of Jesus Christ (Q 4:172, 9:30). Indeed, in one passage (Q 5:72) it seems to threaten Christians with damnation for this belief. How, then, can it be said that Christians and Muslims believe in the same God? What Wheaton College left implicit is stated explicitly by Nabeel Qureshi, a Muslim convert to evangelical Christianity who recently died from stomach cancer at the age of thirty-four. Qureshi, responding to this controversy, points to the Qur'an's polemic against Christian teaching: "Let's start with the obvious: Christians believe Jesus is God, but the Quran is so opposed to this belief that it condemns Jesus worshipers to Hell (5:72). *For Christians, Jesus is certainly God, and for Muslims Jesus is certainly not God.* How can it be said that Christians and Muslims worship the same God?"[24]

Christians are not alone in wondering whether the God of Muhammad is the same God of Christianity. Muslims have asked this question, too, and they've arrived at different answers. This is no surprise, since the Qur'an seems to say two different things about this issue. On one hand, the Qur'an seems to affirm that Christians and Jews ("People of the Book") *do* worship the same God as Muhammad. Qur'an 29:46 declares:

> Do not argue with the People of the Book except in a manner which is best, except such of them as are wrongdoers, and say, "We believe in what has been sent down to us and in what has been sent down to you; *our God and your God is one* [and the same] and to Him do we submit."

On the other hand, the Qur'an also seems to accuse Christians, and even Jews, of having faulty ideas of God. Qur'an 4:171 seems to warn Christians, declaring "Do not exaggerate in your religion." Qur'an 5:64 attacks Jews for what they say about God: "The Jews say, 'God's hand is tied up.' Tied up be their hands, and cursed be they for what they say!"[25]

In light of such passages many Muslims insist that only the Qur'an, and not the Bible, depicts God as he actually is. This helps explain why many Muslim translators of the Qur'an speak not of God but of "Allah." By keeping the Arabic word "Allah" when they render the Qur'an into English, they emphasize the distinctiveness of the Qur'an's God.

Authorities in the Southeast Asian country of Malaysia have taken this even farther. In 2014 a Malaysian federal court ruled that only Muslims are allowed to use "Allah" in print for God (Christians and others were told to use the Malay word). This struck many as a strange decision, as Arabic-speaking Christians and Jews (and Baha'is and others) know of no other name for God than "Allah."

At the risk of angering the Malaysian authorities, in the present book I often refer to God as "Allah." In doing so, however, I don't mean to make a theological or religious statement. I am not concerned with determining whether Muslims and Christians (or Jews, or Sikhs, or anyone else for that matter) worship the same God. My interest is in the Qur'an as a book, and the Bible as a book, and God as a character in both of those books. As I seek to emphasize what is distinctive in the Qur'an's portrayal of God, it is useful to have a proper noun — Allah — to refer only to him.

Still, it should not be forgotten that the word "Allah" is today simply the word for "God" in Arabic, and it is used by people of all faiths who speak that language. There is also good reason to think that "Allah" was not the creation of the Qur'an. There are two prevalent theories about the derivation of "Allah." According to the first, Arabic *allah* comes from the word for God in Syriac, a Christian language that was spread throughout the Middle East at the dawn of Islam: *allaha*. According to the second, it is derived instead from Arabic *al-ilah* (meaning "the god" — similar to the common description of God in Greek as *ho theos*). This term is used for God in inscriptions of Ancient North and South Arabian, languages related to classical Arabic.

In fact, there is evidence from the Qur'an itself that even Muhammad's opponents — who were supposedly polytheists or pagans—recognized a god named Allah. The Qur'an even suggests that his opponents knew Allah to be the creator. This is seen, for example, in two verses from Sura 29. In the first, the divine voice of the Qur'an declares to the Prophet:

> If *you* ask them, "Who created the heavens and the earth and disposed the sun and the moon?" They will surely say, "God [*Allah*]." Then where do they stray? (Q 29:61)

Two verses later we read:

> And if *you* ask them, "Who sends down water from the sky, with which He revives the earth after its death?" They will surely say, "God [*Allah*]." *Say,* "All praise belongs to God!" But most of them do not exercise their reason. (Q 29:63)

Such passages led Toshihiko Izutsu to write, "The concept of Allah that was prevalent among the pre-Islamic Arabs on the eve of the Islamic era was, in general, surprisingly close in nature to the Islamic one."[26] Indeed, the Qur'an goes so far as to declare that when these (supposedly) pagan opponents found themselves in great danger, for example, at sea, they would call on Allah:

> When waves cover them like awnings, they invoke God [*Allah*], putting exclusive faith in Him. But when He delivers them towards land, [only] some of them remain unswerving. No one will impugn Our signs except an ungrateful traitor. (Q 31:32; cf. 29:65, 17:67, 10:22, 6:63)[27]

It's a bit puzzling that the Qur'an uses seafaring as the example to teach a lesson here, for in the accounts of Islamic tradition, Arabs of Muhammad's time and place travel by camel, not by boat. More importantly, however, we see something of the Qur'an's theology here. The Qur'an demands that believers place "exclusive faith" in Allah. They are not to call on him only when it is convenient, as the "pagans" do.

Doing Theology

It is also important to notice the depiction of divine mercy in the "seafaring" passage above. Allah hears the cries of those, even pagans, who call on him. He delivers them from the midst of the storm. Allah, in other words, is not a distant god who remains aloof in a celestial fortress. He is close to humans, closer, according to one verse (Q 50:16), than a human's jugular vein. Yet something of the wrath of God is also evident in this passage, as he speaks of the pagans as "ungrateful traitors."

The goal of this book is to uncover the theology of the Qur'an, to explore the Qur'an's presentation of a God who is both merciful and wrathful. Part of this exploration will involve contrasting the Qur'an with elements of the Bible. This reflects my own academic background, and in particular my research for a previous book on the Qur'an and the Bible.[28] However, this also reflects the Qur'an's own conversation with biblical literature. As we will begin to discover in the next chapter, the Qur'an has its own perspective on biblical figures, from Adam to Moses, to Jesus and Mary. It also has its own perspective on God, and the Qur'an's theology is in part a response to biblical theology.

From a traditional Islamic perspective, it is unusual to speak of a "theology" of the Qur'an. Theology—as the term is generally understood—is a *human* effort to understand God (it is derived from the Greek words *theos,* "God," and *logos,* "word" or "reason"). However, for a pious Muslim the Qur'an has no human element at all. It is not simply a book about God; it is a book *by* God. The Qur'an is what in Arabic might be called a *kashf,* an "unveiling," of the divine.[29]

The present book, however, is written from a scholarly perspective, not a pious, religious perspective, and begins with the simple observation that the Qur'an says things about God, things that can be analyzed for their "theology." From this perspective we get to know the God who is lord to millions of Muslims across the globe.

I
Allah and His Book

1

The Qur'an and the Bible

Know that God is severe in punishment, and that God is Forgiving, Merciful.

—*Qur'an 5:98*

From a traditional religious perspective, the Qur'an is a perfect book, a heavenly book. Its style is matchless, inimitable. Yet from a literary perspective, the Qur'an can be a challenging book to read. It often jumps from one topic to another, and its logical coherence is not immediately evident. As a starting point for our study of the God of the Qur'an, in this chapter we address this challenge by offering a simple introduction to the Qur'an and to its relationship with the Bible.

The Qur'an is divided into 114 chapters known as Suras. These Suras do not proceed from creation to the apocalypse, as the books of the Christian Bible do, or according to a chronology of the Prophet Muhammad's career. Instead, they are more or less organized by size: longer Suras appear near the front of the book (this method of organizing a book is similar to the way the letters of Paul are put together in the New Testament: from longest to shortest). In other words, by reading the Suras from 1 to 114, one cannot follow any clear progression of thought.

Occasionally one hears the opinion that those who are reading the Qur'an for the first time are better off reading it "backwards"—that is, beginning with Sura 114. Behind this opinion is the traditional idea that most of the small Suras toward the end of the text represent Muhammad's earlier proclamations when he was still in Mecca (the traditional dates are AD 610–622), whereas many of the longer Suras toward the beginning of the Qur'an represent his proclamations later in his career in Medina (AD 622–632). Thus by reading the Qur'an "backwards," one can roughly follow the development of Muhammad's thought (so the theory goes).

Scholars (both traditional Muslim scholars and academic scholars) have tried to do better than that. They have sought to establish a precise "chronological" order of the Qur'an's Suras. Certain translations of the Qur'an have even been rearranged so as to follow this supposed order.[1] When you open the cover of one of these translations, you will not find Sura 1, *al-Fatihah* ("The Opening"), but usually Sura 96, *al-ʿAlaq* ("The Sticky Mass"), which according to most traditions was the first Sura revealed to Muhammad by the angel Gabriel.

The idea of rearranging the Suras in a list that would fit a chronology of Muhammad's prophetic career reflects a number of traditional ideas and assumptions: that the entirety of the Qur'an is the work of one man only (or, from a Muslim perspective, one God), that his proclamations were reliably preserved and transmitted, that they were not edited (by anyone other than Muhammad or God), and that early Muslims could still remember which Suras were proclaimed before others. This idea also implies that Suras were more or less proclaimed as units, that is, that Muhammad finished proclaiming one Sura before he began to proclaim the next.

In fact, some scholars grant that the situation might have been more complicated: that Muhammad might have announced different parts of the same Sura at different times, and material from other Suras in between.[2] Nevertheless, even many of these scholars do not hesitate to place the Suras as a whole into a chronological list.[3] For these scholars the Suras become puzzle pieces that can be rearranged and fit together into one long sequence. As I made clear in the introduction, in this book I avoid this "puzzle pieces" approach to the Qur'an.

The Text of the Qur'an

A second problem that occupies scholars is the question of when the Qur'an was first written down.[4] The standard account relates that it was the third caliph, 'Uthman, who put together an official version of the Qur'an (and had other versions burned) around the year 650. The earliest manuscripts are indeed very early (although it is maddeningly difficult to pin them down to a specific date), but they are written in an imperfect form of the Arabic script that allows for a variety of possible readings. In fact, we know that a long series of debates ensued about how exactly that script is to be read.

In some ways those debates ended only in 1924, when a committee appointed by the Egyptian Ministry of Education established a definitive, complete edition of the Qur'an and disposed of variant versions by sinking them into the Nile River.[5] By virtue of the prestige of Egypt as the home of the famous Al-Azhar University in Cairo, this 1924 edition spread throughout the Islamic world and eventually to the West. Today, it is virtually the only edition of the Qur'an that is in circulation. Certain scholars are currently working to establish what is known as a "critical edition" of the Qur'an, that is, an edition based on the most ancient manuscripts.[6] For now, however, the "1924 Cairo Qur'an" is the standard text.

The success of the 1924 Cairo Qur'an gives the impression that there are no variants to the text. In fact, there are many reports of ancient variants to the Qur'an, and in recent years developing work on Qur'an manuscripts (notably an ancient "palimpsest"—a manuscript with writing that had been erased and written over—found in Yemen) has brought to our attention an increasing number of variants. However, the authenticity of such reports is debated, and the variants found in manuscripts tend not to affect the meaning of qur'anic passages. Accordingly, in this book we do not focus on these variants but rather largely stick to the text of the Qur'an that is widespread today.

The Rhetoric of the Qur'an

While we wait for a critical edition, much can still be said about the nature of the Qur'an. To begin with, we might note how different it is from the Bible. The Bible groups together different books, written by different authors, at different times, in different languages, and in different lands.

In addition, many of the biblical books, such as Genesis and the Gospels, are made up of narratives that testify to the ways in which God has acted in human history. These stories are often detailed: they describe principal characters (including at times their appearance: David is "ruddy" and has "beautiful eyes") and the places they go (and sometimes, how they got there: walking with a staff or riding a donkey). A nice example of the narrative quality of the Gospels is the description of John the Baptist found toward the beginning of Mark:

> [4]John the baptizer appeared in the wilderness, preaching a baptism of repentance for the forgiveness of sins. [5]And there went out to him all the country of Judea, and all the people of Jerusalem; and they were baptized by him in the river Jordan, confessing their sins. [6]Now John was clothed with camel's hair, and had a leather girdle around his waist, and ate locusts and wild honey. (1:4–6)[7]

This sort of narrative detail is not found in the Qur'an. In Sura 19, where the Qur'an introduces the character of John (it does not give him the title "the Baptist"), it offers few details:

> [12]"O John!" [We said,] "Hold on with power to the Book!" And We gave him judgement while still a child, [13]and compassion and purity from Us. He was Godwary [14]and good to his parents, not self-willed or disobedient. [15]Peace be to him, the day he was born, the day he dies, and the day he is raised alive!

While the Qur'an mentions John by name, it does not tell us where he lived or what he did, let alone what he wore and what he ate. Instead, it tells us only what is important to the Qur'an's author: John's religious qualities, that he was "Godwary and good to his parents." It is who John was, and not what he did, that matters to the author of the Qur'an.

In other places this "allusive" literary quality leads to

some confusion. For example, Sura 97 (known as "Ordain-ment") begins with the declaration "Indeed We sent it down on the Night of Ordainment." The Qur'an, however, never ex-plains what "it" is. Muslim commentators generally argue that "it" must be the Qur'an—that is, that the Qur'an is here refer-ring to the sending down of *itself* from heaven. However, the reference is so vague that some scholars have argued that "it" is Jesus, and the Qur'an is referring to the sending down of Jesus from heaven. The "Night of Ordainment" in other words, might be Christmas night.

In Sura 9 the Qur'an relates, "Among them there are some who say, 'Give me leave, and do not put me to temptation'" (Q 9:49). However, it never identifies who said this, and why that person said it. Again, the commentators had an answer: these were the words of a "hypocrite" among Muhammad's community in Medina named al-Jadd. When the Prophet asked for volunteers to join a military campaign to the north of Arabia near the Byzantine frontier, al-Jadd came up with an excuse: he claimed that he would not be able to resist the beauty of the Byzantine women, and so he said, "Do not put me to temptation."[8]

Another interesting case of the Qur'an's "allusive" quality is the report in Q 11:71 that Abraham's wife Sarah laughed: "His wife, standing by, laughed as We gave her the good news of [the birth of] Isaac, and of Jacob after Isaac." The Qur'an never explains why Sarah (who is left unnamed in the Qur'an—the only woman named in the Qur'an is Mary, mother of Jesus) laughed. If this passage is read in the light of Genesis 18, we can recognize that she laughed because of the news that she would have a son (Isaac—whose name in Hebrew is related to the word for "laughter") in her old age: "So Sarah laughed to herself, saying, 'After I have grown old, and my husband is old, shall I have pleasure?'" (Gen 18:12).

Muslim commentators, however, did not always rely on the Bible in their reading of the Qur'an. Accordingly, they came up with a wide variety of different explanations for Sarah's laughter, most of which have nothing to do with the birth of Isaac. Some did away entirely with the laughter: they argue that the Arabic word which usually refers to laughing here refers to menstruation. Sarah didn't laugh, they concluded; instead, she had her menstrual period.

The Qur'an as a "Homily"

Yet if the Qur'an is fundamentally different from the Bible—in literary terms, at least—then to what can it be compared? One solution is to think of the Qur'an as a sermon, or a "homily." In a homily a preacher seeks to persuade his or her audience of a religious argument or to impress on them the importance of an ethical lesson from the Bible.

At first glance this seems to be a pretty good description of the Qur'an's rhetoric. The Qur'an has its own distinct message, but it refers regularly to the main characters of the Bible. Adam, Noah, Abraham, Moses, David, Solomon, John, Jesus, and Mary (among others) all appear in the Qur'an. In other words, the Qur'an is actively involved in the *interpretation* of the Bible and biblical traditions. We might think of the Qur'an competing with Jewish commentators and Christian homilists by advancing its own interpretation of biblical stories.

One interesting case of the Qur'an interpreting the Bible is the story of Jonah. In the Book of Jonah the people of Nineveh repent (and are saved) after Jonah proclaims to them an impending divine punishment ("Yet forty days, and Nineveh shall be overthrown!," 3:4). The Qur'an does not retell that story. It doesn't speak of the great fish that swallows Jonah or the other details of the biblical story. It doesn't even mention the name of Nineveh. Instead, it seems to assume that the audience already knows the details.[9]

> [98]Why has there not been any town except the people of Jonah that might believe, so that its belief might benefit it? When they believed, We removed from them the punishment of disgrace in the life of this world and We provided for them for a time. [99]Had your Lord wished, all those who are on earth would have believed. Would you then force people until they become faithful? (Q 10:98–99)

Moreover, the Qur'an uses its references to Jonah to develop a religious idea. In the Bible the story of Jonah is meant to show that the God of Israel has power over the entire world and that he is merciful to all people. The Qur'an, while not rejecting these lessons, adds a new idea: that God has the power to make people believe or disbelieve ("Had your Lord wished, all those who are on earth would have believed").[10]

Thus we might conclude that the Qur'an is not so much interested in retelling biblical stories as much as it is interested in using biblical characters to advance its own message. In this way it seems to be "preaching" a new homily or sermon. There is, however, one major difference between the Qur'an and a homily: unlike a Christian preacher, the Qur'an claims to be speaking with the authority of God.

The Divine Speech of the Qur'an

With a few exceptions, the Qur'an is written in the voice of God.[11] In other words, the rhetoric of the Qur'an is not only homiletic, it is also prophetic.

Here it is worth elaborating a bit more carefully the speakers and "addressees" of the Qur'an. One scholar, Nicolai Sinai, speaks of the Qur'an's "discursive constellation" made up of three points: God (who at times speaks in the first person—singular or plural—and at other times is spoken *about* in the third person), the Prophet Muhammad (or another prophet) to whom God speaks directly, and the audience whom God or the prophets sometimes address (and that audience has different components: believers, unbelievers, Jews, Christians, and hypocrites).[12] The rhetoric of the Qur'an thus is pretty complicated.

In the prophetic books of the Old Testament, prophets narrate the things that God has told them. For example, Ezekiel repeatedly explains that God has spoken to him, saying "the word of the Lord came to me" and then repeating the words of God. In the Qur'an this sort of narration is usually missing. God simply speaks. As Sinai comments perceptively, "Generalising somewhat, one might say that while in the Hebrew Bible it is divine speech that requires an introductory formula, in the Qur'an it is human speech that does so."[13]

In certain places the Qur'an quotes unbelievers (what one scholar calls "counterdiscourse").[14] The impression one gets is that God has been listening in on what they say and tells the Prophet Muhammad how to respond:

> When Our manifest signs are recited to them, those
> who do not expect to encounter Us say, "Bring a

Qur'an other than this, or alter it." *Say,* "I may not
alter it of my own accord. I follow only what is revealed to me. Indeed, should I disobey my Lord, I
fear the punishment of a tremendous day." (Q 10:15)

In other passages God speaks not to Muhammad in particular,
but to anyone who will listen. Sometimes, this sort of address is
combined with declarations about God, as in Q 3:56–57:

As for the faithless, *I will punish them* with a severe
punishment in the world and the Hereafter; and
they will have no helpers. But as for those who have
faith and do righteous deeds, *He will pay them* in
full their rewards, and *God does not like* the wrongdoers.

Non-Muslim observers have sometimes seen the
Qur'an's tendency to move between God's speech and third-
person reports about God as a sort of inconsistency, if not a
defect. Islamic tradition, for its part, gives this shifting a special
name—*iltifat*—and describes it as one element among many of
the Qur'an's "inimitable," or matchless, styles.

One question to be considered is whether the Qur'an's
quotations of what people have said (such as the counterdiscourse in Q 10:15 above) are quoting things that were really
said. After all, the Qur'an also tells us what the unbelievers
will say on the Day of Judgment, or when they are condemned
to the fires of hell.[15] Perhaps every time the Qur'an "quotes"
opponents, it is in fact simply staging a scene. This question
is only one of many that scholars debate fiercely regarding the
rhetoric of the Qur'an.

Qur'anic rhetoric is thus distinct, but its prophetic speech still puts it squarely within biblical tradition. In at least one passage the Qur'an specifically attributes the transmission of the Qur'an to the agency of the angel Gabriel:

> *Say,* "Whoever is an enemy of Gabriel [should know that] it is he who has brought it down on your heart with the will of God, confirming what has been [revealed] before it, and as a guidance and good news to the faithful." (Q 2:97)

The designation of Gabriel as the agent of revelation is biblical. Gabriel is a messenger to Daniel (Dan 8:16, 9:21–27) in the Old Testament and to Zechariah (Luke 1:19) and Mary (Luke 1:26) in the New Testament. The biblical background of the Qur'an's idea of prophecy seems even more evident in light of the Arabic term that the Qur'an uses for prophet, *nabiy,* which is related to the Hebrew term, *nabi,* used for the prophets of the Old Testament.[16]

This is an interesting point, since Islamic tradition insists that Muhammad first began proclaiming the Qur'an in Mecca, which was (again, according to tradition) the center of a pagan and idolatrous culture. The main shrine, the Ka'ba (the black, cube-shaped building around which the Muslim faithful today process during the annual pilgrimage), was supposedly a house of idols.[17] Jews and Christians were, basically, nowhere to be found.

How could it be that Muhammad came from a city and a culture so deeply marked by paganism when the Qur'an is so deeply marked by the biblical idea of prophecy? Islamic tradition has an answer to this question: God called Muhammad from the midst of a pagan people as he once had called Abraham. Just as Abraham lived among the pagans of Ur (something that is suggested by, although not explicit in, the account of Genesis) and heard the call of God, so Muhammad lived among the pagans of Mecca and heard the call of God. This parallel can be extended still further: just as Abraham would eventually leave the pagans of Ur and travel to Harran, and eventually Canaan, so Muhammad would leave the pagans of Mecca and travel to a new city, a largely Jewish city, Medina (originally named Yathrib).

However, there is another explanation: perhaps the original context of the Qur'an was less pagan than the tradition makes it out to be. Perhaps the tradition has portrayed Mecca as a pagan city precisely because it wanted to portray Muhammad as a new Abraham. Perhaps, in other words, the real historical context of the Qur'an's origins included more Jews and Christians than we have been led to believe.

The Qur'an's "Self-Referentiality"

Quite unlike the Bible, the Qur'an has a fascinating tendency to refer to itself. Such "self-references" are often (although not only) found at the beginning of Suras. For example, Q 2:2 declares, "That is the Book, there is no doubt in it, a guidance to the Godwary." Another reference to "the Book" can be found in Q 3:3 (here God is speaking to the Prophet): "He has sent down to *you* the Book with the truth, confirming what was [revealed] before it." Many more such examples could be cited that seem to have the Qur'an talking about the Qur'an.

But can such references to a "Book" actually be references to the Qur'an as we know it with its 114 Suras,[18] or, as Islamic tradition might put it, to "the codex between two covers"?[19] After all, these verses, which are part of that "codex," seem to be referring to something *else*.[20] In fact, the term "Book" (Arabic *kitab*) in the Qur'an may have a more general meaning of revelation—something "written" in heaven but not on earth.

Something similar might be concluded about the appearance of the word "Qur'an" in the Islamic scripture. For example, in Sura 10 we read: "This Qur'an could not have been fabricated by anyone besides God; rather, it is a confirmation of what was [revealed] before it, and an elaboration of the Book, there is no doubt in it, from the Lord of all the worlds" (Q 10:37). The use of Arabic "Qur'an" here leads some readers to assume that the Qur'an is speaking about itself. However, "Qur'an" is simply an Arabic term meaning "recitation." It became the name of the Muslim scripture only later, when subsequent generations of Muslims (precisely on the basis of verses such as these) began to use it as a name for their holy book. In other words, even when it refers to "Qur'an," the Qur'an must be referring to something *else*.

As the French scholar Anne-Sylvie Boisliveau has argued, the Qur'an's repeated insistence that it has come from heaven seems to testify to an environment in which there were skeptics.[21] Apparently, not everyone was convinced by the Prophet's claims that his proclamations came from God or were "written in heaven." In places, the Qur'an presents views that resemble precisely this sort of skepticism. In Sura 6 the Qur'an relates (in a good example of counterdiscourse), "When they come to you, to dispute with you, the faithless say, 'These are nothing but myths of the ancients'" (Q 6:25).[22] The Qur'an's author was clearly intent on responding to these skeptics by insisting that its proclamations were not myths, but prophecies.

Muhammad and the Qur'an

But who is that author? The Qur'an's claim of divine origins raised an interesting dilemma for non-Muslim scholars. They often felt compelled to consider the following question: If Muhammad was not actually visited by an angel, was he at least sincere in the belief that his revelations came from God? In other words, did he consciously *fabricate* his proclamations and seek to pass them off as the word of God (perhaps in order to achieve influence or power through them)? Or did he have a sincere conviction that he was hearing the word of God? Was he, in other words, an impostor?

In the foundational work of Western qur'anic studies, *The History of the Qur'an* (*Geschichte des Qorāns* [1860]), Theodor Nöldeke defends Muhammad's sincerity.[23] He insists that the sort of allegiance and enthusiasm that Muhammad won from his followers could only come from a sincere "inner voice."[24]

Nöldeke, however, was not above criticizing Muhammad. He considers that the Prophet regrettably came to believe that *all* of his thoughts came from a divine source, that he "used the authority of the Koran to issue ordinances that are not at all related to religion."[25] No doubt Nöldeke has in mind those passages, traditionally considered "Medinan," that give decrees on matters such as marriage, divorce, battle tactics (Q 4:101–4), and the sharing of war booty (Q 8:1, 38–41); whether it is permitted to raise one's voice in the presence of the Prophet (Q 49:2); or even whether Muhammad had the right to marry the divorced wife of his adopted son (Q 33:37).[26] By Nöldeke's telling, Muhammad eventually came to believe that his personal convictions had a divine origin, and that is why "mundane" matters are included in the Qur'an.[27]

The question of Muhammad's sincerity arose for scholars such as Nöldeke who assumed that Muhammad is the sole author of the Qur'an. Today, however, some scholars offer different scenarios for the origin of the Qur'an—for example, that it is the culmination of a complicated process involving various sources and layers of editing.[28]

One argument for the possibility that the current shape of the Qur'an owes much to a complicated process of editing is the appearance within it of multiple versions of the same story. To give just one example, the Qur'an relates in seven different Suras an account by which God commands the angels to bow down before Adam (2:34, 7:11–12, 15:28–33, 17:61–62, 18:50, 20:115–16, 38:71–78). A traditional explanation for this repetition would be that Muhammad decided to proclaim (or God decided to reveal) the same account in different circumstances (one modern scholar has compared these repetitions to a politician's "stump speech").[29] An alternative explanation is that initially there was one tradition about angels bowing before Adam, but as this tradition spread orally, different versions of it developed. Eventually, when the Qur'an was written down, seven different versions were all incorporated into the text through a process of editing.

All of this offers some idea of the profound differences in scholarly perspectives on the origin of the Qur'an. This diversity is reflected in the way that various sorts of scholars refer to passages in the Qur'an. Traditional Muslim scholars, who consider the Qur'an to have a divine source, might introduce a qur'anic passage by declaring, "God says. . . ." Earlier generations of Western scholars would do so instead with the words "Muhammad says. . . ." Today, scholars tend to avoid the question entirely by simply saying, "The Qur'an says. . . ."

The Qur'an's Relationship to the Bible

In articulating its message, the Qur'an does not claim to be the first or the only divine book. God has spoken before. In fact, the Qur'an even names books that God has "sent down" to earlier prophets. We can see this in Sura 3:

> ³He has sent down to *you* the Book with the truth, confirming what was [revealed] before it, and He had sent down the Torah and the Evangel ⁴before as guidance for mankind, and He has sent down the Criterion. Indeed, there is a severe punishment for those who deny the signs of God, and God is all-mighty, avenger.

The language the Qur'an uses here for the earlier books that God has sent down is telling. The word rendered here "Torah" represents Arabic *tawrah,* stemming ultimately from Hebrew *torah,* meaning "law" but used in Jewish literature for the first five books of the Hebrew Bible (or the Pentateuch), or even the entire Hebrew Bible. "Evangel" here represents Arabic *injil,* stemming ultimately from the Greek *euangélion,* meaning "gospel."

Elsewhere the Qur'an seems to refer to other elements of biblical tradition. In Q 4:163, and again in 17:55, the divine voice of the Qur'an declares, "We gave David the *zabur,*" a term often translated "Psalms."[30] This declaration suggests that the author of the Qur'an was aware of the traditional association (made by Jews and Christians alike) of David with the Psalms. The identification of *zabur* with the Psalms is also suggested by Q 21:105: "Certainly We wrote in *al-zabur,* after the remembrance: 'My righteous servants shall indeed inherit the earth,'" a verse that seems to be a paraphrase of Ps 37:29: "The righteous shall possess the land, and dwell upon it forever."[31]

Thus the Qur'an claims a certain connection to the biblical tradition. The Qur'an is meant to be a revelation in the tradition of Moses, David, and Jesus.

Yet did the author of the Qur'an ever read the Bible? There are a number of reasons to conclude that he did not. First, and most important, most scholars believe that at the time of the Qur'an's origins the Bible had not yet been translated into Arabic. By that time, many Arabic speakers had become Christians—some tribes had converted en masse—but Arab Christians must have known the Bible only through oral translations from other languages (above all a Semitic language known as Syriac).[32] Indeed, there is some reason to think that part of the appeal of the Qur'an to Arabic speakers in the seventh century was that it offered God's word in their own language. On a number of occasions the Qur'an draws attention to its Arabic language.[33]

Second, the Qur'an tends not to quote from the Bible. The closest thing to a quotation is Q 21:105 (cited above), which is close to—but not a precise quotation of—Ps 37:29. Elsewhere the Qur'an includes other biblical turns of phrase but never precise quotations of biblical passages. The Qur'an (7:40) alludes to the New Testament maxim of a camel and the "eye of the needle"; however, it does not reproduce the version of that maxim in any of the Gospels (Matt 19:23–24, Mark 10:25, Luke 18:25). Something similar could be said about the way the Qur'an speaks of a "mustard seed,"[34] an "uncircumcised heart,"[35] and the "twinkling of an eye."[36] In each case the Qur'an cites a biblical turn of phrase, but to a different effect.[37]

Third, the Qur'an's author tends not to distinguish between material found in the Bible and material found in other texts. When speaking of Jesus, for example, the Qur'an refers both to miracles known from the canonical Bible, such as his healing of lepers or his raising the dead, and to miracles known only from "apocryphal" and other later texts, such as his speaking "in the cradle" or his bringing a clay bird to life (Q 3:49, 5:110). The Qur'an also tells stories about other figures—such as the account of the angels bowing before Adam or Abraham being thrown into a fire (Q 21:68–70, 29:24–25, 37:97–98)—that are found not in the Bible but in assorted Jewish and Christian texts. All of this suggests that in the environment of the Qur'an's author, Jewish and Christian traditions were "in the air"—transmitted orally but not available in writing.[38]

This conclusion might explain why the Qur'an never describes the Bible precisely. It never speaks of the Old or New Testament (or the Jewish division of the Hebrew Bible into Torah, Prophets, and Writings) or, for that matter, any individual book of the Bible (with the possible exception of Psalms). When it speaks of the Torah, it is not clear that the Qur'an has the first five books of the Hebrew Bible in mind. And the Qur'an notably always speaks of "Evangel" or "Gospel" in the singular, and never of the four Gospels of Matthew, Mark, Luke, and John. Apparently, the Qur'an's author had a conception that, just as the Qur'an is a "book" from heaven, so too earlier prophets received "books": Moses the Torah, David the Psalms, and Jesus the Evangel. This brings us a long way from the actual appearance of the Bible, which is not a book given to a Moses, David, or Jesus but a book *about* Moses, David, and Jesus.

The way in which the Qur'an refers to these earlier books led later Muslim scholars to develop a scenario of revelation, which had the advantage of affording them a way to argue against the authenticity of the Bible. According to this scenario God revealed books to certain (but not all) prophets, among them Moses, David, and Jesus. However, at some point (and here Islamic tradition is far from unanimous) these revelations were corrupted, or falsified. That is why the Bible can't be trusted.

The development of this scenario was also a response to certain passages in the Qur'an that criticize Jews (especially) and Christians (also) as poor stewards of revelation. For example, in a qur'anic passage addressed to the Israelites, God says, "Do not mix the truth with falsehood, nor conceal the truth while you know" (Q 2:42). Later in that same Sura the Qur'an declares, "So woe to them who write the Book with their hands and then say, 'This is from God,' that they may sell it for a paltry gain" (Q 2:79). Certain other passages of the Qur'an (e.g., 4:46, 5:14) report that the Israelites "pervert words from their meanings," a turn of phrase that seems to accuse them of "misinterpreting" scripture but is often taken to mean that they have *physically changed* scripture.[39]

All of this led most—although not all—Muslim scholars to develop a hostile perspective on the Bible. From this perspective, the Bible is not equivalent to the Torah, Psalms, and Evangel mentioned in the Qur'an. It is only an inauthentic remnant of original revelations. In a famous tradition a companion of Muhammad declares:

> O community of Muslims, how is it that you seek wisdom from the People of the Book? Your book, brought down upon His Prophet—blessings and peace of God upon him—is the latest report about God. You read a Book that has not been distorted, but the People of the Book, as God related to you,

exchanged that which God wrote [for something else], changing the book with their hands.[40]

Yet when we read the Qur'an carefully, we find another voice, a voice which seems to say that the Jewish and Christian scriptures are not that bad after all. For example, the hadith cited above seems to contradict Q 10:94, in which God tells the Prophet to check with the "People of the Book" when he is in doubt over what God has revealed to him. In another passage the Qur'an commands the "People of the Gospel" to judge according to the things revealed in it (Q 5:47).

The Qur'an's concern with the Torah, Psalms, and Evangel suggests a conclusion that we have already suggested above, namely, that it was proclaimed in a context heavily marked by the presence of Jews and Christians. In order to persuade them of the truth of this new message, the author of the Qur'an chose to associate his own proclamations with those scriptures. This is rather typical in the history of religions. Joseph Smith, the prophet of the Mormons, also acknowledged the Bible in addition to his own revelations. Baha'u'llah, the prophet of the Baha'i faith, acknowledged both the Bible and the Qur'an in addition to his own revelations.

Yet ultimately the negative assessment of the Bible's authority had an important impact on later Muslim attitudes. Most Muslim authorities discourage other Muslims from reading the Bible (except, perhaps, when they are making arguments on the basis of the Bible to convert Jews or Christians to Islam). And while some Muslim scholars have looked to the Bible as a source for understanding the biblical narratives in the Qur'an,[41] the Bible plays no role in Muslim ritual.

God as a Qur'anic Character

In fact there are profound differences between the Bible and the Qur'an. Adam in the Bible is not the Adam in the Qur'an (for instance, only the Qur'an tells the story of angels bowing down before him). Moses in the Bible is not the Moses in the Qur'an (only in the Qur'an is Moses concerned with the resurrection of the body and the Day of Judgment). Jesus in the Bible is definitely not the Jesus in the Qur'an (only in the New Testament is he a divine savior). And all of this brings us to a key question: What about God? Is he the same character in both books?

From a theological perspective, it is difficult to conclude that the God of the Bible is not the God of the Qur'an. After all, in many ways Muslims and Christians (and Jews, along with Baha'is, Sikhs, and other monotheists) share a common understanding of God. All would say that God is the creator, that he is just, that he is merciful, that he is providential (concerned with human affairs), and that in some way he brings humans to an account for their lives. From a theological perspective, one might simply argue that since there is only one God, Muslims, Christians, and other monotheists are all worshipping him together (although this is not really a foolproof argument, since in theory some monotheists could conceive of their "one god" in such an unusual way—say, as a great dragon in the sky—that their belief would not overlap with the beliefs of others).

From a literary perspective, however, the God of the Bible and the God of the Qur'an are both characters like the human protagonists who appear in those books. "Allah" appears in the Qur'an alongside human characters such as Adam, Moses, Mary, Jesus, and Muhammad and alongside angels and other supernatural creatures known as the *jinn*. The author of the Qur'an uses all of these characters, including God, to advance his religious arguments. The God of the Qur'an, in other words, is defined in a distinct way by all of the things the Qur'an says about him.

Another way to think of this is to imagine a list of the "cast of characters" that one sometimes finds at the opening of the text of a play. If such a list were to appear at the opening of the Qur'an, we might assume that the first "character" to be presented would be Allah (after all, the word "Allah" appears about twenty-seven hundred times in the text). But how would he be described? In other words, who is Allah? This is the question we try to answer in the following pages.

2

God and the Prophets

When Allah completed creation, He wrote with Him on His Throne: "My Mercy has preceded My Anger."

—Saying of the Prophet Muhammad

In the mid-1990s I was working at a social justice center that provided English courses and social work services to Arab immigrants in Brooklyn, New York. One night the center held a meeting among local faith leaders and activists. There was a lot of talk of improving relations between the religious communities in New York. About halfway through the meeting a woman in a headscarf stood up and explained: "I want everyone here to know that Islam has no problems with other monotheists. As long as you believe in one god, you are fine by us." At this, another woman—evidently a non-Muslim—stood up and responded: "But why limit this to people who believe in one god? What about people who believe in many gods or no god at all?" The first woman didn't respond, and I realized that this was a sensitive point for her. After all, belief in only one God is the most important point of Islamic theology: it makes up the first part of the profession of faith ("There is no god but Allah . . ."), and it is central to the religious worldview of the Qur'an.

In the New Testament we read of an unforgivable sin: "Blasphemy against the Holy Spirit."[1] The Qur'an, too, has an unforgivable sin, but it is different. The unforgivable sin of the Qur'an is polytheism, or associating something with Allah (Arabic *shirk*). In two different passages of the same Sura we read that God will never forgive this sin:

> Indeed, God does not forgive that a partner should be ascribed to Him, but He forgives anything besides that to whomever He wishes. Whoever ascribes partners to God has indeed fabricated [a lie] in great sinfulness. (Q 4:48; cf. 4:116)

This passage tells us something about the nature of the qur'anic God. He will not tolerate rivals. He is a jealous God.

What else can be known of Allah? Who is he? Sura 7 relates how Moses, while on Mount Sinai, yearns to see God, to look at him. To this request, God responds: "Look at the mountain: if it abides in its place, then you will see Me." When God shows himself to the mountain, the mountain crumbles and Moses falls down prostrate in terror, declaring, "I turn to You in penitence!" (Q 7:143).

Yet if Moses did not see God on the mountain, many Muslim theologians still hold that the blessed might see him in paradise. There is some evidence for this idea in Islamic sources. Qur'an 75:23 speaks of the blessed "gazing upon their Lord." In a hadith attributed to the Prophet Muhammad he tells his followers, as they are looking at a full moon in the night sky, "You will see your Lord in the Hereafter as you see this moon."[2]

Another tradition relates that the Prophet Muhammad saw God already in this life. According to this tradition Muhammad journeyed on a miraculous winged beast (named Buraq) by night from Mecca all the way to Jerusalem. He then ascended to heaven and passed various prophets on different levels. Finally, Muhammad (according to some versions of the account) advanced to the very throne of God. There, God touched Muhammad between his shoulder blades "with cool and comforting hands."[3] According to this version of the account, Allah even has hands. He can reach out and touch a human.

Another tradition goes still further. A medieval scholar named Bayhaqi (d. 1066) has Muhammad report, "I saw my Lord in the form of a curly-haired, beardless young man wearing a green robe."[4] Many Muslim scholars reject this hadith, with one scholar calling this tradition of God as a "curly-haired beardless young man" a "condemned, disauthenticated addition."[5]

Some (notably among Shiʿite Muslims and a school of theology known as the Muʿtazila) consider the very possibility of a vision of God impossible. From their perspective, there is no way to know what God looks like. Or, better, God does not look like anything. Yet even those who would say it is impossible to depict what Allah looks like would still say it is possible to describe him in other ways. Even if God cannot be seen, he can still be known.

In this chapter we begin to get to know Allah as we unveil his character in the Qur'an. In order to do this, we first examine what the Qur'an says about God, including the sorts of names that it gives to God (in other words, "who God is").

We then analyze how the Qur'an portrays God's interactions with humanity ("what God does"). This leads us to examine several qur'anic stories about prophets, those men whom God commissions to model proper human conduct and to deliver his messages.

These two tasks correspond to classical ways of looking at God: the first of these (to use some technical terms) is *ontological*—the way God *is*, independently, essentially; the second of these is *economic* (not in the sense of business but in the sense how God "manages" the world)—the way God is in his relationship with creation, and humanity in particular. In both respects—the ontological and the economic—we will discover a theological tension that will occupy us more and more in this book, namely, that the God of the Qur'an is at once merciful and vengeful.

Allah and the Other Names of God

Perhaps the simplest way to begin an analysis of the God of Islam is to look at the names that the Qur'an gives to him. We have already mentioned the passage in the Qur'an (Q 59: 22–24) that gives God's "beautiful" or "best" names. To Muslims such passages are the key to understanding the God who is lord of the universe. By describing himself with different names (remember that according to a Muslim perspective, God is the author of the Qur'an), God has given humanity a glimpse of his essence. He has unveiled something of his being. The Qur'an, one might say, is God's self-presentation.

When I begin teaching a class, I ask the students to write on a notecard some basic information about themselves (their name, hometown, hobbies; their interest in taking the class) so that I might get to know them better. From a Muslim perspective, we might say that the Qur'an is God's "notecard," which he has written and delivered to humans so that we might get to know him better. It does not say everything that could be said about God (surely, God cannot tell *everything* there is to say about himself in a single book), but it does offer some important insights. The Qur'an, for example, calls God "king" (Arabic *malik*) or "sovereign," "holy," "benign," and "securer." Each of these names defines God a bit more; each term distinguishes the particular Islamic vision of God.

The principal name of God in the Qur'an is, of course, Allah. Muhammad proclaims the Qur'an "in the name of Allah" (Q 1:1). But is "Allah" God's name or simply a word meaning "God"?

In the Book of Exodus in the Bible, God speaks to Moses on Mount Sinai. One of the issues that comes up in their conversation is God's name. Moses asks God, "If I come to the people of Israel and say to them, 'The God of your fathers has sent me to you,' and they ask me, 'What is his name?' what shall I say to them?" (3:13). And God responds, "I AM WHO I AM. . . . Say this to the people of Israel, 'I AM has sent me to you'" (3:14). The Hebrew rendered here "I am who I am" is "Yahweh," and Jewish tradition, on the basis of this passage, took "Yahweh" to be God's "special" or "proper" name. The name "Yahweh" is considered to be so holy that it is generally not to be pronounced or even written (for this reason, one sometimes writes only the consonants and represents the name as YHWH, called the Tetragrammaton).

The Qur'an does not seem to have this same idea with the name Allah. God in the Qur'an can be called Allah, but he can also be called by other names. Notably, the Qur'an often (fifty-seven times, in fact) refers to God simply as "the Compassionate One" (*al-rahman*) (see more on this in Chapter 4). One passage in the Qur'an suggests that Allah and *al-rahman* are both particularly fine alternatives: "*Say,* 'Invoke "[Allah]" or invoke "the All-beneficent" [*al-rahman*]. Whichever [of His Names] you may invoke, to Him belong the Best Names'" (Q 17:110).

But what about the other names that the Qur'an gives to God? It refers to God with a rich and diverse vocabulary. Different lists of God's "ninety-nine" names, with considerable variations, developed through time.[6] The number ninety-nine was established by a prophetic hadith (on the authority of a companion of Muhammad named Abu Hurayra) in which Muhammad declares, "God has 99 names—one hundred minus one—and who ever counts them will enter into paradise."[7] Other traditions relate that God has one hundred names but kept one name a secret.[8]

Together, the names of God allow us to describe the character of Allah in a way that is different from a vague or "lowest common denominator" definition of the divine that might be common to different religious traditions. One of the most common names for God in the Qur'an is "master" (*rabb*). This term appears hundreds of times (never with the definite article). God is said to be *rabb* of humans (Q 79:24, 87:1) and *rabb* of "this house" (Q 106:3; usually thought to be a reference to the Ka'ba in Mecca).

A number of other divine names in the Qur'an also emphasize the quality of God's sovereignty; these include the "self-sufficient" (*al-ghani*), the "self-subsisting" (*al-qayyum*), the "strong" (*al-qawi*), the "mighty" (*al-'aziz*), the "great" (*al-kabir*), and the "high or lofty" (*al-'ali*). Other divine names emphasize other qualities, such as the "wise" (*al-hakim*) or the "knowledgeable" (*al-khabir*).

Still other divine names in the Qur'an allude to the ways or modes with which Allah interacts with humans. He is said to be the "gentle" (*al-halim*), the "forgiving" (*al-ghafur*), the "re-lenting" (*al-tawwab*), and the "benevolent" (*al-latif*) but also the "powerful" (*al-jabbar*) and the "compeller" (*al-qahhar*). One Islamic tradition divides the divine names between the names of beauty (*al-jamal*) and the names of majesty (*al-jalal*).

An echo of these divine names can be heard in the names of Muslims. The name Abdallah means "servant" or "slave" of Allah. Other Arabic names beginning with "Abd" are also found, for example Abd al-Aziz ("slave of the mighty"), Abd al-Halim ("slave of the gentle"), and Abd al-Jabbar ("slave of the powerful"—the name taken by the legendary basketball player Kareem Abdul-Jabbar).

Yet what do these names actually tell us about Allah? In his work *God of Justice* Daud Rahbar criticizes the way in which Western scholars rely on the notion of God's names in order to paint a portrait of Allah. Rahbar makes the important observation that the Qur'an on occasion gives pairs of divine names that would seem to affirm both one thing and its opposite. For example, Allah is "the one who honors" and "the one who humiliates," "the one who grants" and "the one who with-holds," "the one who offers help" and "the one who causes distress," "the one who guides" and "the one who leads astray." In other words, these names simply make the point that God is responsible for everything. They do not define his character or disposition in any particular way. Indeed, they would seem to keep God's nature a mystery.

God and Humans

There is, however, another way to get to know the God of the Qur'an. Instead of focusing on his names, one might instead focus on his actions. In other words, one might learn about

Allah by analyzing those passages that describe not only *who* he is but also *what* he does and how he relates to humans.

What God does above all is demand obedience. In a mysterious passage found in Sura 7, all of the souls of humanity—in some primordial time before their earthly existence—come to acknowledge God's sovereignty:

> When *your* Lord took from the Children of Adam
> their descendants from their loins, and made them
> bear witness over themselves, [He said to them,]
> "Am I not your Lord?" They said, "Yes indeed! We
> bear witness." [This,] lest you should say on the Day
> of Resurrection, "We were indeed unaware of this."
> (Q 7:172)

This verse, known as the *alastu* verse (from the first Arabic words in the question that God poses to humanity), seems to illustrate the Qur'an's conception of the divine-human relationship: the fundamental task of humans is to acknowledge God's lordship.

The same lesson is taught by those passages that describe creation. While the Qur'an argues that God has created things for the sake of humanity, it also insists that he expects something in return. Creation is not an act of pure grace. God expects gratitude and, ultimately, submission:

> It is God who made for you the shade from what
> He has created, and made for you retreats in the
> mountains, and made for you garments that protect
> you from heat, and garments that protect you from
> your [mutual] violence. That is how He completes
> His blessing upon you so *that you may submit [to
> Him]*. (Q 16:81)

The Arabic of the final phrase in this verse is *la'allakum tusli-mun,* an expression that could be read, "that you would be a Muslim." The very name for the Islamic religion comes from those qur'anic passages that speak of "submission"—in Arabic, *islam*—to God.[9]

In the Qur'an the lesson about submission is taught even by the angels. A number of qur'anic passages tell the story of how God commanded the angels to bow before Adam, the first human. All of the angels obey the divine command except for one: "but not the devil: he was not among those who prostrated" (Q 7:11) When asked why he did not bow before Adam, the devil has a logical answer: "'I am better than him,' he said. 'You created me from fire and You created him from clay'" (Q 7:12). This story—which explains how the devil fell from heaven—is known to us from pre-Islamic Christian sources. In those sources the story of the fall of the devil is "Christological"; that is, the point of the Christians who told this story is that just as the angels bowed before Adam (who before his fall bore the perfect image of God), so too they will bow before Christ (see Phil 2:9–10), who is both human and divine.

In the Qur'an, of course, this Christological element is missing: Christ, according to the Qur'an, is not God incarnate and not worthy of angelic worship. Instead, in the Qur'an the story of the angels' bowing is meant simply to teach humans a lesson about obedience. Faced with a divine command, even one that seems to be counterintuitive (why would God command angels to bow before a being made out of clay?), the question is, Will humans obey or disobey? Will they make the choice of the angels or of the devil?

In some ways, the qur'anic character who most distinctly models the human obligation to recognize God's lordship and to obey him is Abraham. In a story that is also known to us in

pre-Islamic writings, the Qur'an relates how Abraham became
a monotheist by observing the stars, the moon, and the sun:

> [75]Thus did We show Abraham the dominions
> of the heavens and the earth, that he might be of
> those who possess certitude. [76]When night dark-
> ened over him, he saw a star and said, "This is my
> Lord!" But when it set, he said, "I do not like those
> who set."
>   [77]Then, when he saw the moon rising, he said,
> "This is my Lord!" But when it set, he said, "Had
> my Lord not guided me, I would surely have been
> among the astray lot."
>   [78]Then, when he saw the sun rising, he said,
> "This is my Lord! This is bigger!" But when it set,
> he said, "O my people, I indeed disown what you
> take as [His] partners." [79]"Indeed, I have turned my
> face toward Him who originated the heavens and
> the earth, as a *hanif*, and I am not one of the poly-
> theists." (Q 6:75–79)

In the final verse of this passage Abraham identifies himself
as a *hanif*, a term that is usually understood to mean a "pure
monotheist" and is frequently associated with Abraham in the
Qur'an.[10] Its meaning is presumably connected with the larger
theme of this passage, in which Abraham wisely discovers by
observing heavenly bodies that nothing but God, the creator,
is to be worshipped.

Yet the point of the Qur'an is not simply that God alone
is to be worshipped by human beings. The God of the Qur'an
wants more than that. He wants their obedience. And Abra-

ham also models obedience to God, most notably in the story of the sacrifice, or the near-sacrifice, of his son.

Readers may be familiar with the story from Genesis 22, known as the *akedah* (or "binding" of Isaac) in Jewish tradition, in which God calls on Abraham to sacrifice Isaac. In the biblical account the tension around this story is connected to God's promise that Abraham would have descendants "without counting" through Isaac, the very son whom God is now demanding Abraham to sacrifice. The test of Abraham's obedience, or his love of God, is thus all the more dramatic. He is faced with a terrible dilemma.

This element is missing from the Qur'an. Unlike Genesis, the Qur'an never describes Isaac as the son through whom a promise will be fulfilled. Indeed, in the qur'anic account it is not even clear that the son to be sacrificed is Isaac. That son is never named, and the majority of Muslim interpreters insist that it is not Isaac but Ishmael (the ancestor of the Prophet Muhammad according to his traditional genealogy).

Yet if the point about Abraham's promise is not to be found in the qur'anic version of this account, the point about a prophet's obedience to God is still prominent. Indeed, in some ways this larger point is accentuated, since in the qur'anic account both Abraham *and* his son declare their willingness to go forward with the sacrifice. In this account, Abraham has a dream of the coming sacrifice. When he describes that dream to his son, the (unnamed) son declares that he is ready to die, saying,

> "Father! Do whatever you have been commanded.
> If God wishes, you will find me to be patient."
> (Q 37:102)

Notably, the son here does not simply say that he will be patient. The son exclaims, "If God wishes," he will be patient. With this exclamation he suggests that God has the ability to intervene in human affairs, or even control human behavior. Whether or not the son will endure the test depends on God's will. This is a point to which we shall return.

As in the account of Genesis 22, in the Qur'an the son does not die. At the last moment, God redeems the son. Genesis 22 speaks of a ram that is caught in a thicket and is sacrificed in the place of Isaac. Qur'an 37 speaks instead of a "great sacrifice" (37:107).[11]

Jesus in the Qur'an

Jesus, too, models obedience to God in the Qur'an. This obedience is seen in a conversation that he carries on with God near the end of Sura 5 (we will return to this conversation in Chapter 6). During the conversation, God asks Jesus whether he told people to worship him—and his mother—as gods. He responds piously:

> Glory be to You! It does not behove me to say what I have no right to. Had I said it, You would certainly have known it: You know whatever is in myself, and I do not know what is in Your Self. Indeed, You know best all that is Unseen. (Q 5:116)

The very idea that he (or his mother) would be equal to God shocks Jesus. He is only a servant of God, or even a slave of God.

In some ways one could imagine that it would be especially important for Jesus to model submissiveness before God in the Qur'an. The Qur'an's author is aware that Christians consider Jesus to be the "son of God." At one point (Q 9:30) the Qur'an declares, "The Christians have said, 'Christ is the son of God'" (that same verse curiously insists that the Jews consider Ezra to be the son of God, too). Indeed, the Qur'an goes out of its way to make the point that Jesus was a prophet, but nothing more than a mortal. The Qur'an presents a simple argument to make this case: Jesus (and his mother) ate food (Q 5:75).

The Qur'an does not deny that Jesus performed miracles—indeed, no figure in the Qur'an is said to perform more miracles than Jesus. However, when reporting the miracles of Jesus, the Qur'an often (although not always) makes the point that he did so with the permission (or "leave") of Allah:

> I have certainly brought you a sign from your Lord:
> I will create for you the form of a bird out of clay,
> then I will breathe into it, and it will become a
> bird by God's leave. I heal the blind and the leper
> and I revive the dead by God's leave. I will tell you
> what you have eaten and what you have stored in
> your houses. There is indeed a sign in that for you,
> should you be faithful. (Q 3:49; cf. 5:109)

Elsewhere the Qur'an makes the same point in a different way. In Sura 18 God declares, "Do not say about anything, 'I will indeed do it tomorrow' without [adding], 'God willing'" (*in sha'a allah;* Q 18:23–24).[12] This verse helps explain the popularity of the well-known expression *inshallah* ("if God wills") in the Arabic and Islamic worlds. Muslims, it implies, should not take anything for granted, since everything depends on the will of God. Muslim theologians have even debated whether one could say "I am a Muslim" without adding *inshallah*.

The Punishment Stories

With the examples of Abraham and Jesus, we have seen how the God of the Qur'an demands human obedience. Yet he does not send prophets only as models of proper human behavior or as moral exemplars. In the Qur'an God also sends prophets with the command to worship and obey God. They transmit God's promise that those who do so will be admitted into paradise and those who refuse to do so will be condemned to hell. This is why the prophet in the Qur'an is called both a bearer of good news (*bashir*) and a bearer of a warning (*nadhir*). This is why the qur'anic message is sometimes called both an incitement to desire a reward (*targhib*) and an incitement to fear punishment (*tarhib*).

At the heart of this dynamic are those passages, concentrated in a number of Suras—notably 7, 11, 26, 37, and 54—that are largely consumed with accounts about civilizations God has destroyed for rejecting the message of the prophets sent to them. These accounts are known (for good reason) in Western scholarship as "punishment stories." They are not part of a sacred history with a grand narrative that develops in stages and leads to a certain culmination with the life of the Prophet Muhammad. Instead, these accounts are different versions of the same scenario. They are meant, collectively, to persuade the Qur'an's audience that it is dangerous to reject the message of a prophet. This threat is stated clearly in Sura 6:

> Your Lord is the All-sufficient dispenser of mercy. If
> He wishes, He will take you away, and make whom-

ever He wishes succeed you, just as He produced
you from the descendants of another people. (6:133)

All of the punishment stories are in Suras that are traditionally classified as "Meccan" (although they are also mentioned
in two "Medinan" Suras: Q 9:70 and 22:42–44).[13] Some, but
not all, of these accounts involve biblical characters such as
Noah, Lot, and Moses (the punishment stories of Q 37 notably
include only biblical characters).

It is interesting to note that these characters in the
Qur'an retain certain characteristics of their biblical narratives. The Qur'an does not, for example, have the people of
Noah's time destroyed by fire instead of water, or the people
of Lot's time drowned in water instead of consumed by fire,
or Pharaoh and his chariots lost in the desert and not thrown
into the sea. However, the role of biblical narratives in shaping
the qur'anic punishment stories might be described as orna-
mental. The Qur'an uses certain distinctive features of those
biblical narratives—perhaps because they were so well-known
that it could not do otherwise. However, those biblical narratives are transformed to fit the standard model of the punishment stories. For the Qur'an is not concerned with teaching
its audience about the personalities of Noah, Lot, and Moses.
Rather, it is concerned with making a religious argument by
asking the age-old question about the disappearance of earlier
peoples: *ubi sunt qui ante nos fuerunt* ("where are those who
were before us?").

Precisely because the Qur'an does not fit these characters into a historical narrative it is able to integrate into the
punishment stories other characters unknown to the Bible, including Hud, Salih, and Shu'ayb, characters who presumably
came from pre-qur'anic Arabian lore. These characters, too,

are poured into the same prophetic mold. All of these stories,
whether they involve biblical or nonbiblical characters, involve
a similar scenario. To show the cyclic nature of these accounts,
I cite here excerpts from six punishment stories, according
to the three principal stages of these accounts (the prophet
preaches, the people reject the prophet, and God destroys the
unbelievers), as they appear in Sura 7:

The Prophet Preaches to His People
1. "[Noah] said, 'O my people, worship God! You
   have no other god besides Him. I indeed fear
   for you the punishment of a tremendous day'"
   (Q 7:59).
2. "[Hud] said, 'O my people, worship God! You
   have no other god besides Him. Will you not
   then be wary [of Him]?'" (Q 7:65).
3. "[Salih] said, 'O my people, worship God! You
   have no other god besides Him. There has
   certainly come to you a manifest proof from
   your Lord. This she-camel of God is a sign for
   you'" (Q 7:73).
4. "[Lot] said to his people, 'What! Do you
   commit an outrage none in the world ever
   committed before you?!'" (Q 7:80).
5. "[Shu'ayb] said, 'O my people, worship God!
   You have no other god besides Him. There has
   certainly come to you a manifest proof from
   your Lord. Observe fully the measure and the
   balance, and do not cheat the people of their
   goods, and do not cause corruption on the
   earth after its restoration'" (Q 7:85).
6. "And Moses said, 'O Pharaoh, I am indeed

an apostle from the Lord of all the worlds. It behooves me to say nothing about God except the truth. I certainly bring you a clear proof from your Lord. So let the Children of Israel go with me'" (Q 7:104–5).

The People Reject the Prophet
1. "The elite of [Noah's] people said, 'Indeed we see you in manifest error'" (Q 7:60).
2. "The elite of [Hud's] people who were faithless said, 'Indeed we see you to be in folly, and indeed we consider you to be a liar'" (Q 7:66).
3. "So they hamstrung the She-camel and defied the command of their Lord, and they said, 'O Salih, bring us what you threaten us with, if you are one of the apostles'" (Q 7:77).
4. "But the only answer of [Lot's] people was that they said, 'Expel them from your town! They are indeed a puritanical lot'" (Q 7:82).
5. "The elite of his people who were arrogant said, 'O Shu'ayb, we will surely expel you and the faithful who are with you from our town, or else you shall revert to our creed.' He said, 'What! Even if we should be unwilling?!'" (Q 7:88).
6. "[Pharaoh] said, 'If you have brought a sign, produce it, should you be truthful'" (Q 7:106).

God Destroys the Unbelievers
1. "So We delivered [Noah] and those who were with him in the ark, and We drowned those who denied Our signs. Indeed they were a blind lot" (Q 7:64).

2. "Then We delivered Hud and those who were
   with him by a mercy from Us, and We rooted
   out those who denied Our signs and were not
   faithful" (Q 7:72).
3. "Thereupon the earthquake seized them and
   they lay lifeless prostrate in their homes. So
   [Salih] abandoned them [to their fate], and
   said, 'O my people! Certainly I communicated
   to you the message of my Lord, and I was your
   well-wisher, but you did not like well-wishers'"
   (Q 7:78–79).
4. "Thereupon We delivered [Lot] and his family,
   except his wife; she was one of those who
   remained behind. Then We poured down upon
   them a rain [of stones]. So observe how was the
   fate of the guilty!" (Q 7:83–84).
5. "So the earthquake seized them and they lay
   lifeless prostrate in their homes. Those who
   impugned Shu'ayb became as if they had never
   lived there. Those who impugned Shu'ayb were
   themselves the losers" (Q 7:91–92).
6. "So We took vengeance on [Pharaoh's people]
   and drowned them in the sea, for they denied
   Our signs and were oblivious to them"
   (Q 7:136).

The way in which the Qur'an tells these stories of warning,
disbelief, and destruction one after another tells us something
about its fundamental concern. The Qur'an seeks to warn *its
own* audience and thereby to persuade them to believe in its
God and in its prophet, Muhammad. Thus in the Qur'an the

prophets of the past *are prophets of the present.* One scholar
has gone so far as to speak of "mono*prophetism*" in the Qur'an
(parallel to its mono*theism*).[14]

The point of these stories is that by hearing them the
Qur'an's audience will make a better choice than those who
chose not to believe in the prophet sent to them. The Qur'an
means to inspire fear of God. One might think of how, in the
Gospel of Matthew, Jesus says, "Do not be afraid of those who
kill the body but cannot kill the soul; rather, fear him who can
destroy both soul and body in hell" (Matt 10:28). Similarly, in
Sura 2 the Qur'an, referring to wrongdoers, exclaims, "So do
not fear them, but fear Me" (Q 2:150).

Tellingly, the prophets not only warn their people of ca-
lamity; they also invite their people to look back at how earlier
generations were destroyed. Thus in Sura 7 Hud refers to the
destruction of the people of Noah, saying:

> [69]Do you consider it odd that there should come
> to you a reminder from your Lord through a man
> from among yourselves, so that he may warn you?
> Remember when He made you successors after the
> people of Noah, and increased you vastly in cre-
> ation. So remember God's bounties so that you may
> be felicitous.

Just as Hud points to the fate of an earlier people in order to
persuade his own people to believe, so the Prophet Muhammad does the same in the Qur'an. Muhammad, one might say,
is the last of the prophets of the punishment stories.[15]

An interesting feature found in Q 26 (but not in the other
Suras that relate punishment stories) is a refrain in which the

prophet demands that his people obey him. Time and again the prophets in Q 26 warn, "Be wary of Allah and obey me!" (Noah, vv. 108, 110; Hud, vv. 126, 131; Salih, vv. 144, 150; Lot, v. 163; Shuʻayb, v. 179). The point of this refrain is clear: the prophet is the representative of God on earth. Just as Muslims are to obey God, they are also to obey the prophet. One can understand why later Islamic tradition developed the doctrine that the prophets are all infallible. If they are to be obeyed, they must be fully trustworthy, they must be perfect.

The punishment stories, however, also leave us with a problem: If God destroyed the earlier peoples who rejected their prophets, why did he not destroy the people of Mecca who rejected Muhammad? Was Muhammad disappointed that God did not come through and send a firestorm or a mighty wind or earthquake to sweep away the Meccans? Certain verses suggest that at some point Muhammad believed that God might destroy them:

> *Say,* "Whoever abides in error, the All-beneficent shall prolong his respite until they sight what they have been promised: either punishment, or the Hour." Then they will know whose position is worse, and whose host is weaker. (Q 19:75)

> We will indeed take vengeance on them, whether We take you away or show you what We have promised them, for indeed We hold them in Our power. (Q 43:41–42)

Another verse seems to promise, incredibly, that *every* town will be punished by God (presumably including Mecca):

> There is not a town but We will destroy it before the
> Day of Resurrection, or punish it with a severe pun-
> ishment. That has been written in the Book. (Q 17:
> 58)

David Marshall offers a solution to this problem. He argues that Muhammad initially expected God to intervene in
human history and punish his enemies in Mecca. This moment passed, however, when Muhammad arrived in Medina
and gathered a force of men who could fight those enemies
in open warfare. In Medina, as Muhammad gathered military
strength, he began to see himself as the rod of divine punishment. Marshall sees this development culminate in one verse
of Sura 9. He writes: "The Medinan paradigm is expressed
nowhere more clearly than at 9:14. . . . Here there is nothing
allusive or indirect about the language used; the believers are
simply commanded: Fight them and God will punish them *at
your hands* and degrade them."[16]

God of Punishment, God of Mercy

So do these punishment stories mean that Allah is merciless or
vindictive? For many Muslims they suggest exactly the opposite. As was explained to me by a Muslim imam at a conference
on religious extremism in Cairo, the most important element
of these stories is that God has gone to the trouble of sending
messengers at all. The end of Q 17:15 declares, "We do not punish [any community] until We have sent [it] an apostle." This
verse suggests that God always sends a warner before he destroys a city. He is not obliged to do so; he does so out of his
mercy.

From a similar perspective the sending down of revelation, of divine books, can be seen as an act of divine mercy.
The Qur'an refers to the book given to Moses in just this way:
"Certainly We gave Moses the Book, after We had destroyed
the former generations, as [a set of] eye-openers, guidance and
mercy for mankind, so that they may take admonition" (Q 28:
43). So too the book that God gave to Muhammad, the Qur'an,
is conceived as an act of mercy. The stories it tells of God's destruction of earlier peoples might be gruesome, but that is the
point. They are meant to frighten, even to terrify, people into
repentance and belief.

But can such a God be called "loving"? In his book *Allah:
A Christian Response,* the Protestant theologian Miroslav Volf
notes that one of the divine names for God is "the lover" (*al-
wadud*). He also argues that the Christian concept of love is
close to the Islamic concept of "mercy" because it is in mercy
that God in Islam *gives* something to humanity, namely, forgiveness.[17] It should be noted, however (and as we will discover in Chapter 4), that Allah's mercy is not for everyone.
Those peoples whom God has destroyed did not receive divine
mercy; they received only divine wrath.

Of course, we should not forget that punishment
stories—such as those of Noah, Lot, and Pharaoh—also exist
in the Bible, but the perspective of the New Testament on
divine love seems to be different. This is noted subtly in the
Christian response (known as the "Yale Response" because it
was principally authored by three scholars from Yale University, including Volf) to the Muslim letter "A Common Word
Between Us and You" (see the introduction). The original
Muslim letter is principally focused on human responsibili-
ties, namely, loving God and loving neighbor. The Yale Re-

sponse makes the point that the love is reciprocal. God also loves humans:

> We find it equally heartening that the God whom we should love above all things is described as being Love. In the Muslim tradition, God, "the Lord of the worlds," is "The Infinitely Good and All-Merciful." And the New Testament states clearly that "God is love" (1 John 4:8). Since God's goodness is infinite and not bound by anything, God "makes his sun rise on the evil and the good, and sends rain on the righteous and the unrighteous," according to the words of Jesus Christ recorded in the Gospel (Matthew 5:45).[18]

The authors of the Yale Response make an implicit distinction between the God of the Qur'an and the God of the Bible, implying that the God of the Bible loves everyone, even the unrighteous. Again, and although they do not say so explicitly, they presumably know that the Qur'an speaks of those whom God does *not* love, including the unrighteous or the wrongdoers (Q 3:57). In fact, the Qur'an pays special attention to the punishment that God will mete out against the wrongdoers on the Day of Resurrection. We now turn to the drama of that day, and to the qur'anic accounts of heaven and hell.

3

Heaven and Hell

And the People of the Left Hand—what are the People of the Left Hand?! Amid infernal miasma and boiling water and the shadow of a dense black smoke, neither cool nor beneficial. Indeed they had been affluent before this, and they used to persist in great sin.

— *Qur'an 56:41–46*

According to a well-known tale, a female Muslim mystic by the name of Rabi'a used to walk the streets of the Iraqi city of Basra with a torch in one hand and a bucket of water in the other. When asked what she was doing, she would reply that the torch was to set paradise on fire and the water to douse the flames of hell. This, she explained, would mean that people would learn to love God for his own sake, and not out of a desire for heaven or out of a fear of hell.

The story of Rabi'a is important for Islamic spirituality. It teaches the lesson that one should love God for his sake alone and not out of personal interest. Yet the message of heaven and hell is nevertheless central to the Qur'an. Time and again the Qur'an asks its audience to consider their own eternal fate: to make a choice that will lead them to paradise and away from the gruesome punishments of hellfire.

The Pakistani-American scholar Mustansir Mir argues that the God of the Qur'an is particularly interested in rewarding the good in heaven. Mir compares the Qur'an's vision of divine judgment with a school: "The primary purpose of establishing a school or university is not to fail students but to pass them."[1] Nevertheless, a schoolteacher might spend quite some time reminding students of the consequences of bad behavior or poor work.

In the previous chapter we began to examine how Allah interacts with humans during their lives. He (mercifully) sends prophets to warn them of punishment, and he (vengefully) punishes those who reject those prophets. Here, we examine how Allah interacts with humanity *after* their lives. The Qur'an insists that one day God will raise humans from the dead and send them either to the pleasures of heaven or the punishments of hell. Still more, the Qur'an describes heaven and hell with vivid detail: heaven is a domain of pleasure and relaxation, and hell is one of excruciating punishment.

Islamic Eschatology

There is no debating that the Qur'an is concerned with eschatology, that is, the events that will happen at the end of time, including the Day of Judgment. Yet scholars have long debated whether Muhammad believed that the end was coming soon.

According to one perspective, the Qur'an speaks so often about the Day of Judgment because Muhammad believed that God was on the verge of punishing the evildoers and infidels of his day in one final, cataclysmic moment.

In the early twentieth century a scholar named Paul Casanova wrote a book in French—*Mohammed et la fin du monde* ("Muhammad and the End of the World")—in which he argued that Muhammad was an apocalyptic prophet, preaching that the end was near.[2] (To defend his argument Casanova noted that Muhammad never appointed a successor to rule after him.) It was only when Muhammad died and the end did not come that his later followers (necessarily!) adjusted his message to make it less apocalyptic. Long neglected, this theory has recently been taken up again by the American scholar Stephen Shoemaker.[3]

In fact, some passages in the Qur'an suggest that the Day of Judgment is not far off. Qur'an 54:1 proclaims, "The Hour has drawn near and the moon is split." It's not clear what is meant by "the moon is split," though Islamic tradition reports that Muhammad really split the moon in two (some Islamic websites display images of the moon to show where a big crack might be found). Some of the shorter Suras near the end of the Qur'an reflect an intense apocalyptic fervor. Sura 82, for example, begins with a series of oathlike predictions:

> [1]When the sky is rent apart, [2]when the stars are scattered, [3]when the seas are merged, [4]when the graves are overturned, [5]then a soul shall know what it has sent ahead and left behind.

Apocalypticism is also found outside of the Qur'an. A number of hadith imply that Muhammad believed the end was coming soon. One hadith reported by a companion of the Prophet named Anas b. Malik expresses this teaching with a story about Muhammad and a boy:

> A young boy of Mughira b. Shuʻba happened to pass by (the Holy Prophet) and he was of my age. Thereupon Allah's Apostle said: "If he lives long he would not grow very old until the Last Hour would come."[4]

The end, of course, did not come, although certain Islamic movements (notably within Shiʻism, but also the extremist group ISIS) are still fascinated with eschatology today. Yet what is to explain this interest in the early Islamic community?

It is often thought that interest in the "Last Hour" is connected to a pious desire to see things set aright. Like believers in other religious traditions, many early Muslims were troubled by problems they saw around them. They asked questions such as, Why do some people still reject Islam? Why is there internal strife and bloodshed even among believers? Why do unrighteous and sinful people go unpunished? The easiest answer to such questions is eschatological: all will be made right when Judgment Day arrives, when God rewards righteous believers and punishes sinners and infidels. This trust in eschatology led early Muslims to believe (or at least to hope) that Judgment Day would come soon.

Eventually, Muslims developed a scenario of all of the events that would happen leading up to the Day of Judgment: apocalyptic battles will take place between Muslims and their enemies, an evil anti-Christ figure known as al-Dajjal ("the liar") will appear and lead people astray, Jesus (not Muhammad) will descend from heaven to kill al-Dajjal and convert the entire world to Islam. Jesus will then live out the rest of his life peacefully in a final, idyllic period of human history before the resurrection of the dead.

The role of Jesus in this eschatological scenario is especially interesting since it seems to give him a special prominence. The Qur'an calls Muhammad the "seal" of the prophets (Q 33:40), and Muslims generally understand this to mean that he is the last prophet. Yet this scenario suggests that he is not the last, that Jesus will come after him. Islamic traditions are usually careful to add that when Jesus returns to earth, he will follow the law, the sharia, of Muhammad. Nevertheless, Jesus is the Muslim prophet of the last times.

Why would the early Islamic community, which was otherwise interested in making the case that Muhammad is more important than Jesus, make Jesus the apocalyptic hero? Why would Islamic tradition create an apocalyptic scenario which is close to that of Christianity?

Two elements of the Qur'an might help us answer these questions. First, the Qur'an (at least according to the standard Islamic reading) seems to deny the death of Jesus. According to Q 4:157–58 Jesus did not die on the cross. Instead, God raised Jesus to himself and *someone else* was transformed to look like Jesus and was crucified in his place. While the Qur'an never denies the death of Jesus explicitly, this passage was taken to mean that because of this "switch," Jesus is alive body and soul in heaven today. And if Jesus is alive—so the logic goes—then God must have a plan for him in the future. God must want Jesus to return to earth someday. This logic is close to that among Jews, who expect Elijah—who never died but went to heaven in a chariot of fire, according to 2 Kings—to return.

Second, one verse of the Qur'an (Q 43:61) can be read to mean that Jesus is "knowledge"—or, according to a variant, a "portent"—"of the Hour." In other words, at least according to the standard interpretation, the coming of the "Last Hour" will be known by the descent of Jesus from heaven. And so it was concluded that Jesus must come back before history will end.

But there is another important point to make about the Islamic "end times" scenario: only after Jesus returns and the dead are raised will souls be sent to heaven or hell. In other words (and unlike Christian thinking), according to the Qur'an the reward or punishment of humans does not take place immediately upon death. At death, the soul falls into a sort of sleep. The period between the death of humans and their resurrection from the dead—a period known as *barzakh* in Islamic tradition—is merely a time of waiting for the Day of Judgment.[5]

This does not mean, however, that nothing will happen to the dead during this time. In fact, certain Islamic traditions relate that a "torture of the grave" will take place during *barzakh*. According to these traditions two angels known as Munkir and Nakir (not found in the Qur'an) will impose punishments upon sinners in their tombs. Some accounts relate that these angels will ask certain questions of the dead about the Islamic faith, and for each wrong answer the angels will strike them with a hammer.

Another tradition relates that while bodies lie in the tomb, souls will be taken away and dwell mysteriously all together under the Dome of the Rock in Jerusalem—in a spot known as the "Well of Souls." One legend reports that if you descend into the chamber below the rock in the dome and put your ear to the rock wall, you will hear the dead speaking.

What the Qur'an itself teaches is that on the Day of Judgment the soul will be awoken, the body will be raised, and the two will be united. At this, the individual, regaining consciousness, will feel as though only a moment has passed. Thus, if most Christians believe in something that might be called "immediate retribution" (that souls will be sent to heaven or hell after an individual judgment after death), most Muslims believe that a "delayed retribution" will take place only after the collective resurrection of the dead on the Day of Judgment.

The Sleep of Souls

This notion that souls will fall "asleep" at death is vividly depicted in two qur'anic stories. The first of these is contained in one verse of Sura 2 and has to do with a man and his donkey:

> Or him who came upon a township as it lay fallen on its trellises. He said, "How will God revive this after its death?!" So God made him die for a hundred years, then He resurrected him. He said, "How long did you remain?" Said he, "I have remained a day or part of a day." He said, "No, you have remained a hundred years. Now look at your food and drink which have not rotted! Then look at your donkey! [This was done] that We may make you a sign for mankind. And now look at the bones, how We raise them up and then clothe them with flesh!" When it became evident to him, he said, "I know that God has power over all things." (Q 2:259)

The man in this story (which is connected to a Jewish tale about Jerusalem)[6] has no sense that a hundred years has passed: he feels as though it has been only "a day or part of a day" since he died, or "fell asleep," so he is surprised to learn that he has slept for one hundred years. According to the Qur'an this is what the experience of death will be like: we will fall "asleep" and will be "woken up" on the Day of Judgment. Yet even if a hundred (or a million) years have passed, we will experience this time as though it were "a day or part of a day."

A similar expression is found in the second story, which involves a number of young men—also accompanied by an animal (this time a dog)—who take refuge in a cave. This story is related to a Christian tale about Ephesus, a city in modern-day Turkey. In the Christian tale the drama surrounds the transformation of the city from a pagan city, with a persecuted Christian minority, into a Christian city filled with crosses. The young men are Christians who flee from persecution (or, more precisely, from being compelled to perform sacrifices to pagan gods) during the reign of the Christ-hating emperor Decius (d. 251). God casts a miraculous sleep upon them until they are "woken" (or raised from the dead) during the reign of the Christ-loving emperor Theodosius II (d. 450). Entering into the town they are amazed to see Ephesus transformed into a city of churches where pagan temples once stood.

In the qur'anic version of this tale all of these details are stripped away (the author of the Qur'an was not interested in the triumph of Christianity), but the lesson about the resurrection of the dead remains. The qur'anic version turns on the experience of a group of young men (and their dog)[7]—their exact number is never specified by the Qur'an. Faced with persecution for their faith in God, these young men seek refuge in a cave where God casts "sleep" upon them (sleep in this story again works as a metaphor for death). Although they wake up 309 years later, their sensation is much like the man with his donkey who slept for one hundred years:

> So it was that We aroused them [from sleep] so that
> they might question one another. One of them said,
> "How long have you stayed [here]?" They said, "We
> have stayed for a day, or part of a day." They said,
> "Your Lord knows best how long you have stayed."
> (Q 18:19)

All of this has happened, the divine voice of the Qur'an explains, not for the sake of the young men, but for the sake of
the people of the city who find them. These people (left unnamed) become witnesses of God's power to raise the dead
when they encounter the young (or actually, very old) men
who have been awoken. They (and thereby the Qur'an's audience) are meant to learn that the threat of the apocalypse—the
"Hour"—is not made in vain: "So it was that We let them come
upon them, so that they might know that God's promise is indeed true, and that there is no doubt in the Hour" (Q 18:21).

This notion of the "sleep of souls" thus stands at the center of the qur'anic scenario of how humans are judged and sent
to their eternal fates. This scenario is brought together neatly
in Q 50:

1. Angels record the merits and faults of humans
   during their lives (vv. 16–18):

   "Certainly We have created man and We know
   to what his soul tempts him, and We are nearer
   to him than his jugular vein. When the twin re-
   corders record [his deeds], seated on the right
   hand and on the left: he says no word but that
   there is a ready observer beside him."

2. Then humans die (v. 19):

"The throes of death bring the truth: 'This is what you used to shun!'"

3. The trumpet of the Day of Judgment is sounded (v. 20):

"And the Trumpet will be blown: 'This is the promised day.'"

4. The dead come forth, escorted by angels (v. 21):

"Every soul will come accompanied by [two angels], a driver and a witness."

5. And they will then be punished (vv. 24–26):

"[The two accompanying angels will be told,] 'Cast every stubborn ingrate into hell, [every] hinderer of good, transgressor and sceptic, who had set up another god along with God and cast him into the severe punishment.'"

6. Or rewarded (vv. 31–34):

"And paradise will be brought near for the God-wary, it will not be distant [any more]: 'This is what you were promised. [It is] for every penitent and dutiful [servant] who fears the All-beneficent in secret and comes with a penitent heart. Enter it in peace! This is the day of immortality.'"

Notably, nothing happens between the death of humans (no. 2) and the sounding of the trumpet on the Day of Judgment (no. 3). Souls are simply "asleep."

Certain elements of this qur'anic end times scenario are

known from the New Testament. For example, the idea that
a trumpet will be blown to announce the Day of Judgment
(v. 20; a role assigned by Islamic tradition to an angel named
Israfil) is found in several New Testament passages.[8] Elsewhere
(Q 27:82) the Qur'an speaks of a "beast from the earth" that
will appear before the Day of Resurrection, something that
seems to be connected to the beasts in Revelation (see especially Rev 13:11). The Qur'an also speaks of "Gog and Magog"
being let loose (Q 21:96) before the end times, names that appear elsewhere in Revelation (Rev 20:7–8). Even the notion of
the "sleep of souls" is not entirely novel. In the Eastern, Syriac-
speaking church—the tradition that gives us the story of the
Sleepers of Ephesus—a similar idea was entertained by certain
writers.[9] Thus, qur'anic eschatology continues some Christian
themes even as it emphasizes certain elements, notably the resurrection of the body.

Arguments for the Resurrection of the Body

The centrality of the resurrection of the body to the Qur'an's
eschatology seems to explain why the Qur'an is so interested
elsewhere in developing logical arguments that God really
can—and really will—raise dead bodies. Few arguments are
more common in the Qur'an than the analogy that it makes
between God's ability to bring a dead body to life and the way
in which rain brings a barren land back to life:

> [17]So glorify God when you enter evening and when
> you rise at dawn. [18]To Him belongs all praise in the
> heavens and the earth, at nightfall and when you
> enter noontime. [19]He brings forth the living from

> the dead and brings forth the dead from the living,
> and revives the earth after its death. Likewise you
> [too] shall be raised [from the dead]. (Q 30:17–19;
> cf. Q 16:65, 43:11, 50:6–11, 57:17)

One can imagine that this argument would be meaningful in the arid climate of the Middle East. In many places, when autumn rains come after a long dry summer, one can see a barren landscape turn dramatically green.[10]

Elsewhere the Qur'an makes a different sort of argument for the resurrection of the body by comparing the original creation of humans with the "new creation" when they are raised from the dead. If God had the ability—so the argument goes—to create humans from dust in the beginning (keep in mind here the story of the creation of Adam from the earth), then he also has the ability to recompose those bodies that have decomposed and again become dust. Thus the Qur'an speaks of the resurrection as a "new creation":

> [98]That is their requital because they denied Our
> signs and said, "What, when we have become
> bones and dust, shall we really be raised in a new
> creation?" [99]Do they not see that God, who created
> the heavens and the earth, is able to create the like
> of them? (Q 17:98–99)

This argument is based on the analogy between the first creation and the resurrection. It might be compared to the words of a woman who appears in the deuterocanonical (or apocryphal) book 2 Maccabees. This woman, a mother, witnesses a number of her sons being martyred for their commitment to the Jewish law. She comforts one of them (soon to be killed too) by arguing that his initial creation by God suggests God's power to bring him back to life:

> [22]"I do not know how you appeared in my womb;
> it was not I who endowed you with breath and life,
> I had not the shaping of your every part. [23]And
> hence, the Creator of the world, who made every-
> one and ordained the origin of all things, will in
> his mercy give you back breath and life, since for
> the sake of his laws you have no concern for your-
> selves." (2 Macc 7:22–23)

Elsewhere in Sura 17 the Qur'an insists again in still more dramatic language on God's ability to re-create humans. God is not limited to "re-creating" from dust—he could remake humans from anything:

> [49]They say, "What, when we have become bones and
> dust, shall we really be raised in a new creation?"
> [50]Say, "[Yes, even if] you should become stones, or
> iron, [51]or a creature more fantastic to your minds!"
> They will say, "Who will bring us back?" Say, "He
> who originated you the first time." They will nod
> their heads at you and say, "When will that be?"
> Say, "Maybe it is near!"

This passage includes an important declaration at the end: *Maybe the resurrection is near!* This line is meant to leave the opponents of the Quran's reader in anxiety about the pros-pects of the coming of the eschatological hour.[11] If God has the ability to resurrect the dead, and if he will judge humans after their resurrection, then humans should know that their judgment could come at any moment. The conclusion is clear: now is the time to repent, not later.

Confronting the Doubters

In such passages we also see the Qur'an exhibiting one of its most typical rhetorical strategies: the "counterdiscourse."[12] The Qur'an quotes its opponents' skepticism and then provides a response. This strategy is again found in Q 19:66–67:

> [66]Man says, "What? Shall I be brought forth alive [from the grave] when I have been dead?" [67]Does not man remember that We created him before when he was nothing?

The use of counterdiscourse in such passages suggests that the Qur'an's author was particularly concerned about certain people who denied the resurrection. He found an effective way to respond to them by first quoting their arguments, and then offering refutations of them. We might compare the way the Qur'an operates in such passages to a trial lawyer who anticipates possible objections from the opposing attorney.

It is possible, of course, that these dialogues are not recordings of actual conversations but rather the Qur'an's own creation. To use a term from one twentieth-century Muslim scholar of the Qur'an, they may be more "literary truth" than "historical truth."[13] Actually, in some passages the Qur'an scripts dialogues that have not even happened yet—dialogues that will occur only on the Day of Resurrection.

In the scripts from the end of time we learn how the damned in hell will repent of their impiety, or their sinfulness, but that their repentance will be too late. In Sura 23 the Qur'an predicts that the damned (described as "those whose deeds weigh light in the scales," since they did not do enough good deeds to be worthy of paradise) will express regret. Their pleas will be rejected by God, who will respond harshly to them:

> [103] As for those whose deeds weigh light in the scales — they will be the ones who have ruined their souls, and they will remain in hell [forever]. [104] The Fire will scorch their faces, while they snarl, baring their teeth. [105] "Was it not that My signs were recited to you but you would deny them?" [106] They will say, "Our Lord! Our wretchedness overcame us, and we were an astray lot. [107] Our Lord! Bring us out of this! Then, if we revert [to our previous conduct], we will indeed be wrongdoers." [108] He will say, "Get lost in it, and do not speak to Me!"

The point of these passages is to persuade the Qur'an's audience that the time to repent and believe is now. Repentance on the Day of Judgment will be too late. The mercy of God will be exhausted, and only his wrath will remain.

Hell

The intensity of God's wrath is apparent in the images of hell the Qur'an paints. Not only does it describe hell as a place of painful torment (whether or not hell is a place of *everlasting* torment is an unresolved question to which we will return), it gives vivid details of what that torment will be like.

The Qur'an speaks of hell as "the punishment of the burning" (Q 22:9). Elsewhere, however, we learn that hell is not only about burning; the damned in hell will be compelled to eat of a terrible tree named Zaqqum, a tree with fruit like the heads of devils. They will also have a hot (very hot) drink to wash down their meal:

> [62]Is this a better reception, or the Zaqqum tree? [63]Indeed, We have made it a punishment for the wrongdoers. [64]It is a tree that rises from the depths of hell. [65]Its blossoms are as if they were devils' heads. [66]They will eat from it and gorge with it their bellies. [67]On top of that they will take a solution of scalding water. [68]Then their retreat will be toward hell. (Q 37:62–68)

In another passage—as though to increase the terror—the Qur'an even has hell speak: "The day when We shall say to hell, 'Are you full?' It will say, 'Is there any more?'" (Q 50:30).

Islamic tradition, perhaps influenced by a qur'anic passage (Q 15:44) which declares that hell has seven "gates," would eventually develop the idea that hell has seven levels. Each level was given a name based on terms for punishment found in qur'anic passages.[14] One of these, *jahannam,* is particularly interesting since it is connected to biblical vocabulary. *Jahannam* is related to the Greek New Testament term *geenna* or "Gehenna"—derived ultimately from the Hebrew term *ge hinnom,* "the valley of Hinnom"—the name of a valley on the outskirts of Jerusalem where pagan sacrifices once took place.

The vividness of the qur'anic hell is not shared with the New Testament, in which Jesus refers only in allusive ways to the punishment of the afterlife. The closest the Gospels get to descriptions of the punishment of hell are those passages that speak of "fire," "wailing," and "gnashing" of teeth. In the ex-

planation of the Parable of the Weeds (or "Tares") told in the
Gospel of Matthew, Jesus explains the following:

> [40]Just as the weeds are gathered and burned with
> fire, so will it be at the close of the age. [41]The Son
> of man will send his angels, and they will gather
> out of his kingdom all causes of sin and all evil-
> doers, [42]and throw them into the furnace of fire;
> there men will weep and gnash their teeth. (Matt
> 13:40–42)

The way that the Qur'an describes hell in particularly
vivid, gruesome terms brings us back to something we mentioned in Chapter 1, namely, that the Qur'an in many ways is a
"homiletic" work, a work written like a homily or sermon. The
Qur'an's intention is not simply to declare that those who disobey God will be punished, but to describe that punishment
in a way which brings the awfulness of hell to life. Similarly,
homilists in the early centuries of Christianity expanded dramatically on the New Testament allusions to hell. In a sermon
attributed to John Chrysostom (d. 407) we read a description
of hell with the sort of detail that we find in the Qur'an:

> It is a sea of fire—not a sea of the kind or dimen-
> sions we know here, but much larger and fiercer,
> with waves made of fire, fire of a strange and fear-
> some kind. There is a great abyss there, in fact, of
> terrible flames, and one can see fire rushing about on
> all sides like some wild animal. . . . There will be no
> one who can resist, no one who can escape: Christ's
> gentle, peaceful face will be nowhere to be seen.[15]

Heaven

The vividness of the Qur'an's descriptions of hell is matched by the vividness of its descriptions of heaven. To enter the Islamic heaven (at least, according to the standard idea) is not to enter into some vague spiritual state of communion with the divine but to enter into a real place, a garden, with physical pleasures. The Qur'an regularly refers to heaven as *janna*, which is related to the Hebrew term *gan*, meaning "garden." Indeed, in a number of places the Qur'an speaks of heaven as the "garden of Eden" (*jannat 'adn*).[16]

In doing so it seems likely that the Qur'an is not simply comparing heaven to the biblical garden of Eden. Instead, the Qur'an means quite literally that the blessed will return to the very same garden in which Adam and Eve dwelled. There is reason to believe that the Qur'an conceives of this garden also existing in the heavenly realm (and not somewhere in Mesopotamia, as the Book of Genesis—which speaks of the Tigris and Euphrates rivers flowing through Eden—would suggest), for when it relates the expulsion of Adam and Eve (and the devil) from the garden, it has God send them *down* from the garden into the world.

While this does not match what we find in Genesis, it does match the way in which later Christians began to think of things. The Eastern church father Saint Ephrem (d. 373) thought of Eden as existing on the top of a "cosmic" mountain, the peak of which reached into heaven:

> With the eye of my mind
> I gazed upon paradise;
> > the summit of every mountain
> > is lower than its summit,

the crest of the Flood
reached only its foothills;
    these it kissed with reverence
    before turning back,
to rise above and subdue the peak
of every hill and mountain.
    The foothills of Paradise it kisses
    while every summit it buffets.[17]

Ephrem, like the author of the Qur'an, also thought of Eden as the destiny of the blessed after divine judgment. In the same work quoted above, *Hymns on Paradise,* Ephrem writes, "In the world there is struggle / in Eden a crown of glory."[18]

The Qur'an also refers to heaven with the fascinating term *firdaws,* a term that comes from Greek *paradeisos* (which itself comes from a Persian term)—from which we derive the English word "paradise." Originally, *firdaws* seems to have meant a walled garden. Here too we can find a certain connection with the New Testament. When Christ in Luke's Gospel says to the "good thief," "Today you will be with me in paradise," the word for paradise is none other than *paradeisos.*

Those who make it to the Islamic paradise will find there not only trees and rivers and the sort of things one might expect in a garden, but also a banquet. Elsewhere in the Gospel of Luke, at the Last Supper, Jesus says to his disciples, "I tell you that from now on I will not drink of the fruit of the vine until the kingdom of God comes." This suggests, of course, that there will be drinking of wine in paradise. Tellingly, while Islam forbids the drinking of alcohol during this life (although whether the Qur'an itself does so is less clear than it may seem), the Qur'an indeed promises that believers will be able to drink wine in the next life. For example, Sura 56 presents the blessed in the heavenly garden as follows:

> [15]On brocaded couches, [16]reclining on them, face to face. [17]They will be waited upon by immortal youths, [18]with goblets and ewers and a cup of a clear wine, [19]which causes them neither headache nor stupefaction.

This is not all that the blessed will enjoy in paradise. They will also be served "such fruits as they prefer and such flesh of fowls as they desire" (Q 56:20–21).

Javed Ahmad Ghamidi, a contemporary Muslim scholar from Pakistan, adds the following details to the qur'anic descriptions of paradise on the basis of hadith:

> The Prophet has further explained that the dwellers of Paradise shall eat and drink but will neither spit nor need to urinate or defecate; neither will there be any fluid coming out of the nose nor will there be any saliva and cough; even their sweat will smell of musk.[19]

The Qur'an's portrayal of paradise might be seen as a development of the New Testament idea of heaven as a wedding banquet. In Matthew 22 Jesus compares the "kingdom of heaven" to a man who gives a wedding banquet for his son. The Qur'an presents that wedding banquet in all of its detail, with wine, fruit, and poultry.

Yet one element of the qur'anic portrayal of the heavenly banquet seems to distinguish the Islamic scripture from the Bible—the notion that certain servants, called "immortal youths," will be at the banquet. What is more, if we read a bit farther in Sura 56, we find that female servants are also in paradise—and these females, apparently, are not there only to serve food: "and big-eyed houris like guarded pearls, a reward for what they used to do" (Q 56:22–24). The term "houri" is a simple transliteration of the Arabic term *hur* that appears here and elsewhere to refer to heavenly females who are apparently present for the sexual pleasure of male believers.[20] Here they are described as a "reward" for the believers. Elsewhere the Qur'an declares that God will "marry" the believers to these women (Q 52:20).

The term "houri" means "white." The use of this term to refer to the maidens of paradise is usually explained as a reference to the white in the eyes of these maidens (the idea being that their eyes are large—thought of as a beautiful feature—and so the whites show distinctly), but it is not clear that this is exactly what the Qur'an means. One scholar—writing under a pseudonym because he believed his ideas were too controversial—argued famously that "white" here is not connected at all to eyes or even to women. The Qur'an, he believed, is referring to "white *grapes*." By his telling, it is only fruit, and not females, that the believers will receive in paradise.[21] This opinion has not caught on among scholars, in part because the Qur'an refers to these maidens of paradise with terms other than "houri" as well. Later in the same Sura we find them described as "spouses": "and noble spouses. We have created them with a special creation, and made them virgins, loving, of a like age" (Q 56:34–37).

The appearance of maidens of paradise in the Qur'an led early Muslim men to all sorts of speculation about what exactly those maidens are like. Some traditions relate that they have the name of God inscribed on one breast and the name of the believer for whom they are waiting in paradise on the other. Other traditions insist that God grants these maidens virginity anew whenever they have sex with their designated believer (a view connected to the interpretation of Q 56:36, "and made them virgins," quoted above). Another hadith relates, "If a woman from among the people of Paradise were to look at the people of this earth, she would light up all that is in between them and fill it with fragrance."[22] In an online juridical opinion, or fatwa, on the topic, one Muslim scholar reports that men will have a special power to enjoy these maidens in paradise: "A man will be given the strength of a hundred men to eat, drink, feel desire and have sexual intercourse."[23]

Certain currents of Islamic thought, notably the Ash'ari school (about which we will learn more in later chapters), insist that there is also another, more spiritual pleasure to be had in paradise: a vision of God himself. As we have seen, Q 75:23 speaks of the blessed as "gazing upon their Lord" and could be used to defend this teaching. On the other hand, Moses is twice told in the Qur'an (Q 6:104 and 7:143) that he will not be able to see God. Those who defend the doctrine of the "vision" (Arabic ru'ya) of God often turn to the hadith. One hadith relates that the veil between the believers and God will be lifted on the Day of Resurrection so that the faithful will gaze upon God's face.[24]

To certain scholars this experience of divine vision is greater than the material pleasures of paradise. It is a "spiritual reward higher than the material fulfilment of personal desires and wishes."[25] For the most part, however, even those who follow the idea that there will be a spiritual reward in paradise do not deny that there will also be physical delights.

But what about Muslim women in paradise? If the men have maidens, what will women have? The Qur'an is clear that

women will also be admitted into paradise: "God has promised the faithful, men and women, gardens with streams run-
ning in them, to remain in them [forever], and good dwellings in the Gardens of Eden" (Q 9:72). According to one
widespread opinion, Muslim women will be transformed into
young women and thereby please their husbands anew. This
much is suggested by a story, quoted by the Qur'an commentator Zamakhshari (d. 1144), about an old woman who asks
the Prophet Muhammad to pray that she might go to paradise:

> An old woman said to the Messenger of God: "Ask
> of God that he will bring me into the heavenly gar-
> den." He said, "No old woman may enter the heav-
> enly garden." So she went away crying. Then he
> said, "Tell her that on that day she will no longer be
> an old woman!"[26]

We might note how all of these traditions are meant to
make humans yearn for paradise and fear hell. The Qur'an,
from this regard, is a profoundly psychological work. Like a
Christian preacher, like John Chrysostom or Saint Ephrem,
the author of the Qur'an speaks of heaven and hell to persuade
his audience to repent and believe. He does so in a way, however, that is distinct—emphasizing physical pain and physical pleasure in order, apparently, to make a greater impression
on his audience. He puts a terrible tree into hell and young
women in paradise.

All of this detail about heaven and hell, however, still
leaves a very important question unanswered: How does a person end up in one and not in the other? We begin to answer
this question in the following chapter.

II
Mercy

4

Divine Mercy

*The Lord God in Islam does not pursue His creatures with bellig-
erance and enmity as do the Gods of Olympus in their outbursts
and fits of fury as is depicted in Greek tales. He does not arrange
vengeful schemes against them as in the counterfeit tales of the
Old Testament.*

— *Sayyid Qutb,* In the Shade of the Qur'an

An Islamic tradition tells the story of prisoners of war
who were brought before the Prophet Muhammad.
One captive woman among them was nursing an
infant. When the Prophet noticed what she was
doing, he took the opportunity to teach a lesson about divine
mercy:

> "Do you think that this lady can throw her son in
> the fire?" We replied, "No, if she has the power not
> to throw it (in the fire)." The Prophet then said,

"Allah is more merciful to His slaves than this lady
to her son."[1]

This tradition in some ways reflects the spirit of the Qur'an,
which frequently calls God "the Compassionate, the Merciful
[al-rahman, al-rahim]." These two names usually appear first
in the lists of God's ninety-nine "beautiful" names.

The twentieth-century Indian politician and scholar Abu
Kalam Azad (d. 1958) writes that the Qur'an calls God both al-
rahman and al-rahim because it wants to "stamp" mercy "on
man's memory as the most obvious and conspicuous attribute
in the idea of God."[2] The contemporary scholar Mustansir
Mir puts things even more dramatically in a recent article on
mercy: "I would like to begin by making a statement that, I
hope, will not be taken as too radical, namely, that the God of
the Qur'ān has, essentially, only one attribute—that of mercy."[3]

In this chapter we evaluate Mir's claim, asking not so
much whether it is radical, but whether it is accurate. We
ask: What does the Qur'an mean exactly when it speaks of
God's mercy? Does God's mercy have any limits? How do the
Qur'an's declarations of God's mercy go together with its references to his vengefulness? Our answers to these questions will
show that the nature of divine mercy in Islam (as in other religions) is more complicated than it may seem at first.

In imagining that mercy is the only attribute of God, Mir
joins a trend in recent studies that emphasize God's gentleness, compassion, and providence and set aside his wrath or
judgment.[4] This does not mean that the notion of divine mercy
was not important to premodern Muslim thinkers as well. Mohammad Hassan Khalil notes that certain prominent classical
Muslim theologians emphasized God's mercy to the point of
predicting the salvation of non-Muslims (see Chapter 6).[5]

Among certain modern thinkers, however, one can detect a distinctive method of reading the Qur'an that avoids emphasizing divine judgment or wrath. For example, in *Major Themes of the Qur'an* the Pakistani scholar Fazlur Rahman (d. 1988) writes: "[God's] very infinitude implies not a one-sided transcendence but equally His being 'with' His creation; note that He is nearer to man than is man's jugular vein."[6] This image of the "jugular vein" comes straight out of the Qur'an, and Rahman uses it to suggest that the God of the Qur'an has a providential care for humans.

Yet when we actually read the qur'anic passage of the "jugular vein," we find that the message is more complicated than Rahman lets on:

> [16]Certainly We have created man and We know to what his soul tempts him, and We are nearer to him than his jugular vein. [17]When the twin recorders record [his deeds], seated on the right hand and on the left: [18]he says no word but that there is a ready observer beside him.
>
> [19]The throes of death bring the truth: "This is what you used to shun!" (Q 50:16–19)

The point of God's nearness in this passage is not providential care, but rather judgment. God is so near to humans that none of their misdeeds escape him.

This is not the only place where Rahman quotes the Qur'an out of context. Elsewhere he cites a famous passage (from Q 7:156) in which God declares, "My mercy embraces all things."[7] Rahman, however, leaves out the first part of the verse, which includes a divine threat: "Said He, 'I visit My punishment on whomever I wish, but My mercy embraces all things.'" Far from a clear statement on mercy, here the Qur'an offers us a theological paradox. On one hand, God insists that he punishes whomever he wishes, but on the other, he adds that his mercy "embraces all things." In what follows we will seek to unravel this paradox.

A God Named "the Compassionate"

The Qur'an is proclaimed in the name of God, "the Compassionate, the Merciful [al-rahman al-rahim]." Yet what this invocation means precisely is a bit of a problem. How are the terms *rahman* and *rahim*—terms that come from the same Arabic root—to be distinguished from each other? Mir argues that one term simply intensifies the other, as in the English phrase "pitch black."[8] On the other hand, certain classical Muslim scholars argue (with no clear evidence in the qur'anic text) that *rahman* refers to the mercy of God for all people (principally in the good things of nature), and the related term *rahim* refers to the mercy of God for believers only (principally in the forgiveness of sins).[9] A tradition involving Jesus expresses the same idea in a different way: Jesus declares that God is *rahman* in relation to things of this world and *rahim* in relation to things of the next world.[10]

But references to divine mercy abound elsewhere in the Qur'an as well. The Qur'an names God "forgiving" no fewer than ninety-one times.[11] It also uses a series of nouns to refer to the mercy of God, including favor (*ni'ma*), bounty (*fadl*), and forgiveness (*maghfira*).[12] On four occasions the Qur'an describes God as "Most merciful of the merciful."[13]

Most tellingly, perhaps, on fifty-six occasions the Qur'an simply names God *al-rahman,* "the Compassionate." This would seem to suggest that the Qur'an's idea of God is deeply intertwined with the concept of mercy. A closer analysis, however, complicates this suggestion in three ways. First, the name *al-rahman* is used for God in a number of verses in which God is *not* merciful.[14] This is the case with Q 19:45, in which Abraham tells his (pagan) father, "I am indeed afraid that a punishment from *al-rahman* will befall you, and you will become Satan's accomplice." This paradoxical use of *al-rahman* appears again in Q 21:42, where God commands the Prophet: "*Say,* 'Who can guard you, day and night, against [the punishment of] *al-rahman.*'"[15] Second, in the Qur'an the term *al-rahman* always appears with the definite article (*al*) and never as a simple adjective. And third, whereas *rahim* is used to refer to things other than God (e.g., in Q 9:128 Muhammad is *rahim*), *al-rahman* is used only to refer to God.

Together these things suggest that the Qur'an's author meant to use *al-rahman* principally as a proper noun for God. This possibility seems more likely in light of what we know from the evidence left behind on rocks by monotheists who lived in Arabia before Islam. Pre-Islamic Arabian rock inscriptions often refer to God, or God the Father in the Christian Trinity, with a version of the name *al-rahman*. In South Arabian the name appears as *rahmanan*.[16]

In North Arabia, too, God, or a god, was referred to as "the merciful." A North Arabian inscription (in a variety of Ancient North Arabian known as Safaitic) includes an appeal to a god who is referred to with a term related to Arabic *rahim* and *rahman*.[17] Thus, *al-rahman* (or other versions of it) seems simply to have been a typical way to refer to God in Arabia.[18]

God "Has Made Mercy
Incumbent upon Himself"

So is *al-rahman* "just a name"? If so, does this mean that the
Qur'an does not actually conceive of God as merciful? On the
contrary! The point is that the Qur'an emphasizes *both* divine
mercy and divine judgment. This is seen in Q 6:12:

> *Say,* "To whom belongs whatever is in the heavens
> and the earth?" *Say,* "To God. He has made mercy
> binding for Himself. He will surely gather you on
> the Day of Resurrection, in which there is no doubt.
> Those who have ruined their souls will not have
> faith."[19]

The reference here to God's mercy is sandwiched between
two other statements: first, that God possesses everything in
heaven and earth; and second, that God will gather everyone
together (presumably, to judge them) on the Day of Resurrection.[20] Something similar can be said about the second appearance—later in the same Sura—of a similar statement:

> When those who have faith in Our signs come to
> *you, say,* "Peace to you! Your Lord has made mercy
> incumbent upon Himself: whoever of you com-
> mits an evil [deed] out of ignorance and then re-
> pents after that and reforms, then He is indeed all-
> forgiving, all-merciful." (Q 6:54)[21]

Here, too, context is important. The Qur'an makes God's forgiveness conditional: God forgives those who have done evil
out of ignorance and who repent and reform themselves.

The God of the Qur'an may be merciful, but he is not un-conditionally forgiving.

In a passage related to a story found in Genesis, the Qur'an describes in Sura 15 how messengers came to give Abraham good news of a son (Isaac) in his old age. After receiving the good news Abraham exclaims, "Who despairs of his Lord's mercy except the astray?!'" (Q 15:56). The message is clear: some people, the "astray," *should* despair of God's mercy. This point is punctuated by what happens next in Qur'an 15: the "visitors" to Abraham continue on to the people of Lot, "a guilty people" (Q 15:58), and destroy them (an account related to the story of the destruction of Sodom and Gomorrah with "brimstone and fire" in Genesis 19). Thus some people receive God's mercy; others know only his wrath.

Types of Divine Mercy in the Qur'an: Creation

In his work *God, Muhammad and the Unbelievers*, David Marshall argues that divine mercy in the Qur'an is communicated in three different ways: through creation itself, through the sending of prophets, and through the forgiveness of sins.[22] Let's examine these categories more closely, beginning with creation.

According to the Qur'an the way in which God created the natural world is an expression of mercy. The Qur'an calls on its audience to recognize the good things in the world as blessings given by God.[23] A passage in Q 79 emphasizes the blessings of God in creation:

> [27]Is your creation more prodigious or that of the heaven He has built? [28]He raised its vault and fash-

ioned it, ²⁹and darkened its night, and brought forth
its daylight. ³⁰Thereafter He spread out the earth,
³¹bringing forth from it its water and pastures, ³²and
setting firmly its mountains, ³³as a [place of] suste-
nance for you and your livestock.

Humans are not simply to enjoy the fruits of the earth; they are
to think about them and recognize that they come from God.
They are even to think about their food:

> ²⁴Let man consider his food: ²⁵We pour down plen-
> teous water [from the sky], ²⁶then We split the earth
> making fissures in it ²⁷and make the grain grow in
> it, ²⁸as well as vines and vegetables, ²⁹olives and date
> palms, ³⁰and densely-planted gardens, ³¹fruits and
> pastures, ³²as a sustenance for you and your live-
> stock. (Q 80:24–32)

An Islamic saying attributed to Jesus sums up the
proper response to divine goodness in creation: "Even if God
Almighty had not decreed torment for sinning against Him,
it would [nonetheless] be fitting that He should not be disobeyed, out of gratitude for His bounty."²⁴

Izutsu comments that the proper human response to
divine signs is thankfulness (Arabic *shukr*). He calls this "the
human counterpart of the initial Divine goodness."²⁵ Failure
to be thankful has consequences. Tellingly, we find that the
above passage is followed by a description of divine judgment:

> ⁴⁰and some faces on that day will be covered with
> dust, ⁴¹overcast with gloom. ⁴²It is they who are the
> faithless, the vicious. (Q 80:40–42; cf. 16:79–84)

The Qur'an even calls on people to consider their own qualities as human beings. It describes human faculties as gifts from God. In Sura 16 the Qur'an declares:

> God has brought you forth from the bellies of your mothers while you did not know anything. He made for you hearing, eyesight, and hearts so that you may give thanks. (Q 16:78)

The Qur'an thus implies that humans should not take for granted their ability to see, or to hear, or to think and feel (if this is how we should understand the reference to hearts). These are all gifts of God, gifts that he was not obliged to give to humans, and gifts for which we should be thankful.

Elsewhere the Qur'an insists that humans tend *not* to be grateful for these gifts:

> *Say,* "It is He who created you, and made for you hearing, eyesight, and hearts. Little do you thank." (Q 67:23)[26]

Like spoiled children, humans tend to focus on what they don't have and ignore the many things they've been given and for which they should be thankful.

Sura 76 describes the creation of humans as a test, and a test with serious consequences:

> [2]We indeed created man from the drop of a mixed fluid so that We may put him to test, so We endowed him with hearing and sight. [3]We have indeed guided him to the way, be he grateful or ungrateful.

⁴We have indeed prepared for the faithless chains, iron collars and a blaze.

⁵Indeed, the pious will drink from a cup seasoned with camphor, ⁶a spring where God's servants will drink, making it gush forth as they please.

In other words, creation in the Qur'an is not simply an act of mercy or grace. The gifts of hearing and sight, we might say, come with strings attached. Humans better use them well, or else.

The qur'anic idea of creation as a sign might be compared to the perspective of Paul in the letter to the Romans. Paul insists that God and his power are evident to all in nature: "Ever since the creation of the world his invisible nature, namely, his eternal power and deity, has been clearly perceived in the things that have been made" (Rom 1:20). Like Paul, the Qur'an makes it clear that the good things of nature are evident to everyone. Some people recognize these blessings, and some do not. This scenario is played out in a verse on nature in Sura 16:

⁸¹It is God who made for you the shade from what He has created, and made for you retreats in the mountains, and made for you garments that protect you from heat, and garments that protect you from your [mutual] violence. That is how He completes His blessing upon you so that you may submit [to Him].

The Qur'an declares that humans, upon recognizing these blessings, should "submit" to God (the Arabic for "submit" is *tuslimun,* a term that can also mean "become Muslim").

One might compare these passages to the declaration of Jesus in the Gospel of Matthew according to which God shares the blessings of nature with both the good and the evil: "But I say to you, Love your enemies and pray for those who persecute you, so that you may be sons of your Father who is in heaven; for he makes his sun rise on the evil and on the good, and sends rain on the just and on the unjust" (Matt 5:44–45). In Matthew, Jesus asks that his audience imitate the goodness of God, which is given to *everyone* in nature. As God has blessed even the wrongdoers, so humans should love even their enemies.

Types of Divine Mercy in the Qur'an: Prophets

A second element of Allah's mercy is his choice to send prophets.[27] As a popular online mufti, or jurist, puts it, "One aspect of the Mercy of Allah to His slaves is that He sent the Messengers and revealed the Books and laws to organize their lives according to the ways of wisdom."[28]

God sends the prophet to humanity as a "warner" (Arabic *nadhir*) and a "herald of good news" (*bashir*) in order that humans might heed his message and go to heaven instead of hell. The divine voice of the Qur'an declares to Muhammad, "Indeed We have sent you with the truth, as a herald of good news and as a warner" (Q 2:119a; cf. Q 11:2–3, 22:48–51). By sending prophets, God offers humans a final chance to save themselves. If humans do not heed the signs they see in nature, perhaps they will heed the signs they hear recited by a prophet. Before he destroys unbelieving and wrongdoing peoples, God warns them, thereby giving them a chance to repent. This idea is found in Q 17:15, in which God says, "We do not punish [any community] until We have sent an apostle."

In a verse in Sura 21 God describes the "sending" of Muhammad himself as a kind of mercy: "We did not send you but as a mercy to all the nations" (Q 21:107). The Qur'an does not mean that Muhammad always acted with mercy (indeed, on occasion he was not merciful with his adversaries) but that Muhammad's prophetic ministry itself is a sort of mercy: he warned humans about hell and thereby helped them to get to heaven.

Here's another way to think about this: from the Qur'an's perspective, God had no obligation to send prophets—he had already given humans signs of his existence in nature. He could have left them alone to figure things out for themselves. But instead he chose to help humans still further by sending prophets to warn them of the dire consequences of a wrong decision. He chose to speak.

From this perspective one can also see how even the Qur'an's rhetoric on the gruesome punishments of hell, rhetoric that may be jarring to a first-time reader, can be seen as an expression of divine mercy. One might compare qur'anic rhetoric on divine punishment to films that a driving school might show of the terrible accidents and injuries caused by drinking and driving. When I was learning to drive, I was upset by such disturbing footage, but I learned the lesson about drinking and driving precisely because the films were disturbing. Similarly, it is not very pleasant to read the qur'anic descriptions of the torments of the damned in hell, but they serve as a warning and may save one's soul.

All of this does not take us very far from the way in which classical Muslim theologians thought of divine grace (Arabic *lutf*). Qadi 'Abd al-Jabbar (d. 1025), a theologian from a school known as the Mu'tazila, argues that God is obliged by his just nature to help humans fulfill the commands that he has im-

posed on them.[29] He classifies all of the things that God does
to this end under the category of *lutf*.[30] Among these things are
"health, wisdom, the use of reason, prophecy, and the provi-
sion of holy books."[31] The point of *lutf* is that it helps humans
to believe and repent without *compelling* them to do so. The
threat of hell does just that. Thus 'Abd al-Jabbar writes: "As
for the threat of hell, it is a favor (*lutf*) to humans tasked with
obedience from God Most High, as is the repeating of it in the
book of God Most High, and as are the statements with mention of the exhorting servants, blaming them, and reproaching
them, in the rest of the Book, in the ways that they appear in
the Qur'an. This is a favor (*lutf*) and a goodness."[32] Even hell,
then, becomes an element of divine mercy.

The notion that God's sending of prophets is an expression of his mercy is emphasized by the prominent twentieth-
century Indian scholar Abu l-Hasan 'Ali Nadwi. For Nadwi the
souls admitted to paradise "could not attain this coveted place
by dint of their own intelligence, academic accomplishment or
personal effort." This is why God sends prophets: "Allah does
not descend to the earth to guide each and every human being.
Nor does He take anyone's hand in His in order to show him
the way to Paradise. Instead, He has devised certain ways for
man's guidance. Of these the most prominent is His arrange-
ment of sending down His Messengers who come with the
truth." Without the prophets, Nadwi concludes, "Man would
have been lost in error."[33]

This perspective leads to certain theological questions,
namely, why God did not send more prophets to more peoples,
and why God did not send any prophets after Muhammad. In
2014 I discussed the "punishment stories" in the Qur'an as part
of a lecture at the University of Oxford. During the question-
and-answer period the Muslim chaplain of the university cited

an Islamic tradition (not found in the Qur'an) that God has sent 124,000 prophets to earth. His point was that God gave humans plenty of chances to repent before destroying them. Now the Qur'an claims that God sent a prophet to every group of people ("There is an apostle for every nation" [Q 10:47]), but in reality many peoples (say, in the Amazon Basin) have never heard of Islam, let alone a Muslim prophet. And even if God had sent a prophet to each nation, would one prophet be enough? One wonders why other generations of that nation (earlier or later) would not receive a prophet. One might also ask about the fate of children and others in the cities that were destroyed: Were they also swallowed up in divine wrath? These are perhaps questions best left for Muslim theologians concerned with "theodicy"—the problem of evil—to contemplate.

Types of Divine Mercy in the Qur'an: Repentance and Forgiveness

Divine mercy is not exhausted with the sending of prophets. The Qur'an also speaks of a third aspect of God's mercy: forgiveness of sins.

Sura 40—known under the title "the Forgiver"—speaks of God as "Forgiver of sins and acceptor of repentance, severe in retribution, [yet] all-bountiful" (Q 40:3a). Here, divine forgiveness is tied up with a number of other concepts, including repentance and even the notion of God's "retribution" (something we will get to in Chapter 8). Later in Sura 40 the angels are interceding for humans. Notably, however, they do not ask that God forgive *all* humans:

> Those who bear the Throne and those who are around it celebrate the praise of their Lord and have

faith in Him, and they plead for forgiveness for the
faithful: "Our Lord! You embrace all things in Your
mercy and knowledge. So forgive those who repent
and follow Your way and save them from the punishment of hell." (Q 40:8)

Thus the angels ask God to forgive those who "repent."
Here and elsewhere the notion of repentance is expressed in
the Qur'an with the root *t-w-b*.[34] The related noun *tawba* is
perhaps best thought of as a sort of "return." This perspective
helps explain why the Qur'an uses the verbal phrase *taba ila*
for humans who "return" to God and the verbal phrase *taba
'ala* (e.g., Q 3:128 and 33:24) for God's return to humans. God's
desire for repentance is found in the divine name *al-tawwab*
(Q 4:64, 9:118, 24:11, 29:12), "the oft-returning" (also used of
humans [Q 2:222] who repent repeatedly). God, in his very
nature, desires to "return" to humans. The idea is expressed in
dramatic fashion in a hadith which suggests that God actually
values sin because it allows him to forgive: "If you had no sins
for God to forgive, God would have brought another people
who have sins so that He might forgive them."[35]

While the Qur'an usually relates that humans need to
"return" to God in order for him to "return" to them, Q 9:118
puts things the other way around. Speaking of three believers
who disobeyed God (most traditional reports identify them as
three men who refused to join Muhammad on a distant military campaign), the Qur'an relates, "[God] turned clemently
toward them so that they might be penitent." God, in other
words, acted first.

In places, the Qur'an suggests that even the prophets are
in need of repentance and divine forgiveness: God returns to
Adam (Q 2:37, 20:122); Abraham and Ishmael pray that God

will return to them (Q 2:128); Moses repents for asking God to show himself (Q 7:143); Jonah seems to repent for his anger against God in a declaration of regret (Q 21:87).

In Q 4:17–18 we find the necessity of human penitence as a condition of divine forgiveness stated clearly:

> [17][Acceptance of] repentance by God is only for those who commit evil out of ignorance and then repent promptly. It is such whose repentance God will accept, and God is all-knowing, all-wise. [18]But [acceptance of] repentance is not for those who go on committing misdeeds: when death approaches any of them, he says, "I repent now." Nor is it for those who die while they are faithless. For such We have prepared a painful punishment.

Here the Qur'an suggests not only that God refuses to forgive the unrepentant, but also that he refuses to forgive those who repent on their deathbeds. This idea found its way into a hadith in which Muhammad declares, "God (powerful and mighty) will accept the repentance of a servant until the moment when he gurgles" (the sound of a dying person in their final moments or death throes).[36] Sinners or unbelievers on the verge of dying are already condemned. It is too late for them.

Thus the third type of mercy, forgiveness, is for sinners who repent and unbelievers who convert (and don't wait too long to do so).[37] Forgiveness is their reward.

Put otherwise, "repentance" for unbelievers—and also for "hypocrites" (Q 4:145–46, 9:74) or apostates (Q 3:86–90)—means coming to believe in God. Earlier in this book we learned about the "unforgivable sin" of the Qur'an—*shirk*, that is, polytheism, or the association with God of something that is not God. If polytheism is an unforgivable sin, then it makes sense that we find Jesus declare in the Qur'an that those guilty of this sin are condemned to hell: "Indeed, whoever ascribes partners to God, God will forbid him [entry into] paradise and his refuge will be the Fire, and the wrongdoers will not have any helpers" (Q 5:72).[38]

Who, then, can be forgiven? Not everyone. Indeed, and as David Marshall concludes, God's forgiveness in the Qur'an is principally for believers: "Although God is prepared to forgive the unbelievers if they repent, considered as unbelievers they are worthless in his sight."[39]

Believers and Unbelievers

But there is a suggestion in the Qur'an of a special way by which some can be saved. Sura 4:64 seems to hint that Muhammad could play a role in interceding for those who would otherwise face condemnation on the Day of Judgment. Here the Qur'an's audience is told not only to ask God for forgiveness, but also to ask the prophet to ask God to forgive them:

> We did not send any apostle but to be obeyed by God's leave. Had they, when they wronged themselves, come to *you* and pleaded to God for forgiveness, and the Apostle had pleaded forgiveness for them, they would have surely found God clement and merciful.

Passages like this one would lead to the development of a whole series of traditions, some of which are set on the Day of

Judgment, that give Muhammad a special role in interceding for sinful believers (more on this later in the book).

Yet there are certain people for whom Muhammad cannot intercede. In Q 63:6, a passage that refers to hypocrites (those who pretend to believe while hiding their disbelief), the divine voice of the Qur'an tells the Prophet: "It is the same for them whether *you* plead for forgiveness for them, or do not plead for forgiveness for them: God will never forgive them. Indeed, God does not guide the transgressing lot."[40] In Q 4:88 God seems to reprimand Muhammad for wanting to lead back to the light those whom God has led away into darkness: "Do you desire to guide someone God has led astray?" Qur'an 9:80 insists that God will not forgive unbelievers even if the Prophet intercedes on their behalf:

> Whether you plead forgiveness for them or do not plead forgiveness for them, even if you plead forgiveness for them seventy times, God will never forgive them because they defied God and His Apostle; and God does not guide the transgressing lot.

This passage is especially interesting because it seems to have an echo in the Gospels. In Matthew 18 we find the following dialogue:

> [21]Then Peter came up and said to him, "Lord, how often shall my brother sin against me, and I forgive him? As many as seven times?" [22]Jesus said to him, "I do not say to you seven times, but seventy times seven."

There does not seem to be a direct relationship between Q 9:80 and Matt 18:21–22. In the Qur'an the question is whether God will forgive an unbeliever; in Matthew the question is whether believers should forgive those who sin against them. However, one assumes that the Qur'an is indirectly connected to this Gospel passage (why else, one might ask, would the Qur'an's author decide on the number "seventy"?).[41]

Muhammad is not the only one who is supposed to refrain from praying for unbelievers. According to the Qur'an *all* believers should refrain from praying for the forgiveness of unbelievers.[42] In Sura 9, the Qur'an declares that one should not even pray for unbelieving members of one's own family: "The Prophet and the faithful may not plead for the forgiveness of the polytheists, even if they should be [their] relatives, after it has become clear to them that they will be the inmates of hell" (9:113). In the next verse the Qur'an, as though answering a possible objection, explains why Abraham did at one point pray for his unbelieving father (named Terah in the Bible, Azar in the Qur'an):

> [114]Abraham's pleading forgiveness for his father
> was only to fulfill a promise he had made him. So
> when it became clear to him that he was an enemy
> of God, he repudiated him. Indeed, Abraham was
> most plaintive and forbearing.

Abraham's prayer for his pagan father, which the Qur'an quotes in other places, is thus an exception that proves the rule.[43]

The qur'anic teaching on prayer for unbelievers is followed by later Islamic tradition, according to which Muslims may pray for the *guidance* of unbelievers, that is, for their conversion to Islam, but not for their forgiveness.[44] The medieval Muslim scholar al-Wahidi (d. 1075) relates a poignant story about the Prophet Muhammad that is meant to illustrate the Qur'an's teaching of not praying for unbelievers:

> The Messenger of Allah went out one day to look at the graveyards and we went out with him. He ordered us to sit and then proceeded across until he stopped at one particular grave. He spoke to it for a long time and then the Messenger of Allah wept loudly and we wept for his weeping. After a while, he came toward us and was met by 'Umar ibn al-Khattab [the second caliph] who asked him: "O Messenger of Allah, what has made you cry, for we also cried and we were also scared?" He came toward us, sat with us and then said: "My weeping made you scared?" We said: "Yes, O Messenger of Allah!" He said: "The grave you saw me talking to is the grave of Aminah bint Wahb [Muhammad's mother]. I sought permission from my Lord to visit her and He allowed me to do so. Then, I asked His permission to pray for her forgiveness and He did not grant it. The words of Allah . . . were revealed and I was seized by the tenderness which a son has toward his mother. This is the reason why I wept."[45]

According to this story, the Qur'an's teaching on unbelievers was challenging even for Muhammad. It brought him to tears, but he still obeyed God.

In some places the Qur'an's teaching seems to go beyond not praying for unbelievers and include not befriending them, even if they are among one's own family: "You will not find a people believing in God and the Last Day endearing those who oppose God and His Apostle even though they be their own parents, or children, or brothers, or kinsfolk" (Q 58: 22a; cf. 9:23). Qur'an 60:1 illuminates this idea still further, explaining that unbelievers are the enemies of God: "O you who have faith! Do not take My enemy and your enemy for allies, [secretly] offering them affection" (cf. Q 3:28). If these unbelievers are the enemies of God, it follows that they should be the enemies of believers as well.

Today many commentators read these passages as reflections of a time when the Prophet Muhammad's community was engaged in military conflict with nonbelievers. In that context there was no possibility of forming alliances with the enemy. But now, they would say, things are different: when Muslims are not at war with their non-Muslim neighbors, there is no problem being friends with them.[46]

Divine Signs and Divine Guidance

David Marshall concludes that according to the Qur'an unbelievers are in a "paradoxical position."[47] Inasmuch as they are part of the human race, they receive the first two types of divine mercy (the blessings of nature and the ministry of prophets), but inasmuch as they have refused to believe, they are cut off from divine forgiveness, the third type of divine mercy. One way of resolving this paradox is to conclude that the first two sorts of mercy—creation and the sending of prophets—are only provisional.

God gives the blessings of nature to humans *in order that* they might reflect on those blessings and believe. On creation, Toshihiko Izutsu writes, "The Koran may be regarded in a certain sense as a grand hymn in honor of Divine Creation."[48]

Yet the Qur'an points to creation not simply to emphasize its
marvels or to give glory to the creator. It points to creation
in order to evoke a human response. Creation is a sign (Arabic *aya*). The Qur'an refers to creation always and only for the
sake of its larger argument about obedience to God (and his
Prophet). Elsewhere Izutsu seems to capture this idea when
he writes: "Just as a waymark must not cause a traveler to rivet
his eyes on itself, but direct him towards a certain place which
is the real destination of his travel, so every natural phenomenon, instead of absorbing our attention, as a natural phenomenon, and transfixing it immovably to itself, should act always
in such a way that our attention be directed towards something
beyond it."[49]

Similarly, God sends prophets to humans *in order that*
humans might listen to them and have faith. Prophets, then,
also provide "signs" (note that a verse in the Qur'an is also
named *aya*).[50] In Sura 7 the Qur'an describes the revelation
that the Prophet has brought as a mercy, but tellingly it makes
this revelation a mercy *only* for those who have faith: "Certainly We have brought them a Book which We have elaborated
with knowledge, as guidance and mercy for a people who have
faith" (Q 7:52).[51] The commentary known as *Tafsir al-Jalalayn*
appropriately defines mercy (*rahma*) as "to want what is good
for those who deserve it."[52]

The notion of divine "signs" might help us understand
the interest of the Qur'an in another category: *jahl*. This
term is usually translated as "ignorance," but it is not simple
ignorance. It is above all an inability to recognize the signs
of God.[53] It is in this sense that the era of the pagan Arabs is
called *Jahiliyya* ("era of ignorance").[54] This term doesn't mean
that the pre-Islamic Arabs were "ignorant" in the sense of lack-
ing knowledge or understanding. They weren't stupid. But they

did not recognize the signs of the one true God in creation. Of course, the history of these pre-Islamic Arabs was written from the perspective of later Muslims who sought to glorify Islam and vilify paganism. We can only imagine that the pre-Islamic Arabs themselves would object to the category of *jahl* that Islamic tradition attributed to them.

Thus from the perspective of the Qur'an the mercy of Allah is not about universal forgiveness. It is principally about the sending of "signs." These signs are "the concrete expression of the Divine intention to guide mankind to the right path."[55] God's mercy, one might say, is largely equivalent to his guidance.[56] However, in what follows we will see that Allah does not only guide. He also leads astray.

5

Allah and the Fate of Sinners

Muslims must realize that all their actions are being watched by Allah Who is the embodiment of mercy and compassion.

—*Abu l-Hasan 'Ali Nadwi*, Guidance from the Holy Qur'an

On the road from Jeddah to Mecca in Saudi Arabia, travelers arrive at a point where a large blue sign instructs non-Muslims to turn off the road and continue in a different direction. All Muslims, however, are welcome in the Islamic holy city, whether or not they are righteous or pious. Whether they will also be welcome in the Islamic paradise is another question.

In the previous chapter we learned that the God of the Qur'an is merciful but that his mercy is not boundless. This chapter and the next concern those who seem to be left out of the Qur'an's promises of eternal bliss. In the next chapter we consider the fate of non-Muslims; here, we consider the fate of sinful Muslims.

One might object that the question of their fate might interest only theologians; but much of the recent violence in the Islamic world is justified by extremist groups which hold that certain Muslims are legitimate targets since—because of their teachings or practices—they have effectively become infidels. Yet the Qur'an never clearly addresses the fate of those who fall outside of the broad categories of "sinful unbelievers" and "righteous believers." The fate of those "in between," as Mohammad Hassan Khalil describes them, is unclear.

Two qur'anic passages are sometimes cited in this regard. Qur'an 35:32 simply refers to some people who are "average" (apart from those who do evil and those who do good works), without commenting on their fate. Qur'an 7:46–49 depicts a scene of the afterlife that includes a group of people who are with neither the inhabitants of heaven nor the inhabitants of hell. They are rather "on the heights." This "third" group of people might be *in between* heaven and hell, although it is also possible that they might be in an especially high and lofty position ("on the heights") *within* paradise. Alternatively, some Muslim scholars think of the "heights" as a sort of chamber where souls await entrance into heaven.[1]

With almost nothing to go on in the Qur'an, the problem of the in between was largely left to the speculation of Muslim scholars.[2] One solution they devised is thinking that although hell is a place of punishment, it is not a place of *permanent* punishment. Instead, it is a place of temporary, *therapeutic* punishment, where people are punished in order to be purified of their sins—akin to the Catholic idea of purgatory. This solution allowed scholars to imagine that certain sinners (or even certain unbelievers) would remain in hell for some amount of time as punishment for their sins but eventually would be set free. Hell is just a stop on the road to heaven.

Some scholars went even further and argued that all sinners, and all unbelievers, would eventually escape hellfire. By their view, hell will one day be empty.

Many Muslim scholars who considered these questions accordingly emphasized the role of divine mercy. The well-known theologian and mystic Abu Hamid al-Ghazali (d. 1111), for example, maintained that God's mercy is so vast that it cannot be judged with the "scales of formal reasoning."[3] This view of the ultimate triumph of divine mercy is consistent with a well-known hadith in which Muhammad speaks of an inscription above the throne of God: "When Allah created the creation, He wrote in His Book, which is with Him above the Throne: 'My mercy prevails over My wrath.'"[4]

Big Sins, Little Sins

The declarations in the Qur'an that God will punish sinners, or that he does not love wrongdoers, left Muslim theologians with an enigma. Are not all believers guilty of some sins? Certainly *everyone* cannot be doomed, as then what would be the point of paradise? How much sin is too much sin?

In addressing this enigma Muslim theologians tended to distinguish between major sins (*kaba'ir*) and minor sins (*sagha'ir*). Most Muslim theologians agreed that God might forgive believers who are guilty only of minor sins and admit them into paradise. This consensus was based in part on Q 53: 31–32:

> [31]To God belongs whatever is in the heavens and whatever is in the earth, that He may requite those who do evil for what they have done and reward those who do good with the best [of rewards].

> [32]Those who avoid major sins and indecencies,
> apart from [minor and occasional] lapses. *Your*
> Lord is indeed expansive in [His] forgiveness.

The problem, then, was the status of sinners guilty of major
sins. In the classic work on the subject Muhammad Shams al-
Din al-Dhahabi (d. 1348) identifies seventy major sins (the first
of which is "unbelief" itself).[5] Classical Muslim scholars debated fiercely the question of whether Muslims who are guilty
of major sins, but who continue to declare their faith in Islam,
fall into the category of unbelief (*kufr*) and are therefore hell-
bound and excluded from the mercy of God.

The early Muslim sect known as the Kharijites seems to
have asserted that this was the case.[6] The theological movement known as the Murji'a countered that sinners are still believers and insisted that it was God's right to forgive or punish
them in the afterlife as he wills. Another prominent theological
school, the Mu'tazila, held to what they called the "intermedi-
ate position," between the Kharijites and the Murji'a, insisting
that grave sinners can be called neither unbelievers nor believers (although they affirmed that these sinners would be punished in hell).

Eventually, the Kharijites, the Murji'a, and the Mu'tazila
would be largely overcome by still another theological school,
the Ash'ariyya, whose views we examine more closely below.
The Ash'ariyya agreed with the Murji'a that sinful Muslims are
still to be counted among the believers (although they also affirmed that such Muslims might be punished in the afterlife).
This position is articulated in the creed of the school's founder,
Ash'ari (d. 935), where he comments that faithful Muslims "do
not declare any of the people of the *qibla* [that is, Muslims who
pray toward Mecca] an unbeliever because of a sin which he

commits, such as adultery, theft and similar great sins."[7] This view seems to fall in line with certain hadith which declare that *all* true monotheists will go to heaven. For example, a hadith in the collection attributed to Muslim has one of Muhammad's companions ('Uthman—the third caliph) report, "The Messenger of Allah said, 'Whoever dies knowing that there is nothing worthy of worship except Allah, he will enter paradise.'"[8]

One can imagine that this theological position was constructed in part to avoid disorder in Islamic societies. According to Islamic doctrine, unbelievers are not simply to be spurned or reviled. Muslims are called on to fight them. Ash'ari, namesake of the Ash'ariyya (and a former Mu'tazilite), writes that Muslims "affirm the duty of Jihad against the polytheists from the time of God's sending of His Prophet until the last band which fights the Dajjal [the anti-Christ] and after that."[9] While this declaration is anyway problematic (especially if you are a polytheist), it would be especially so if all gravely sinful Muslims were suddenly to fall within the category of unbelief. The possibilities for civil strife would be endless.

Tradition-minded scholars associated with the Hanbali legal school, sometimes referred to as *ahl al-hadith* ("the Party That Adheres to Prophetic Tradition"), tended to be still less capacious than the Ash'ariyya in their definitions of the community of believers. Many scholars in this movement held that certain sects that claim to be Muslims—including Shi'ites (to whom they may refer with the derogatory term "Rafida," or "those who reject")—are unbelievers. Some contemporary Salafis, those fundamentalist Muslims who may or may not identify with the Hanbali school, are even more restrictive. The Saudi imam Muhammad al-Munajjid, for example, considers any Muslims who do not pray to have crossed over the line into unbelief.[10] They are not simply sinners or wrongdoers; they are infidels.

In some contemporary discourse these ancient theological schools of Islam have become relevant again. In their efforts to delegitimize radical groups such as ISIS, certain Muslim scholars—including Ibrahim al-Hudhud, former president of Al-Azhar University in Cairo, have compared them to the Kharijites.[11] Their point is that by declaring so many Muslim groups to be apostates, or unbelievers, ISIS has followed the precedent of the Kharijites, who considered grave sinners to have left the fold of Islam.

The propaganda agents of ISIS have responded in the following way: unlike the ancient Kharijites, they do not consider all grave sinners to be apostates; their problem is with those who have false *beliefs* or who have abandoned the "pillars" of Islamic practice (profession of faith, prayer, almsgiving, fasting, and pilgrimage).[12] Thus old theological arguments have returned in the modern day.

The Fate of Sinful Muslims

As for those groups who hold that believers guilty of major sins remain in the fold of Islam, they are still left with the problem of how such sinners will be judged in the next life. The Qur'an, after all, seems to make it clear that those who refuse to act righteously will be condemned for their sin: "We shall say to those who did wrong, 'Taste the punishment of the Fire which you used to deny'" (Q 34:42; cf. 39:24). The Qur'an makes the "tree of hell" known as Zaqqum (see Chapter 3) "a punishment for the wrongdoers" (Q 37:63). Elsewhere the Qur'an describes the punishment of wrongdoers with dramatic language:

Even if the wrongdoers possessed all that is on the
earth and as much of it besides, they would offer it
on the Day of Resurrection to redeem themselves
with it from a terrible punishment, and there will
appear to them from God what they had never
reckoned. (Q 39:47)

Such passages seem to leave little, if any, hope for the salvation of wrongdoers. The Muʿtazila held that God has clearly
made his judgment known in the Qur'an and that humans,
who are rational beings capable of understanding God's word,
are to be judged according to their obedience to that word.
All of this implied that it is possible to know who is going to
heaven and who is going to hell, a principle known among the
Muʿtazila as "the Promise and the Threat." As Marcia Hermanson relates, this principle "asserted that an individual's eternal
fate may be at least to some extent rationally ascertained on the
basis of God's promise to reward the good person and punish
the evildoer."[13]

Yet the Qur'an also insists that God has the right to punish and forgive whomever he pleases (see more below). Qur'an
17:54 declares: "Your Lord knows you best. He will have mercy
on you if He wishes, or punish you, if He wishes."[14] This sort of
declaration seems to lead to the opposite conclusion, namely,
that God's judgment is ultimately inscrutable, precisely the
conclusion of those Muslim theologians who had a limited
view of the human capacity to understand God and his ways.

On the fate of sinful believers Hanbalis tended to affirm
God's prerogative to save whom he wills. An early Hanbali
creed (ʿaqida) attributed to the namesake of the school, Ahmad
b. Hanbal (d. 855), reports a hadith in which Muhammad says,
"If someone meets (God) persisting in his sin and not repent-

ing of it, then his affair is for God (to decide); if He wills, He punishes him, and if He wills, He pardons him, provided he died adhering to Islam and the Sunna."[15]

On this point the Ash'ariyya tended to agree. Ash'ari himself unambiguously defended the right of God to punish or forgive a believer guilty of grave sins. He writes the following about the teaching of orthodox Muslims:

> They do not bear witness of Hell (being certain) for any great sinner, nor do they say that Paradise (is certain) for any monotheist, until it comes about that God has placed them where He willed. They say that the affair of these (people) belongs to God; if He wills, He punishes them, and if He wills, He forgives them.[16]

A similarly agnostic position on the fate of the sinful believer is found in the creed of another Sunni thinker, a contemporary of Ash'ari named Tahawi (d. 933):

> We hope for Paradise for the believers who do good, but we are not certain of it, and do not bear witness to them (as having attained it). We seek forgiveness for their evil deeds and we fear for them, but we do not despair of them. Certainty (of Paradise) and despair both turn people away from the religion, and the way of truth . . . lies between them.[17]

As the last line here suggests, this position is in part motivated by a concern to encourage piety. The key to piety is uncertainty. Muslims should hope for paradise and fear hell but be certain of neither.[18]

A Bridge over Hell

Yet what exactly will happen when the time for judgment arrives, when the trumpet is blown and the dead are raised? In answering this question many Muslim scholars began with Q 19:71–72:

> 71There is none of you but will come to it: a [matter that is a] decided certainty with your Lord. 72Then We will deliver those who are Godwary and leave the wrongdoers in it, fallen on their knees.

The phrase "come to it" was generally understood to mean that on the Day of Judgment all people will be brought to the verge of hell.[19] There, on the edge of hellfire, judgment will unfold.

Certain hadith relate that a bridge (known as the *sirat*) will appear above the fires of hell, and each person will be forced to walk across it, beginning with Muhammad and his community:

> On the Day of Resurrection, people will be gathered and He will order the people to follow what they used to worship. So some of them will follow the sun, some will follow the moon, and some will follow other deities; and only this nation (Muslims) will be left with its hypocrites. Allah will come to them and say, "I am Your Lord." They will say, "We shall stay in this place till our Lord comes to us and when our Lord will come, we will recognize Him." Then Allah will come to them again and say, "I am your Lord." They will say, "You are our Lord." Allah will call them, and As-Sirat (a bridge) will be

laid across Hell and I (Muhammad) shall be the first amongst the Apostles to cross it with my followers.[20]

Not everyone will make it to the other side of this bridge (which according to other traditions will be set up above the Kidron Valley in Jerusalem, between the Mount of Olives and the Temple Mount). Unbelievers and certain sinful Muslims will be pulled down by "hooks" into hell, but not all of them will be doomed forever. Angels will dive into the fire and seek out those sinful Muslims who nevertheless prayed to God. The angels will recognize them by marks on their foreheads formed from their repeated prostrations in prayer:

> Some people will be ruined because of their evil deeds, and some will be cut into pieces and fall down in Hell, but will be saved afterwards, when Allah has finished the judgments among His slaves, and intends to take out of the Fire whoever He wishes to take out from among those who used to testify that none had the right to be worshipped but Allah. We will order the angels to take them out and the angels will know them by the mark of the traces of prostration (on their foreheads) for Allah banned the fire to consume the traces of prostration on the body of Adam's son.[21]

In some places of the Islamic world today it is considered a sign of piety to have a callus on one's forehead from repeated prostrations in prayer. In some Arab countries this scar, or "bump," is known as a *zabiba*, a "raisin." According to this hadith, this "raisin" may save one on the Day of Judgment.

However, the "bridge" hadith leaves to the inscrutable will of God the question of which, or how many, sinful believers will be saved. Certain Muslim theologians took the position that *all* Muslims will be saved from hell. In one place Ghazali writes that true monotheists "will be taken out of Hell after punishment. By the grace of God no monotheist will remain in Gehenna and no monotheist will be everlastingly in Hell."[22]

Another hadith suggests that very few people will escape the fires of hell. According to this hadith God will tell Adam on the Day of Resurrection, "O Adam, send forth from your progeny the party of the Fire." Adam will ask, "How many, my Lord?" And God will respond, "999 out of every 1000."[23] Some Muslim thinkers, however, understood this hadith to mean that many of those who are cast into hell will eventually be taken out. How could a merciful God save so few among the people whom he created? Only one of every thousand? Ghazali argues that the "party of the Fire" in this hadith does not refer to "unbelievers who will remain in the Fire" but only to those who will be temporarily in the fire.[24]

Ghazali has a similar argument in his commentary on another hadith, according to which the Prophet said that his community will be divided into "seventy-odd" sects (the precise number differs in different versions of the hadith), "only one of which will be saved."[25] For Ghazali, however, what distinguishes this "one" sect is that its members will never encounter hell. Members of all the other sects will enter hell, but many will ultimately depart from it.[26]

Intercession of the Prophet

For most Ash'ari theologians, it is not only the mercy of God that will save Muslim sinners from hell; they will receive help from their Prophet in the form of intercession by Muhammad, or others (Arabic *shafaʿa*). Tahawi, for instance, says that certain sinful Muslims, thanks to intercession, will experience the punishment of hell for only a limited amount of time: "If He wills, out of His justice He punishes them in hell to the measure of their offence; then in His mercy, and at the intercession of the intercessors among the people obeying Him, He removes them from Hell and raises them to His paradise."[27]

The Qur'an sends mixed signals on the question of intercession. A number of qur'anic passages insist that no soul can bear the burdens of another, which might imply that intercession is not possible.[28] However, other passages allude to the possibility of intercession with the permission of God (Q 2:255). The Qur'an also relates that certain groups *do* intercede for humans, including angels (Q 53:26), "witnesses" (Q 43:86), and "those who have made a covenant with God" (Q 19:87).

Not surprisingly, other Muslim groups came to different conclusions on intercession. Most Muʿtazila, with their strict understanding of divine justice, generally held that humans are to be judged strictly on the basis of their individual deeds. Humans will have a record on the Day of Judgment, and God will judge them according to that record alone. God could not be swayed to overlook certain sins simply because an angel or a prophet asked him to do so.

Thus, for example, the Muʿtazilite Qur'an commentator Zamakhshari specifically argues against this concept in his comments on Q 11:107: "They will remain in [hell] for as long as the heavens and the earth endure—except what *your* Lord may wish." While some Sunni observers felt that the exception in this verse ("except what your Lord may wish") refers to the possibility that the damned may be saved through intercession, Zamakhshari disagreed: "One is not to be deceived here by the assertion of the Mujbira [a pejorative name for Ash'aris] (who maintain) that the exception means that the people of grave sins will be brought out of the hell-fire through intercession."[29]

Hermanson sees something lamentable in this Mu'tazilite vision of God: "The Mu'tazilite alternative here, as on some other issues, seemed to reduce God to a calculating, merciless automaton, unresponsive to human prayer."[30]

The opponents of the Mu'tazila, those Muslim theologians who were open to the idea of God being swayed by intercession, had on their side other hadith that speak of the special right of the Prophet Muhammad to intercede for his community on the Day of Judgment:

> On the Day of Resurrection the Believers will assemble and say, "Let us ask somebody to intercede for us with our Lord." So they will go to Adam and say, "You are the father of all the people, and Allah created you with His Own Hands, and ordered the angels to prostrate to you, and taught you the names of all things; so please intercede for us with your Lord, so that He may relieve us from this place of ours." Adam will say, "I am not fit for this (i.e. intercession for you)." . . . [The believers then go to Noah and Abraham, but neither accepts the task.] So they will go to [Moses] and he will say, "I am not fit for this undertaking." And he will mention (his) killing a person who was not a killer,[31] and so he will feel ashamed thereof before his Lord, and he will say, "Go to Jesus, Allah's Slave, His Apostle

and Allah's Word and a Spirit coming from Him."
Jesus will say, "I am not fit for this undertaking. Go
to Muhammad the Slave of Allah whose past and
future sins were forgiven by Allah." So they will
come to me and I will proceed till I will ask my
Lord's Permission and I will be given permission.
When I see my Lord, I will fall down in Prostration
and He will let me remain in that state as long as
He wishes and then I will be addressed: "(Muhammad!) Raise your head. Ask, and your request will
be granted; say, and your saying will be listened to;
intercede, and your intercession will be accepted."[32]

The point of this hadith is not only to confirm the possibility of
intercession, but also in part to elevate Muhammad above all
other prophets. According to the hadith, Adam, Noah, Abraham, Moses, and Jesus will not be able to intercede—only
Muhammad.[33]

God's Right to Judge as He Chooses

Ultimately, however, the standard Ash'ari/Sunni Muslim position on the salvation of sinners is not only about Muhammad's
intercession. Those who held to this position, including Ash'ari,
Tahawi, and others, also held a certain conviction about God's
prerogative to judge as he pleases. If God is Lord, if God is sovereign, does he not have the right to forgive sinners? Or, more
ominously, can he not condemn whomever he chooses to condemn? In other words, is God's job on the Day of Judgment
only to read the ledger of good and evil deeds and to calculate
where each person stands? Can he not respond in a personal

way to the fate of each soul who comes before him? This sentiment is captured in a hadith reported by the Prophet's beloved
wife Aisha in which he declares to his followers: "One's good
deeds will not make him enter Paradise." They respond by asking him, "Even you, O Messenger of God?" And Muhammad
says, "Even I, unless and until God bestows His pardon and
Mercy on me."[34]

Certain qur'anic passages indeed announce that God will
punish or forgive whomever he chooses. Qur'an 76:31, for example, declares that God "admits whomever He wishes into
His mercy." Qur'an 48:14 says, "To God belongs the kingdom
of the heavens and the earth: He forgives whomever He wishes
and punishes whomever He wishes, and God is all-forgiving,
all-merciful" (cf. Q 5:40). In Q 5:18 the Jews and Christians
claim to be the "children" and "beloved ones" of God. The
Qur'an, which doesn't speak of God as father and does not call
humans "children" of God, responds by insisting that they are
mere *creatures* of God who are subject to his will:

> The Jews and the Christians say, "We are God's chil-
> dren and His beloved ones." *Say,* "Then why does
> He punish you for your sins?" No, you are humans
> from among His creatures. He forgives whomever
> He wishes and punishes whomever He wishes.[35]

A number of further verses could be cited to this effect.[36] Particularly striking is Q 6:125:

> Whomever Allah desires to guide, He opens his
> breast to Islam, and whomever He desires to lead
> astray, He makes his breast narrow and straitened
> as if he were climbing to a height. Thus does Allah

lay [spiritual] defilement on those who do not have faith.

The Qur'an's affirmation of God's inscrutable right to judge as he pleases might seem to compromise the notion of perfect justice. If one cannot affirm that God will judge according to some standard, then how can one say that his judgment is just? What is the meaning of justice if it is nothing more than God's will?

Ash'ari recognized this problem but refused to seek a solution. Holding both that God is just and that his judgment is inscrutable, Ash'ari argued that humans could not (or, better, should not) speculate on how these two things go together. Faithful Muslims, as he puts it, "do not say 'How?' or 'Why?'"[37] Instead, they accept the traditions and doctrines that have been passed down to them and thereby avoid disputations on contentious issues (once again we see how a concern with the welfare of Islamic society shapes theological doctrine).[38]

On the other hand the Mu'tazila, the school to which Ash'ari belonged during his youth, insisted that God acts according to a category of justice that can be known and understood. His will does not surpass this justice; it is consistent with justice. As Khalid Blankinship puts it, "The Mu'tazila stated that God, having declared Himself to be just (Qur'an 6:115; 16:90; 21:47; 57:25), was constrained to follow His own declaration."[39]

This view of God's justice, incidentally, did not mean that the Mu'tazila held to a more "gentle" view of divine judgment. As we have seen, they tended to teach that, because of his commitment to a standard of justice, God would not (or perhaps could not) forgive the grave sinner. He had no right to do so because doing so would violate his justice. Blankinship writes caustically that the Mu'tazilite perspective "presented God as a kind of cosmic justice machine, rather than a free and conscious being."[40]

While Blankinship seems to caricature the views of Mu'tazilites, it is true that from an Ash'ari perspective the views of the Mu'tazila implied that God was constrained or limited. He could not judge each case individually and forgive or condemn humans according to his will. He was obliged to judge each case "justly." Blankinship (who seems to agree with the Ash'ari perspective) writes, "Mu'tazilism tended to lean towards portraying God as a dharmic force, rather than as the personal deity most Muslims conceived Him to be."[41] Dharma is a Hindu notion of a cosmic law, and by invoking this concept Blankinship seems to question the (Islamic) authenticity of Mu'tazilite doctrine.

From a Mu'tazilite perspective, however, all of this makes perfect, rational sense. Given two cases that are effectively similar, God would treat them the same. If two women, one named Maya and one named Mary (both believers), came before God with the same register of good and evil deeds, God would not send Maya to heaven and Mary to hell. But this way of reasoning things out is distinctively Mu'tazilite. They have a high regard for the capacity of the human intellect to understand how things work with God.

To Ash'aris one simply cannot reason this way about God. We humans do not have the ability, or the right, to determine how God should judge. Our job is to affirm his right to judge as he pleases and to live in fear and trembling before him, never sure of our own salvation. This Ash'ari position would triumph in the later development of Islam (although the doctrines of the Mu'tazilites live on in some Shi'ite schools of thought).

The Inscrutable Divine Judgment

But does the Ash'ari position imply a sort of divine capricious-
ness? Is God's judgment so inscrutable that humans are left in
the dark regarding its logic? Are we, in other words, helpless
before the mysterious judgment of an all-powerful, mysterious God?

These are some of the concerns that Pope Benedict XVI
raised in an address he gave in Regensburg, Germany, in 2006.
In the course of that address—which caused controversy when
he quoted a medieval Christian polemic that accuses Muhammad of bloodshed[42]—Benedict noted the emphasis in Islamic
theology on the inscrutability of divine judgment (he obviously
had in mind standard Sunni theology and not the views of the
Mu'tazila or the Shi'a). He declared: "But for Muslim teaching,
God is absolutely transcendent. His will is not bound up with
any of our categories, even that of rationality."[43]

A response to Benedict's observation came in the form
of a letter written by a group of thirty-eight Muslim scholars
who defended Muhammad from the accusation of bloodshed
and took on the question of God's transcendence. The authors
insisted that some things can be definitely known about God.
The Qur'an, they note, gives God certain names:

> To say that for Muslims "God's Will is not bound
> up in any of our categories" is also a simplifica-
> tion which may lead to a misunderstanding. God
> has many Names in Islam, including the Merci-
> ful, the Just, the Seeing, the Hearing, the Know-
> ing, the Loving, and the Gentle. Their utter convic-
> tion in God's Oneness and that There is none like
> unto Him [Q 112:4] has not led Muslims to deny

God's attribution of these qualities to Himself and
to (some of) His creatures. . . . As this concerns His
Will, to conclude that Muslims believe in a capricious God who might or might not command us
to evil is to forget that God says in the Qur'an, Lo!
God enjoins justice and kindness, and giving to
kinsfolk, and forbids lewdness and abomination
and wickedness.[44]

Benedict never wrote a response to this "Open Letter"
(he did, however, initiate a series of dialogues in response to
the controversy), but one could imagine what he would have
said. Benedict's point in his address was that bloodshed in the
name of God (who, in the Christian understanding, is the creator and father of all people—who loves believers and unbelievers, monotheists and polytheists) is always wrong *and* that
this insight is something that can be known *rationally* and not
only by recourse to scripture. Reason should guide our reading of scripture, including those passages (which are found in
both the Old Testament and the Qur'an) that glorify bloodshed. Benedict was criticizing the prominence in Islamic theology of a view (which is indeed dominant among some Sunni
theologians) that is opposed to this sort of rationality, a view
that would have us say that God could command bloodshed
and yet still be called good and that we should affirm these two
things "without asking how."

Still, the authors of the Open Letter made an important
point. The God of the Qur'an is not totally mysterious. He does
not leave humans with no clue as to how to please him. He has
disclosed the sort of things that will lead humans to salvation
or damnation.

We have, then, an interesting theological tension. On one

hand Allah has disclosed the standards of his judgment, and on the other, he still insists on his right to reward and punish whomever he wills. This tension gave birth to the idea among later theologians of a "temporary stay" in hell, thus satisfying the need for divine justice while still allowing for God's mercy. The Islamic hell was thus turned into a purgatory.

But if Allah is merciful enough to save sinful believers in the end, could his mercy extend to unbelievers?

6

Allah and the Fate of Unbelievers

I heard Allah's Messenger (when his uncle, Abu Talib, had been mentioned in his presence), saying, "Maybe my intercession will help him on the Day of Resurrection so that he may be put in a shallow place in the Fire, with fire reaching [only to] his ankles."

— *Tradition attributed to Muhammad*

In a popular Pakistani English-language newspaper (the *Express Tribune*), a teacher at a prestigious school named Hussain Nadim wrote the following about a discussion he had with his students:

> A heated argument in my class erupted when I asked a simple question to my students:
> "Is Mother Teresa going to heaven?"
> To my surprise, more than 80% of this educated elite answered the question with a vehement

"no." All of those who answered in the negative explained that while Mother Teresa was a noble woman, she was not a Muslim and, hence, could not enter heaven. This ideology is the first step towards the action of violence and brutality.

Below is a dialogue with one of my students who represented this school of thought:

"So, Mother Teresa is not going to heaven?"

Student: "No, since she was not a Muslim."

"But she saved thousands of lives."

Student: "Well, she was to be rewarded for that in this world, but one can't enter heaven until he/she says the Kalima [the Muslim profession of faith]."

"So you're saying only the Muslims are going to heaven, no matter how evil they are?"

Student: "Yes, evil Muslims will be punished for some time, and will be sent to heaven after the punishment."

"So, when you die, you're going to go to heaven no matter what you do in this world, just because you were *born* a Muslim?

Student: "Yes, precisely!"[1]

We can notice from Nadim's record of this conversation that his students were aware of Islamic doctrine on the salvation of sinful Muslims, that such Muslims might enter heaven after a temporary stay in hell (as we discussed in the last chapter). We might also notice their considerable reluctance to grant that a non-Muslim, even a woman like Mother Teresa, might make it to heaven. Faith, for these students at least, is more important than works.

On the other hand the class was not unanimous—some students thought that a righteous non-Muslim might go to heaven. What is more, Nadim evidently thought that to be the case (as the discussion continues, he attempts to persuade the students of his position). This division over the possible salvation of non-Muslims reflects the classical Islamic sources.

In the previous chapter we saw how certain Muslim theologians entertained the possibility that sinful believers will eventually be saved from the fires of hell. Indeed, some held that *all* Muslims will eventually be rescued from hell (with most scholars attributing their salvation to the intercession of the Prophet Muhammad). In this chapter we examine a still more radical possibility: that even non-Muslims, according to the Qur'an, might be saved from hell.

This might seem like a surprising conclusion in light of what we have seen of the limits of divine mercy, but it is not in fact a novel idea. Indeed, the idea that non-Muslims might be saved is found among some of the most unusual suspects.[2]

It was inevitable, one might say, that Muslim scholars would be divided over the question of whether non-Muslims could be saved, since the Qur'an is not clear about their fate. Certain verses in the Qur'an seem to condemn both Jews and Christians. In Q 5:13, for example, God declares that he has "cursed" the Jews. Later in that same Sura (Q 5:72) Christians are condemned for their doctrine on Jesus, by none other than Jesus himself. And yet a verse in that same Sura paradoxically seems to assure Jews, Christians, and others that they will be saved, telling them that they need not have any fear of God's punishment: "Indeed, the faithful, the Jews, the Sabaeans, and the Christians—those who have faith in God and the Last Day and act righteously—they will have no fear, nor will they

grieve" (Q 5:69; 2:62 is almost identical).[3] Thus the question of
the fate of non-Muslims is especially difficult to answer.

A Conversation Between
God and Jesus

As we have seen, one point that the Qur'an affirms consistently
is that God can reward or punish whomever he chooses. This
point is exhibited in a passage near the end of Sura 5, one of the
most extraordinary passages of the Qur'an, which involves a
conversation between God and Jesus (Q 5:116–18). Where and
when this conversation takes place is not clear. At one point
Jesus refers to his life in the past tense, which suggests that
the conversation took place (or will take place) in heaven after
Jesus's life. It is possible, although not certain, that the Quran's
author imagines this to be a conversation between God and
Jesus on the Day of Judgment.

The conversation opens with a question that God asks of
Jesus: "O Jesus son of Mary! Was it you who said to the people,
'Take me and my mother for gods besides God'?" The ques-
tion might strike us as peculiar: Why would the Qur'an have
God ask about Jesus, his mother, and God when the Chris-
tian idea of the Trinity involves Jesus, the Holy Spirit, and the
Father? Some scholars believe it is possible that Muhammad
was simply confused, that he imagined the Trinity to be some-
thing like a family: father, mother, and son.[4] Be that as it may,
Jesus answers the question with pious indignation:

> Immaculate are You! It does not behoove me to say
> what I have no right to. Had I said it, You would
> certainly have known it: You know whatever is in

> my self, and I do not know what is in Your self. In-
> deed, You know best all that is Unseen. (Q 5:116)

Here we find Jesus modeling the attitude of the pious believer.
He proclaims the absolute sovereignty of God and acknowl-
edges God's omniscience. In the following verse Jesus seems
almost to wash his hands of Christians:

> I did not say to them [anything] except what You
> had commanded me [to say]: "Worship God, my
> Lord and your Lord." And I was a witness to them
> so long as I was among them. But when You took
> me away, You Yourself were watchful over them,
> and You are witness to all things. (Q 5:117)

Although the Qur'an does not say so explicitly, this passage
suggests that Christians *did* hold that Jesus and his mother
were two gods other than Allah, that they *did not* listen to
Jesus's counsel to "worship Allah, my Lord and your Lord."

The heart of the theological problem here is the nature
of Christ, or "Christology." In the centuries preceding the rise
of Islam, various Christian communities debated questions of
Christology fiercely. For the Melkites (who held the position of
the Council of Chalcedon of AD 451) Jesus had a human and
a divine nature. According to the Jacobites, or monophysites,
Jesus had one nature, comprising his humanity and divinity.
According to the East Syrians (or Nestorians) Jesus had two
natures, but they were so distinct as to be almost two "persons"
(e.g., only the human nature "was born" and "died"; only the
divine nature forgave sins and performed miracles).

The Qur'an enters into this debate by offering a new
Christological position: Jesus had only one, human nature. In

other words, from the perspective of the Qur'an, Jesus is not "Emmanuel," he is not "God with us." He is not the son of God who emptied himself of his divinity and took the form of a servant. Jesus is a prophet and, like other humans, a servant of God. He is not God become man but a human whom Christians have made into a god.

In this way, Christians seem to be guilty of the great sin, according to the theology of the Qur'an, of associating something with Allah or, in Arabic, *shirk*. In Sura 4 (vv. 48, 116), as we have seen, this sin is considered to be "unforgivable."

The Pakistani scholar Javed Ghamidi suggests that *shirk*, associating a partner with God, leads to damnation. He does so by alluding to Q 7:40, a verse related to the famous Gospel maxim about a camel and the eye of a needle:

> At all places the Qur'an has stated this professing faith to be the very first condition for salvation. The reason for this is that if a person deliberately rejects the Almighty and His signs or invents a lie upon Him by associating partners with Him, then this is arrogance, and about arrogance the Qur'an has clearly said that a camel can enter the eye of a needle but an arrogant person cannot enter Paradise [Q 7:40].[5]

Elsewhere the Qur'an seems explicitly to accuse Christians of *shirk:*

> They have taken their scribes and their monks as lords besides God, and also Christ, Mary's son; though they were commanded to worship only the One God, there is no god except Him; He is far too

immaculate to have any partners that they ascribe
[to Him] [*'amma yushrikun*]! (Q 9:31)

In light of all of this it is surprising to find what comes
next in the remarkable conversation at the end of Sura 5. When
Jesus is put on the spot, he refuses to condemn Christians to
hell. Instead, he insists that their fate rests entirely in the hands
of God: "If You punish them, they are indeed Your servants;
but if You forgive them, You are indeed the All-mighty, the All-
wise" (Q 5:118).

We can draw two lessons from this conversation between God and Jesus. First, and consistent with what we have
already seen in this book, the God of the Qur'an, Allah, insists
on his absolute prerogative to judge as *he chooses*. The eternal
fate of humans is wholly dependent on Allah's will and cannot
be known. Second (and this point is connected), if the fate of
humanity depends on the will of God, then no one can be excluded from the possibility of divine mercy. Even Christians,
whom the Qur'an considers to be guilty of a grave theological
crime, might be saved. (Of course, this also means that no one
can be excluded from the possibility of divine wrath, but that's
a topic for the next chapter.)

In other words, Christ does not deign to know whether
Christians will be saved or damned because it cannot be
known: all humans are servants of God and subject to their
master's mysterious will. The point is not that Allah is necessarily gentle and kind, or that he is wrathful and vindictive, but
that Allah has the right to do as he pleases.

Innocent Infidels?

The idea that the God of Islam might save non-Muslims could sound like the wishful thinking of modern-day pluralists (or this non-Muslim). Would any medieval Muslim scholar have dared to propose that a Jew or a Christian could go to heaven? The answer, surprisingly, is yes.

Muslim scholars recognized that non-Muslims too might perform good works, and they were aware of Q 99:7: "So whoever does an atom's weight of good will see it [their good]." Doesn't such a verse (which, after all, says *whoever*) suggest that non-Muslims might have some sort of reward? One way out of this problem is found in the conversation of Pakistani students over Mother Teresa at the opening of this chapter: a non-Muslim could be rewarded in this life but not in the next. A second way out is offered by the classical Qur'an commentator al-Baydawi (d. 1286). In his Qur'an commentary he explains that the righteous acts of unbelievers will not be enough to get them into paradise, but they might be enough to make their punishments (in hell) less severe: "Perhaps the good deed of the unbeliever . . . will bring about some lessening of punishment."[6]

Others, however, went further. In his work *Islam and the Fate of Others,* Mohammad Hassan Khalil notes that Ghazali—who believed that God's mercy is "all-encompassing"—also believed that at least *some* infidels might make it to heaven. Ghazali was particularly interested in the case of those unbelievers who never had a chance to hear the message of Islam. In Q 17:15 God declares, "We do not punish [any community] until We have sent [it] an apostle." In light of this verse, how could one conclude that God would punish Christians or Jews (or others) who never heard Muhammad's message? How could "innocent infidels" be punished for rejecting a prophet they've never heard about?

Something similar seems to be suggested by a well-regarded hadith, preserved in the collection of Muslim, in which the Prophet says: "By Him in Whose hand is the life of Muhammad, he who amongst the community of Jews or Christians hears about me, but does not affirm his belief in that with which I have been sent and dies in this state (of disbelief), he shall be but one of the denizens of Hell-Fire."[7] This hadith suggests that there is a fundamental difference in the destiny of unbelievers who have heard and rejected Muhammad's message and those who have never heard it at all. Ghazali accordingly concludes that the key to evaluating the fate of non-Muslims is whether they ever knowingly rejected Muhammad. In his work *The Decisive Criterion for Distinguishing Islam and Heresy*, Ghazali explains that those who live far away from the land of Islam—he has in mind the Byzantine Christians and the pagan Turks of his day—and who never knowingly rejected Muhammad might be saved.[8]

Moreover, he adds another group to this category of "innocent infidels." Not only might those who have never heard of Muhammad or Islam be saved, so too those who have heard only lies about Muhammad might be saved as well. That means that Christians (and other non-Muslims) who live side by side with Muslims have some hope of salvation.

In the end Ghazali systematically identifies three different sorts of unbelievers. The first are those who have never heard about Muhammad at all. The second are those (Khalil names them "blasphemous unbelievers") who have heard accurately about Muhammad and know about all of his miracles (Ghazali mentions, among other things, how Muhammad split the moon in two, how water sprang forth from his fingertips, and how he miraculously proclaimed the Qur'an). The third are those who are "in between," those who have heard mistruths about Muhammad, who knew nothing of his attributes and were led to believe that he was a liar who only claimed to be a prophet.[9]

According to Ghazali's perspective this third group, which might include Jews or Christians living among Muslims (or, perhaps, Jews and Christians today who hear about Muhammad from the internet), are effectively in the same boat as the first group. Both groups will benefit from divine mercy. The only non-Muslims who will suffer from divine wrath are those who knowingly and consciously reject Muhammad after learning about his miracles, his "signs" of prophethood.

According to Khalil, Ghazali is even open to the salvation of certain polytheists. His conclusion in this regard is related to a conviction that matters of religion are known through revelation, that they are not immediately accessible to unaided human reason. Accordingly, polytheists who have never heard of religious obligations from a prophet can't be blamed for neglecting them: "Ghazali held that in the absence of revelation, one is under no obligation to thank God or to know Him truly."[10]

This is a remarkable stance, since certain hadith seem to declare clearly that there is no hope for polytheists in the afterlife. A chapter of Muslim's collection of hadith is called "Evidence That One Who Dies an Idolator Is One of the People of Hell and No Intervention Can Save Him from That." It includes a number of hadith that describe how Muhammad's uncle Abu Talib rejected on his deathbed his nephew's pleas to accept Islam.[11] Abu Talib was a friend to Muhammad during his life but never embraced his nephew's religion. This hadith maintains that he, and anyone else who refuses to accept Islam,

is condemned. If Abu Talib, the friend and uncle of Muhammad, won't be saved, how could a non-Muslim have any hope?

It is interesting to note that Ghazali's way of thinking
through this question is not unlike the thought process of
many Christians. On the popular evangelical website Christianity Today, a preacher named Dawson McAllister gives two
answers to the question "What if someone never hears about
Jesus?" First, he writes (quoting Rom 1:19–20) that people have
a natural ability to come to know God ("much like the way we
instinctively reach for water when we're thirsty"). Second, he
writes that there is still hope for those who never get the opportunity to hear about Jesus, the savior: "We can be assured
that God, who is loving and just, is still in control. God is sovereign, and he will always do what is right."[12] McAllister arrives
at a conclusion not unlike that of Ghazali almost a thousand
years earlier, but in relation to Jesus rather than Muhammad.

Ghazali's attitude, however, leaves us with a logical problem. In certain passages the Qur'an seems to say simply that
those who do not believe in God and the Prophet are going to
hell. Quran 38:64, for example, calls unbelievers the "inmates
of the Fire." How could one both be condemned to hell and
yet still hope for God's mercy? The answer for Ghazali is related to a teaching we discovered in the previous chapter: like
sinful believers, "innocent infidels" will indeed go to hell, but
not forever.

The End of Hell?

In *The Decisive Criterion* Ghazali seems to conclude that un-
believers might be saved (ultimately) by the vast mercy of God.
They will be inmates of hell, but their sentence is not eternal:
"God's mercy will encompass many bygone communities as

well, even if most of them may be briefly exposed to the [Fire] for a second or an hour or some period of time, by virtue of which they earn the title, 'party of the [Fire].'"[13] Ghazali accordingly concludes that it will be "rare for one to dwell in the Fire forever."[14]

As Khalil notes, however, Ghazali stops there. He is not a "universalist"—that is, he does not argue that *all* people will go to heaven.[15] *Some* unbelievers are beyond the pale and will be eternally doomed. Their punishment in hell will not expiate their sins. The only good that their punishment will serve is that it will help the people of paradise appreciate still more the pleasures of the heavenly garden.

However, the idea of universal salvation is not unheard of in Islam. A tradition associated with a companion of the Prophet named 'Abdallah b. 'Amr b. al-'As (d. 682) relates that all people, even unbelievers, will eventually be saved: "A day will come when the gates of hell will be closed and no longer will anyone be inside." The Qur'an commentator Zamakhshari—who was associated with the Mu'tazila school, which focused on divine justice—refused to accept a literal reading of this tradition, writing, "This and similar (views) are clear deceptions, from which may God preserve us!"[16]

Zamakhshari has a different explanation for what this tradition teaches. It does not mean that eventually all people will eventually escape punishment. It simply means that the *sort* of punishment will change: the damned will be moved out of a place where they are tortured by fire into a different place where they will be tortured instead by cold. Zamakhshari writes: "If the Tradition according to Ibn al-'As is sound, then its meaning can only be that the unbelievers will come out of the heat of the fire (and) into the cold of severe frost."[17]

Other scholars, however, defended the view found in the

tradition of 'Abdallah b. 'Amr b. al-'As. Remarkably, these include two scholars often associated today with fundamentalism: Ibn Taymiyya (d. 1328)—who in many ways is the ideological godfather of modern Salafism, or Wahhabism—and his student Ibn Qayyim al-Jawziyya (d. 1350). Both scholars were known for their polemical stance against all of those movements that fell outside of their strictly defined notion of Sunni Islam. Ibn Taymiyya in particular engaged in violent polemics against Christians, philosophers, Shi'ites, Sufis, and others. In fact, his first known work was a legal text in which he argued that a Christian accused of insulting the Prophet should be condemned to death (although that Christian later converted to Islam).

Moreover, Ibn Taymiyya was what might be called a supersessionist. In *The Splendid Reply to Those Who Exchanged the Religion of Christ,* his massive polemical work against Christianity (penned as an answer to a letter from Christians who wrote from the island of Cyprus), Ibn Taymiyya argues that Muhammad came to set things straight and correct the errors of Christianity.[18] Christians, from Ibn Taymiyya's perspective, falsified the teachings of Christ by divinizing him and disobeying his commands. So God sent Muhammad to fix all this, to establish the definitive religion that replaces everything that came before.

For his part, Ibn Qayyim al-Jawziyya wrote a work against both Jews and Christians.[19] In other words, these two scholars were no friends to non-Muslims. Indeed, today their views are often cited to justify bigotry among extremists.

Yet when it comes to eschatology (the "last things"), Ibn Taymiyya and Ibn Qayyim al-Jawziyya emphasized divine mercy. Ibn Taymiyya held—like Ghazali before him—that only those who had received the Islamic message could be held accountable for it on the Day of Judgment. This conclusion was based in part on Q 6:19: "*Say,* 'God is witness between me and you, and this Qur'ān has been revealed to me in order that I may warn you thereby and whomever it may reach.'"[20] All those who had heard the message about Muhammad (including not only humans but the invisible creatures known as *jinn*—the genies of the Arabian Nights) were obliged, under pain of hell, to accept Islam. Yet those who had not heard the message had no such obligation.

Ibn Taymiyya and Ibn Qayyim al-Jawziyya, moreover, were particularly interested in the question of whether hellfire would last forever. According to an anecdote preserved in a work of Ibn Qayyim al-Jawziyya titled *Healing of the Sick,* Ibn Qayyim raised this subject with Ibn Taymiyya near the end of the latter's life. When he asked Ibn Taymiyya whether the punishment of hell is permanent, Ibn Taymiyya responded, "This issue is very great!" and said nothing further.

It is perhaps not a coincidence, however, that one of the last works that Ibn Taymiyya composed—titled *Response to Whoever Says That the Garden and the Fire Will Pass Away*—addresses the eternal nature of divine reward and punishment.[21] Most likely Ibn Taymiyya wrote this work from his jail cell in Damascus—before his jailors took away his pen and paper in April or May of the year 1328 (he died later that year). Ibn Qayyim al-Jawziyya would later follow the opinion of his master closely when he composed two works, *Spurring the Souls* and the aforementioned *Healing of the Sick.*[22]

In evaluating the views of these two scholars it is important to appreciate that the very concept of hell was at stake. What was God's purpose in creating hell? Was it simply to punish those who failed the test given to them in their earthly lives, or was it to prepare sinners and unbelievers for heaven?

Most scholars held to the former view and taught that unbelievers will be punished in eternal hellfire because of their disbelief. This position was widely considered to have been definitively determined by the consensus of the Islamic community.

Yet not everyone agreed. Ibn Taymiyya and Ibn Qayyim al-Jawziyya operated outside of the standard circles of Sunni theology. They were suspicious of the classical Islamic science of theology and believed that religious questions should be worked out by relying only on the Qur'an and the hadith, and the opinions of the first three generations of pious Muslims (known as the Salaf), and not on principles such as "consensus."[23] Their reading of the Qur'an and the hadith led them to the conclusion that the point of hellfire—even for polytheists and "associators" (even for atheists)—is not punishment but *purification*. Hellfire is therapeutic, and all humans who are sent to hell are merely passing through. As Jon Hoover puts it, for these two scholars hellfire is "a great remedy that purifies and reforms even unbelievers and associators."[24]

Ibn Taymiyya—even though he was a firebrand in his preaching against infidels and heretics—thus concludes that non-Muslims will eventually be saved. Indeed, if one follows his argument to its logical conclusion, one arrives at the notion that hell will disappear. This is a position that Ibn Taymiyya taught clearly in his final work. Ibn Qayyim al-Jawziyya inclines toward this position in *Spurring the Souls* and *Healing of the Sick* and endorses it completely in a work titled *The Thunderbolts Sent Out*. At the end of his life, however, Ibn Qayyim al-Jawziyya seems to have retreated, perhaps because of a conflict with an influential judge in Damascus (whom we will mention below).[25]

It is interesting to note that the idea of an "end to hell" was not unknown to the early Christian church. In Greek, it was known as *apokatastasis* and associated—wrongly or rightly—with the church father Origen (d. 254), who is said to have argued that even the devil will eventually be redeemed.[26] This doctrine was formally condemned at the Second Council of Constantinople in 553.

Interestingly, both Ibn Taymiyya and Ibn Qayyim al-Jawziyya also held the position that unlike hellfire, the heavenly garden will *not* pass away. Heaven will last eternally because God's mercy is greater than his wrath.[27] In defending this position, Ibn Taymiyya refers to a well-known hadith (a version of which is the epigraph to Chapter 2) in which God says, "My mercy overcomes my anger."[28]

Both Ibn Taymiyya and Ibn Qayyim al-Jawziyya advanced their arguments about hellfire with reference to a qur'anic passage from Sura 11:

> [106]As for the wretched, they shall be in the Fire: their lot therein will be groaning and wailing. [107]They will remain in it for as long as the heavens and the earth endure—except what *your* Lord may wish; indeed your Lord does whatever He desires.[29]

The phrase "except what *your* Lord may wish" led both men to argue that if God so desires, if he wills, he may save all of those who are condemned to hell. This phrase suggests that God's will trumps any human notion of justice.[30]

Another tradition that influenced the thinking of Ibn Taymiyya and Ibn Qayyim al-Jawziyya was attributed not to Muhammad but to the second caliph, 'Umar b. al-Khattab (d. 644). He is reported to have said, "Even if the People of the Fire stayed in the Fire like the amount of sand of 'Alij [a vast desert region in Arabia] they would have, despite that, a day in which they would come out."[31] According to the logic of this hadith, the damned might have to wait a long time to escape hell (I've never been to 'Alij—but I'm sure there is plenty of sand there). Eventually, however, they will do so.[32]

The opponents of Ibn Taymiyya and Ibn Qayyim al-Jawziyya—those who held that the punishments of hell would be eternal—countered this opinion with Q 4:169 (cf. 33:65), which declares that the faithless will be *khalidin fiha abadan*—a phrase usually understood to mean "eternally in [hellfire]." Ibn Taymiyya, however, insists that this phrase might simply mean that the damned will be in hellfire as long as hellfire lasts. Hellfire, however, will not last forever.[33]

Pluralists, Inclusivists, Exclusivists

The views of Ibn Taymiyya and Ibn Qayyim al-Jawziyya were forcefully opposed by one of the latter's contemporaries, a powerful Sunni judge in Damascus by the name of al-Subki (d. 1355). Ibn Qayyim al-Jawziyya and al-Subki clashed over a number of questions of Islamic law—from the permissibility of horse races to divorce.[34] As for the question of hell, al-Subki wrote a book in 1348 to respond to the views of Ibn Taymiyya (but perhaps also to send a warning to Ibn Qayyim al-Jawziyya). In it he argues that those who believe that hellfire will pass away have become unbelievers (and the consequences of such an accusation are serious—leaving Islam is punishable by death).[35] It was quite possibly this treatise of al-Subki that led Ibn Qayyim al-Jawziyya to retreat from his earlier endorsement of the position that hell will pass away.[36]

In fact, the standard Islamic position today is that hellfire is indeed eternal. More than one Muslim scholar has sought to redeem Ibn Taymiyya from his "heterodox" view on hellfire.[37]

However, none of this changes the fact that classical Muslim scholars had a diversity of views regarding the fate of the non-Muslim other. In sorting out the various positions of Muslim scholars on this issue, Khalil introduces categories that are known from the world of Christian theology: pluralist, inclusivist, and exclusivist.[38] One way to define these terms is in regard to soteriology, that is, in regard to what they imply about salvation:

> Pluralism: All people, whatever their religious
> tradition, might be saved by their own faith.
> Inclusivism: Those outside of one's faith
> community may be saved *despite* their own
> faith.
> Exclusivism: Those outside of one's faith
> community are damned.

As Khalil explains, scholars such as Ghazali and Ibn Taymiyya (for different reasons) fall somewhere in the category of inclusivism. Al-Subki falls into the category of exclusivism. Very few classical Muslim scholars (with the notable exception of certain philosophically inclined scholars such as the Isma'ili Shi'ite Abu Hatim al-Razi [d. 934]) could be described today as "pluralists," that is, affirming the value of non-Islamic religions for their own sake.

There are a number of parallels in Christian and Islamic thought in this regard. A Jesuit cardinal named Juan de Lugo (d. 1660) argued that Muslims' ignorance of the Gospel, together with their knowledge of true revelation (that which passed into the Qur'an from the Bible or Christian tradition), might mean that they could still be saved. Muslims might be free of the charge of rejecting the Gospel (since they have not truly known it) and still have a sort of salvific faith because of the remnants of Christian truth in the Qur'an. The key to their salvation was the idea that they are "invincibly ignorant" (to use the technical phrase) of the Gospel. His opinion is remarkably close to the "inclusivism" of Ghazali more than five centuries earlier.

De Lugo's "inclusivist" position (Muslims can be saved but they are saved because of Christianity) was later echoed in the twentieth century by another Jesuit theologian, the German Karl Rahner (d. 1984). Rahner proposed the idea that certain nonbelievers could be thought of as "anonymous Christians" if they embraced ethical concepts close to the Gospel and showed a genuine desire to discover truth (of course, believers in other traditions might not want to be thought of as "anonymous Christians"). Rahner went a bit further than De Lugo by arguing that Christ, through the Holy Spirit, was operative in other religions. Still, his position would fall generally within the category of inclusivism.

Today, a number of theologians, such as John Hick and Paul Knitter, embrace religious pluralism. A modern Islamic movement known as perennialism, associated with the Swiss scholar Frithjof Schuon, includes members of other religious traditions and could be described as pluralist.

One complication of this Muslim inclusivist (and pluralist) line of thinking is presented by the modern Syrian Qur'an commentator Rashid Rida (d. 1935). To Rida the human capacity to reason works as something like a divine messenger. He believes that *all* humans—whether or not they are aware of Islamic revelation—should be able to work out rationally that Islam is the true religion. Their failure to do so is a moral defect not unlike the rejection of a prophet.[39] As we have seen, Ghazali, by contrast, was less confident in humanity's ability to work out religious truths through reason alone. This led him to the position that certain infidels are indeed innocent.

Divine Sovereignty

Perhaps there is another way to think about the salvation of non-Muslims. Instead of imagining that God is going to determine the fate of infidels on the basis of what they had heard of Muhammad (as Ghazali does), we might simply note that the Qur'an places no limits on God's ability to forgive.

In Sura 29 the Qur'an develops a legend that Jews and Christians told about Abraham's childhood in the pagan city of Ur.[40] In it, Abraham confronts and condemns his unbelieving people for their idol worship. In the middle of that story is a paragraph (vv. 19–23) — perhaps a later addition — that addresses how God deals with unbelievers. The first thing the Qur'an declares is that God has the right to do as he chooses: "He will punish whomever He wishes and have mercy on whomever He wishes, and to Him you will be returned" (Q 29:21).

Allah is not subject to any code of law, or even any code of justice. This is seen in Q 5:18, where the Qur'an addresses the claims of Jews and Christians to be "the sons of God and His beloved."[41] To the Qur'an this claim is insolent: God is not to be thought of as a "father," and no one can claim to have the special status of being his "sons." In response, two arguments are advanced: First, the Qur'an turns to the Jews and Christians and asks them: "How could this be when He is punishing you for your sins?" (It's not clear exactly what punishment the Qur'an is referring to here.) Second, the Qur'an declares to these insolent Jews and Christians that no one can be certain of God's decree: "You are among the people whom He has created. He forgives whomever He wishes and He punishes whomever He wishes."

In other words, if Jews and Christians are being punished in this world, their fate in the next world is entirely dependent on the will of God. To borrow the language of Khalid Blankinship, the God of the Qur'an is a "free and conscious being."[42] This means that the door of mercy is always open. Allah may forgive Jews, Christians, or others and ultimately admit them into paradise. But this also means that Allah may *not* forgive them. Next to the door of mercy is the door of wrath.

III

Vengeance

7

Divine Wrath

Prophets do not offer philosophy. They offer wisdom of a type, a wisdom which has a dominant note.

—*Daud Rahbar,* God and Man in the Quran

In a well-regarded hadith, one of the wives of the Prophet Muhammad—his beloved wife Aisha—relates how she woke up one night and found that her husband was no longer next to her:

> I noticed that the Messenger of Allah was not in the bed one night, so I searched for him, and my hand fell on the sole of his foot. He was in the mosque, with his feet held upright, and he was saying: "O Allah, I seek refuge in Your pleasure from Your wrath. In Your forgiveness from Your punishment. I seek refuge in You from You. I cannot praise You enough; You are as You have praised Yourself."[1]

This hadith offers us a vivid scene illustrating Muhammad's fear of God's wrath. God is both Muhammad's hope and Muhammad's fear. He prays to God, "I seek refuge in You *from You.*" God, in other words, is both the source of danger and one's ultimate protection.

Muhammad is not the only prophet to be overwhelmed by the fear of God. A tradition related by a ninth-century scholar named Ahmad ibn Hanbal relates, "Whenever the Hour was mentioned, Jesus used to cry out in anguish like a woman."[2]

In Islam, God is the threat, and God is also the salvation. In some ways this perspective reflects a "problem" with monotheism. Dualist religions such as Zoroastrianism have a god (for Zoroastrians this is Ahura Mazda) who is responsible only for good and a second god (Ahriman) who is responsible only for evil. Zoroastrians might then "take refuge" in the good god from the bad god.

What is to be done, however, if there is only one god? The first Sura of the Qur'an has the believer pray to God, "Guide us on the straight path (*sirat*)" (Q 1:6). This prayer makes sense because God is capable of guiding humans elsewhere. In fact, in Sura 37 we find God (speaking of the wrongdoers—and their wives) telling the angels, "Guide them on the path (*sirat*) of hell" (Q 37:23). God's power to lead astray or to guide is brought together in Q 13:27: "Surely God leads astray whomever He pleases and guides to Himself whoever turns (to Him)."

The Japanese scholar Toshihiko Izutsu comments: "The God of the Koran shows two different aspects that are fundamentally opposed to each other. For a pious, believing mind these two aspects are but two different sides of one and the same God, but for the logic of ordinary reason, they would seem contradictory."[3] Izutsu here is alluding to the basic problem, if not the paradox, that is at the heart of the present book: the God of the Qur'an is not simply a God of mercy or a God of vengeance. He is both.

Having already examined the mercy of God and what that mercy means for the salvation of sinners and unbelievers, we now turn to the vengeful side of God. We analyze the qur'anic references to God's anger, investigate the sorts of things that lead God to wrath, and examine how the Qur'an juxtaposes divine wrath and divine mercy.

All of this is meant to show that Allah is deeply involved in human affairs. He does not simply observe the world from on high. He is not the god of the philosophers, the "self-thinking thought" or "unmoved mover" of Aristotle. Allah gets involved with the world. As Izutsu puts it, the God of the Qur'an does not "stand aloof from mankind."[4]

Yet the God of the Qur'an not only gets involved with the world by offering grace and mercy to his creatures; he also actively plots against unbelievers, wrongdoers, and hypocrites. In other words, Allah does not simply judge and condemn them in the next life. He also works against them *in this life* to prevent them from believing, repenting, and thereby saving themselves.

At one point the Qur'an asks rhetorically: "Do they feel secure from God's devising (*makr*)? No one feels secure from God's devising except the people who are losers" (Q 7:99).[5] In the very next verse God threatens his audience with the sealing of their hearts: "Does it not dawn upon those who inherited the earth after its [former] inhabitants that if We wish We will punish them for their sins and set a seal on their hearts so they would not hear?" (Q 7:100).[6]

Allah leads astray the unbelievers.[7] He causes hypocrisy to enter the hearts of those who disregard him (Q 9:76–77), and he increases the sickness in the hearts of those who seek to deceive him (Q 2:10). He is not emotionless or "impassible." He is a God who grows angry and takes action.

Whom Does God Love?

All of this implies that the God of the Qur'an does not love unconditionally or without distinction. He loves some people, and he does not love others. God's love depends on human action. He "loves " (*yuhibbu*) the virtuous (Q 2:195, 5:13), the penitent (Q 2:222), those who keep clean (Q 2:222), the God-wary (Q 3:76; 9:4, 7), those who trust in him (Q 3:159), the just (Q 5:42, 49:9, 60:8), and those who fight in his way (61:4).

On the topic of God's love the Pakistani scholar Daud Rahbar writes: "The word *yuhibbu* in all these verses does not necessarily mean 'loves,' for the word can equally well be rendered as 'likes' or 'approves.' All these verses represent the idea of God's conditional love or approval. They do not say that God loves all men, and therefore they do not convert God into a lenient sovereign." Rahbar adds, "We have shown that there is not a single verse in the Qur'an that speaks of God's unconditional love for mankind."[8]

There are indeed those whom the God of the Qur'an does not love. "God does not love any sinful unbeliever" (Q 2:276). "God does not love the faithless" (Q 3:32; cf. 30:45).[9] God also does not love the wrongdoers (Q 3:57, 140; 42:40), the transgressors (Q 2:190, 5:87, 7:55), the arrogant (Q 4:36, 16:23, 31:18, 57:23), the proud (Q 4:36, 31:18, 57:23), the wasteful (Q 6:141, 7:31), the treacherous (Q 8:58, 22:38), the corrupt (Q 5:64, 28:77), and the boastful (Q 28:76). One passage of the Qur'an even speaks of God's "hate" (*maqt*) for the unbelievers (Q 40:10).

Miroslav Volf, in his work *Allah: A Christian Response,*

argues that the Qur'an's distinction between those whom God loves and those whom he doesn't love is a response to the stance that humans take toward God.[10] This is only partially true. The list of those whom God loves includes "those who keep clean" and "those who fight," and the list of those whom God does not love includes "the arrogant," "the proud," and "the wasteful." In other words, humans have qualities that lead God to love, or not to love, them.[11]

In this regard it is perhaps telling that the Qur'an never describes God as "father," though in other ways the Qur'an's portrait of God is close to that of the Bible. As in the Bible, God in the Qur'an creates the world in six days. As in the Bible, God in the Qur'an judges his creatures and sends them either to heaven or to hell. The qur'anic image of God sitting on a throne matches biblical imagery. However, the biblical language of God as "father"—found throughout the Old and New Testaments—is nowhere found in the Qur'an.[12] Could this departure from biblical language be merely a coincidence?

To some scholars the Qur'an avoids this language because its author understood the notion of father literally. If God were "father," in other words, he must have had sex to produce offspring—an unthinkable concept! Other scholars argue more generally that the Qur'an means to emphasize the transcendence or otherness of God and to elevate him beyond human categories. The medieval Muslim intellectual al-Jahiz (d. 869) declares, "God Most High is too great that fatherhood would be among his attributes. Humans are too contemptible that childhood of God would be their lineage."[13]

In one place the Qur'an indeed declares, "Nothing is like Him" (Q 42:11). Yet elsewhere the Qur'an uses different human categories to describe God, such as a king (Q 20:114, 23:116, 59: 23) or a judge (Q 6:114, 10:109, 11:45, 12:80, 95:8).

Perhaps what is at stake is the relationship that the Qur'an imagines between God and humans. A king may punish a disobedient subject, and a judge can condemn wrongdoers, but a father loves his children even when they are disobedient or do wrong. The God of the Qur'an, however, does not love wrongdoers (Q 3:57, 140; 42:40).

Divine Emotions

In the first Sura of the Qur'an, believers pray that they will not be guided on the path of those "upon whom there is anger" (Q 1:7; cf. 4:93; 5:60; 7:71, 152; 8:16; 16:106; 20:81; 42:16; 48:6; 58:14; 60:13).[14] This suggests that God does not simply withhold his love. He is also capable of growing angry.

Yet how are we to understand the notion of divine anger? Rahbar warns us not to think of Allah as having arbitrary "moods,"[15] as though his behavior toward humans depends on what kind of day he is having. In fact, certain passages in the Qur'an describe God as "self-sufficient," which implies a sort of elevation above human nature.[16] Yet if Allah does not have moods, he does have emotions, including anger. In Q 4:93 — which deals with those who commit murder — we see that God does not simply send murderers to hell; he also grows angry with them: "Should anyone kill a believer intentionally, his requital shall be hell, to remain in it [forever]; God shall be wrathful at him and curse him and He will prepare for him a great punishment."

But if Allah responds to human behavior with emotions, can he be truly just? A strict notion of divine justice would imply that God would judge humans in a perfectly mechanical fashion. He would not let emotions get in his way.

Rahbar argues just that in his 1960 book *God of Justice.*[17]

He insists that the God of the Qur'an follows a strict code of punishing sinners and rewarding the righteous. God does not let his mercy or his wrath interfere with his strict judgment of humanity. Mercy and wrath are subservient to justice.[18]

In support of his argument Rahbar emphasizes the way in which descriptions of heaven are almost invariably followed, or preceded, by descriptions of hell.[19] Similarly, declarations of God's mercy in the Qur'an are frequently followed by descriptions of God's punishment.[20] This is seen, for example, in Sura 6: "But if they impugn *you, say,* "Your Lord is dispenser of an all-embracing mercy, but His punishment will not be averted from the guilty lot" (Q 6:147). The concluding verse of Sura 76 is similar: "He admits whomever He wishes into His mercy, and He has prepared a painful punishment for the wrongdoers" (Q 76:31). Commenting on such verses Rahbar writes: "God is mentioned as the compassionate and the violent punisher in the same breath. Such descriptions of God are reminders of reward and punishment and of God's justice."[21] Toward the end of his work, Rahbar writes the following: "In the present study we have seen that God's forgiveness, mercy and love are strictly for those who believe in Him and act aright. Wherever there is an allusion to God's mercy or forgiveness in the Qur'an, we find that within an inch there also is an allusion to the torment He has prepared for the evildoers."[22] God does not punish humans in hell who deserve paradise, but neither does he reward humans with paradise who deserve hell. Little room is left for mercy.

Rahbar's belief in the strict justice of the God of the Qur'an also leads him to refute the possibility that he is capricious. Rahbar denies that Allah might condemn humans to hell, or reward them with heaven, in a manner that is ultimately inscrutable and unpredictable, or that human destiny is completely subject to the arbitrary divine will. In developing this idea, Rahbar sees himself as responding to a misrepresentation of Allah by Western scholars: "It is a fact well-recognised in scientific scholarship that Fear of God is the dominant sentiment in Qur'anic morality. But that the roots of this sentiment are in *God's stern justice* and not in the preponderant malignance of the arbitrary will of a capricious sovereign is a fact scarcely recognised."[23]

It is not my intention in the present work to argue that Allah is a tyrant, or a "capricious sovereign." I do question, however, whether Rahbar is right in his emphasis on "God's stern justice." There are two important points here.

First, as we saw in the previous two chapters, the God of the Qur'an insists on his right to judge as he chooses. He does not simply weigh human actions against an independent and unchanging standard. He cannot, in other words, be compared to a judge in a court of law whose principal role is to *apply* the law. It is perhaps telling that the Qur'an calls God a judge (*hakam*) one time (Q 6:114) and "best of judges" three times (Q 7:87, 10:109, 12:80), but it calls him "lord" (*rabb*) 130 times. Allah insists on the right to rule according to his own will. Indeed, it is the very unpredictability, the very mystery, of divine judgment that is meant to lead humans to the fear of God.

Second, Allah does not simply observe humans. He plays an active role in human history: he blesses humans, curses them, and avenges himself against them. As we will see in the next chapter, he is not above using plots and trickery to do so. Allah's judgment of humans is not simply an act of scorekeeping.

Understanding God's Anger

Yet is the notion of divine wrath an invention of the Qur'an? Not by any means! The Bible also speaks of the anger of God. When in the Book of Exodus Moses stands before the burning bush and hesitates to accept his call, "the anger of the Lord" is "kindled" against Moses (Exod 4:14). Later, God passes before Moses and says of himself, "The Lord, the Lord, a God merciful and gracious, slow to anger, and abounding in steadfast love and faithfulness" (Exod 34:6). Here, God insists that he is *slow* to anger, but he does not deny that he can grow angry.

And indeed we read in later books of the Pentateuch that God frequently grows angry with Israel. In Numbers 11 God's anger is "kindled" (v. 1) and "blazes" (v. 10) against the Israelites when they complain. By the end of the chapter God grows so angry that he strikes the people with "a very great plague" (Num 11:33). In 2 Samuel 6 a man named Uzzah reaches his hand out to steady the Ark of the Covenant when the oxen leading it stumble. God's anger is "kindled" against him, and he strikes poor Uzzah down.

Divine anger is also a feature of the New Testament. When John the Baptist sees the Pharisees and Sadducees coming to him for baptism, he warns them of God's anger: "You brood of vipers! Who warned you to flee from the wrath to come?" (Matt 3:7; cf. Luke 3:7). In the Gospel of John, Jesus insists that those who refuse to obey "the Son" will be subject to divine wrath: "He who believes in the Son has eternal life; he who does not obey the Son shall not see life, but the wrath of God rests upon him" (John 3:36). In his letter to the Romans Paul speaks of the wrath of God against those who have failed to repent after having seen the signs of God: "For the wrath of God is revealed from heaven against all ungodliness and wickedness of men who by their wickedness suppress the truth" (Rom 1:18). In the Book of Revelation (15:7, 16:1) we read of cosmic bowls filled with divine "anger" that are to be poured out over earth.

Thus both the Qur'an and the Bible depict God as having emotions. The God of the Qur'an may be transcendent in some ways. Allah may not have become incarnate, he may not have a son, and he may not be called "father"; but in other ways he is anthropomorphic. He is, as Khaled Blankinship puts it, a "personal deity."[24] Or, one might say that the God of the Qur'an has personality.

For many Muslims it is important to insist that God is infinitely beyond, or above, humans. In defense of this idea, as we have mentioned, one can cite Q 42:11, which declares, "Nothing is like Him." Muhammad Asad comments that this clause "implies that He is fundamentally — and not merely in His attributes — 'different' from anything that exists or could exist, or anything that man can conceive or imagine or define."[25]

Yet the Qur'an frequently attributes the very human emotion of wrath or anger (Arabic *ghadab*) to God.[26] As we have mentioned, in the first Sura of the Qur'an believers pray that they will not be guided in the path of those who have incurred God's wrath (*al-maghdubi 'alayhim;* v. 7). The Qur'an refers to divine anger on twenty other occasions.

In a particular way the Qur'an speaks of God's wrath against the Israelites (fourteen of the twenty-one references to divine anger involve them). In Q 2:61 it describes how the Israelites complained to Moses about receiving only one sort of food (manna). It then relates, "So they were struck with abasement and poverty, and they earned God's wrath (*ghadab*)."[27] Later in that same Sura the Qur'an condemns the Jews for refusing to listen to God's prophets, for killing the prophets (2:87), and for declaring that their hearts are covered, or, literally "uncircumcised" (2:88).[28] It then declares:

> Evil is that for which they have sold their souls, by defying what God has sent down, out of envy that God should bestow His grace on any of His servants that He wishes. Thus they earned wrath upon wrath, and there is a humiliating punishment for the faithless. (Q 2:90)

Again in Q 3:112 the Jews are accused of killing the prophets, and God's wrath is invoked. In Q 5:60 the Qur'an seems to have the Jews in mind when it speaks of a people "whom God has cursed" and with whom he is wrathful. In the Qur'an God also warns the Israelites of his wrath if they disobey his commands (Q 20:81), and it speaks of God's wrath against them when they do so by worshipping the golden calf (Q 7:150, 152; 20:86).[29]

In Sura 20, God warns the Israelites that they should not violate the food laws he has imposed on them. By doing so they would anger him and put their lives at risk: "Eat of the good things We have provided you, but do not overstep the bounds therein, lest My wrath should descend on you. And he on whom My wrath descends certainly perishes" (Q 20:81). God's wrath is deadly.

Yet God's wrath is not limited to the Israelites. He is also wrathful against those who commit murder (Q 4:93), against polytheists (Q 7:71, 16:106), against hypocrites (Q 48:6), against those who turn their backs in battle (8:16), and against adulterers (Q 24:90). Qur'an 40:10 refers to God's "hate" (*maqt*) of unbelievers.[30] This notion of divine "hate" may be jarring to modern readers, but in the Qur'an it seems to act as a perfect inversion of God's love for believers.

The Qur'an's emphasis on the wrath of God was not lost on later Muslim storytellers. A scholar by the name of Abu al-Layth al-Samarqandi (d. 983) tells a story in which a mountain weeps out of fear of the judgment of God. Jesus then intervenes to save the mountain from divine punishment:

> Jesus was passing by a village where there was a mountain from which came sounds of weeping and wailing. Jesus asked the villagers, "What is this weeping and wailing in this mountain?" The villagers replied, "Ever since we have lived in this village, we have heard the sounds of weeping and wailing coming from this mountain." Jesus said, "O God, let this mountain speak to me." God made the mountain speak and say, "What do you want from me, Jesus?" "Tell me why you weep," asked Jesus. The mountain replied, "I was the mountain from which idols were carved and then worshiped instead of God. I fear that God will cast me into hell-fire, for I have heard God say, 'And fear the flame whose fuel consists of men and stones.'" God inspired Jesus to tell the mountain, "Be at peace, for I have saved you from hell."[31]

A Case of Divine Anger (and Trickery): The People Transformed

Creative accounts of divine wrath do not belong only to later storytellers. The Qur'an itself tells the "People of the Sabbath" story, in which God's wrath leads to a fate worse than death. Sura 7 describes how God punishes a people who fail to keep the Sabbath by transforming them into apes:

> [163] Ask them about the town that was situated on the seaside, when they violated the Sabbath, when their fish would come to them on the Sabbath day, visibly on the shore, but on days when they were not keeping Sabbath they would not come to them. Thus did We test them because of the transgressions they used to commit. . . .
>
> [165] So when they forgot what they had been reminded of, We delivered those who forbade evil [conduct] and seized the wrongdoers with a terrible punishment because of the transgressions they used to commit.
>
> [166] When they defied [the command pertaining to] what they were forbidden from, We said to them, "Be you spurned apes."

The logic of this account is as follows: The people of a certain town by the sea (most Muslim classical scholars identify this town as Ayla, a town near the modern-day Jordanian city of Aqaba on the Red Sea) were sinners. God tested them by having fish come to them on the Sabbath when they were not allowed to fish; the fish disappeared on the other days of the week, when they were allowed to fish. Sure enough, the people failed the test by collecting fish on the Sabbath. For this, God cursed them in an unusual way, by turning them into apes.

Another passage in the Qur'an (5:60) speaks of God's transforming a people into both apes and pigs as a result of divine wrath:

Say, "Shall I inform you concerning something worse than that as a requital from God? Those whom God has cursed and with whom He is wrathful, and turned some of whom into apes and swine."[32]

This verse seems to be connected to the story of the People of the Sabbath in Sura 7, although Muslim scholars question whether the People of the Sabbath were transformed into apes and some other people were turned into pigs (the usual suspects are certain people whom Jesus cursed).

The Qur'an's People of the Sabbath account may ultimately be a development of Num 15:32–36, an Old Testament passage that tells the story of a man among the Israelites who is condemned and stoned to death for gathering wood on the Sabbath. A closer parallel is found in the Jewish text known as the Talmud, which tells the story of a people who were caught fishing on the Sabbath. They were declared outcasts and eventually renounced Judaism (b. Qidd. 72a). Neither of these accounts includes the theme of humans being changed into animals, but they do include the theme of divine anger over violation of the Sabbath. The notion that God would transform people into animals as a punishment may be connected to another tradition in the Talmud (b. Sanh. 109a) where some of the conspirators guilty of building the tower of Babel are turned into apes (among other creatures).[33]

The Qur'an's interest in the People of the Sabbath story is certainly not to encourage its audience to keep the Sabbath. Nowhere does the Qur'an make keeping the Sabbath a religious responsibility.[34] In fact, the Muslim day of prayer is Friday, not Saturday, and for Muslims it is a day of prayer but not of rest (the notion of God's resting on the seventh day after creation, to which Sabbath observance is linked, is not found in the Qur'an). Instead, this story is meant to inspire fear of a God who is capable of stratagems. In it, God sets a trap for the evildoers, by "tempting" them to fish on the Sabbath when the fish appear. The People of the Sabbath cannot withstand this temptation. They are trapped by God's trick, much as their fish are caught in nets. They already are in the habit of committing transgressions (v. 163), and so they commit one more by collecting fish on the Sabbath.

Some Muslim commentators resist the conclusion that God physically transformed people into animals. The Qur'an commentator Tabari (d. 923) reports a tradition from the early Muslim scholar Mujahid (d. 720) by which their "hearts were transformed but they were not actually transformed into apes." Tabari, however, notes that Q 5:60 seems to state clearly that God made (Arabic *ja'ala*) some people into apes and pigs. He therefore concludes, "The statement of Mujahid is in contradiction to the clear indication of the Book of God."[35]

Indeed, this account is not out of keeping with the Qur'an, which seems to have a particular interest in miraculous accounts involving animals. The Qur'an relates how a group of youths and their dog slept for 309 years (Q 18:25), how a man and his donkey were brought back to life after a hundred years (Q 2:259), how a dead fish that Moses and his companion carried came back to life (Q 18:61), how the prophet Salih was accompanied by a "camel of God" (Q 7:73, 11:64, 91:13; cf. 26: 155, 54:27), and how a fish swallowed and later spat up Jonah (Q 21:87–88, 37:139–48), a story also included in the Bible.

The Lord-Servant Relationship

Another way to understand the People of the Sabbath story is to remember that humans, according to the Qur'an, are not simply meant to love God. They are to obey him. God is "lord" (*rabb*), and humans are "servants" (*'ibad*).[36]

In the *alastu* verse on the primordial covenant between God and all of humanity (Q 7:172), discussed in Chapter 2, God's question to the souls gathered before him is simply, "Am I not your Lord?" This verse makes it clear that in his relationship to humans, God is above all "lord." Humans are to obey him and to worship him in a way that befits a servant (the qur'anic term for proper worship of God is literally the "act of a servant," *'ibada*). This is why, as Toshihiko Izutsu explains, the sorts of dispositions that the Qur'an asks of humans include "humbleness, modesty, absolute obedience, and other properties that are usually demanded of a servant."[37]

This might help us understand better why the Qur'an so often calls on its audience to have a disposition of "pious fear" or "God-consciousness" (*taqwa*) before God or "to submit" themselves to God. The Arabic term for "submission" is, of course, *islam*, and early Muslims would eventually take this term as a name for their religion (being influenced by verses such as Q 3:19, 85 and 5:3). However, in the Qur'an itself the term *islam*, and the corresponding verb *aslama*, is not used to designate a religious movement, but rather a proper religious disposition.

This disposition is encouraged by Q 39:54: "Turn penitently to Him and submit (*aslimu*) to Him before the punishment overtakes you, whereupon you will not be helped." In the Qur'an Abraham is a model of this sort of submission: "When his Lord said to him, 'Submit,' he said, 'I submit to the Lord of all the worlds'" (Q 2:131). Accordingly, Abraham is elsewhere (Q 3:67) called a *muslim,* a "submitter" (although he cannot be thought of as a Muslim with a capital "M," as he lived before Muhammad).

The original meaning of *islam,* then, concerns the disposition of the believer before God; it concerns the responsibility of humans, as servants, to be completely submissive to their master. Regarding this Izutsu writes, "The primary function of a servant consists naturally in serving his master faithfully, paying constant and careful attention to the latter's wishes whatever he wishes, and obeying without murmuring his commands."[38]

Does Allah Grieve?

We have seen examples of Allah's anger at human disobedience. But does this disobedience also cause him sadness?

In certain biblical passages God is saddened by the disobedience of his people. In the prologue to the story of the flood, for example, we read that God was "grieved" by the wickedness of humanity: "The Lord saw that the wickedness of man was great in the earth, and that every imagination of the thoughts of his heart was only evil continually. And the Lord was sorry that he had made man on the earth, and it grieved him to his heart" (Gen 6:5–6). The root Hebrew word behind "grieved" is *'asab,* which can even have the sense of "to hurt" or "to pain."

In Jeremiah God expresses both anger and sadness at the disobedience of Israel:

> My grief is beyond healing,
> my heart is sick within me.

Hark, the cry of the daughter of my people
      from the length and breadth of the land:
"Is the Lord not in Zion?
      Is her King not in her?"
"Why have they provoked me to anger with their graven
    images,
      and with their foreign idols?"
"The harvest is past, the summer is ended,
      and we are not saved."
For the wound of the daughter of my people is my heart
    wounded,
      I mourn, and dismay has taken hold on me.

Is there no balm in Gilead?
      Is there no physician there?
Why then has the health of the daughter of my people
      not been restored?
O that my head were waters,
      and my eyes a fountain of tears,
that I might weep day and night
      for the slain of the daughter of my people!
      (Jer 8:18–9:1)

What about Allah? Does he grieve over human sin or infidelity? The Qur'an insists that there is nothing that unbelievers can do that could hurt God:

[176]Do not grieve for those who are active in unfaith; they will not hurt God in the least: God desires to give them no share in the Hereafter, and there is a great punishment for them. [177]Those who have bought unfaith for faith will not hurt God in the

least, and there is a painful punishment for them.
(Q 3:176–77; cf. 9:39, 47:32)

David Marshall, who refers to Gen 6:5–6 quoted above, notes how the Qur'an insists that God is not affected by the disobedience or the wickedness of humanity. He concludes: "It might be accurate to say that sin, or human disobedience towards God, is indeed a problem in the Qur'an, but it is a problem for human beings, and apparently not for God."[39]

Marshall's perspective is partly correct. It is true that the God of the Qur'an is not hurt or harmed by human sin; he is, however, affected by it. Sin *is* a problem. What is different is the nature of God's response to sin. He does not respond with sadness; he responds with anger. Allah responds to disobedience with an emotion befitting a king. And he does not only get angry; he gets even.

8

The Avenger

The standpoint of the Koran is not that of pure logic; the Koranic thought unfolds itself on a plane which is essentially different from that of the logic of human freedom.

—*Toshihiko Izutsu,* God and Man in the Koran

In December 2017 Italian television broadcast a conversation between Pope Francis and an Italian prison chaplain in which they discussed the Lord's Prayer, or the "Our Father" prayer, line by line. When they arrived at the line usually translated (in Italian as in English) "do not lead us into temptation," Pope Francis expressed some concerns: "I'm the one who falls. But it's not (God) who pushes me into temptation to see how I fall. No, a father does not do this. A father helps us up immediately." The pope continued: "The one who leads us into temptation is Satan, that's Satan's job."[1]

In fact, that line of the Lord's Prayer had already been modified in most French-speaking countries so that it reads,

"Do not let us enter into temptation" ("Ne nous laisse pas entrer en tentation"). In English-speaking countries, however, the news broke that Pope Francis was trying to "change" the Lord's Prayer, and some Catholics responded with shock.

Meddling with the wording of a dearly beloved prayer can cause confusion, but Pope Francis was following a long tradition of Catholic theology by which God is responsible for guidance and goodness only. The devil or human concupiscence is responsible for sin. This idea already has firm grounding in the New Testament letter of James:

> [13]Never, when you are being put to the test, say, "God is tempting me"; God cannot be tempted by evil, and he does not put anybody to the test.
>   [14]Everyone is put to the test by being attracted and seduced by that person's own wrong desire. (1:13–14)

In Islamic theological tradition the origin of evil is deeply contested. The Mu'tazilite school hesitated to make God, who is just, responsible for leading humans astray. And yet much of Islamic tradition accepts that God is no friend to unbelievers or sinners. He doesn't simply judge them or condemn them; he actively opposes them. Among most traditional lists of God's "beautiful" names is one that might surprise some readers: *al-muntaqim*, the "avenger." The presence of this name among others that speak of God's forgiving or gentle nature is jarring. At least one major Muslim scholar insists that it has no place among God's beautiful names.[2]

And yet, "the avenger" is there in the Qur'an. On three occasions God says in the Qur'an that he will "take vengeance" (Arabic *inna muntaqimun*: Q 32:22, 43:41, 44:16). Elsewhere, after referring to peoples whom he has destroyed, God declares, "We have taken vengeance" (*intaqamna;* Q 7:136; 15:79; 30:47; 43:25, 55). In Sura 7 the Egyptians promise Moses that if only Allah will remove a plague from them, they will believe in him and let the Israelites go. When they are not true to their word and break their promise (Q 7:135), the divine voice proclaims, "So We took vengeance on them [*intaqamna*] and drowned them in the sea, for they impugned Our signs and were oblivious to them" (Q 7:136).³ In Sura 43 the Qur'an refers again to the story of Moses, describing how Pharaoh persuaded his people to reject Moses's claims. Allah then declares, "So when they roused Our wrath, We took vengeance on them [*intaqamna*] and drowned them all" (Q 43:55).

Some Muslim commentators, those opposed to the idea that God could be an avenger, suggest that the Arabic term rendered as "vengeance" (*intiqam*) actually works in the Qur'an as a simple synonym for divine punishment.⁴ And yet, as testified in Q 43:55, God's vengeance follows when his "wrath" is "roused."

Like the notion of divine anger, that of divine vengeance is not new. In Deuteronomy 32 we find a vivid picture of God's anger with the Israelites for their worship of other gods, along with declarations of his plans to avenge himself:

> ²²For a fire is kindled by my anger,
>   and it burns to the depths of Sheol,
> devours the earth and its increase,
>   and sets on fire the foundations of the
>   mountains.
>
> ²³And I will heap evils upon them;
>   I will spend my arrows upon them;

²⁴they shall be wasted with hunger,
     and devoured with burning heat
     and poisonous pestilence;
and I will send the teeth of beasts against them,
with venom of crawling things of the dust.

Psalm 10 describes the furtive plots of evildoers and implores God to take vengeance against them: "Break thou the arm of the wicked and evildoer; seek out his wickedness till thou find none" (Ps 10:15). In the next chapter we explore more closely this relationship between the vengeance of God in the Bible and in the Qur'an. Here, we focus on stories that are distinct to the Qur'an.

A Table from Heaven

Toward the end of Sura 5, disciples ask Jesus for a special kind of miracle: "The Disciples said, 'O Jesus son of Mary! Can your Lord send down to us a table from the sky?'" (Q 5:112a). This question seems curious. Of all the things to ask for, why would the disciples request a "table from the sky"?

Some scholars have argued that this passage could be connected to the story of the multiplication of fish and loaves in the Gospels, as both stories have to do with the miraculous gift of food. Others think that it might be connected to a story in Acts 10 in which Peter sees a sheet come down from heaven with animals in it for him to eat (although Jesus plays no role in that story).

The most convincing explanation has to do with Psalm 78. In the midst of this Psalm, the author refers back to the story of the Israelites' wanderings in the desert and proclaims:

^{18}They tested God in their heart
>   by demanding the food they craved.
^{19}They spoke against God, saying,
>   "Can God spread a table in the wilderness?"

Both Psalm 78:19 and Q 5:112 speak of "Israelites" (in the latter case they are the disciples of Jesus) asking for a "table."[5] The Gospel of John is connected here too. In it, the crowds around Jesus demand that he perform a sign, harkening back to the manna that Moses provided their ancestors: "So they said, 'What sign will you yourself do, the sight of which will make us believe in you? What work will you do? Our fathers ate the manna in the wilderness; as it is written, "He gave them bread out of heaven to eat"'" (John 6:30–31).

In all three cases the demand for a table, or a sign, appears to be insolent.[6] In the Qur'an Jesus hesitates to ask God for this table. Instead, he tells the disciples, "Be wary of God, if you be faithful" (Q 5:112b). But they press on with their demands, and Jesus relents:

> ^{113}They said, "We desire to eat from it, and our hearts will be at rest: we shall know that you have told us the truth, and we will be among witnesses to it."
> ^{114}Said Jesus son of Mary, "O God! Our Lord! Send down to us a table from heaven, to be a feast for us, for the first ones among us and the last ones and as a sign from You, and provide for us; for You are the best of providers." (Q 5:113–14)

What is particularly interesting for us is the way God responds to Jesus after his back and forth with the disciples. God is willing to grant Jesus's request, but he adds a terrible threat, saying, "should any of you disbelieve after this, I will indeed punish him with a punishment such as I do not punish anyone in all creation" (Q 5:115). The disciples thus receive a special "sign" from heaven, a table. Precisely because of this, they will be held especially accountable. Allah threatens to punish the disciples with a punishment *unlike any other*. A tradition preserved in the commentary *Tafsir al-Jalalayn* describes this punishment in a way that may be familiar to us: "It is said that the Table sent down from heaven consisted of bread and meat, and they were commanded not to be treacherous and [not] to store anything for the next day: but they were and they stored some of it, and were [consequently] transformed into apes and swine."[7]

The Crucifixion of Jesus

The second story involving Jesus relates to the end of his life. In a well-known verse in Sura 3 the Qur'an insists that God tricks those who try to trick him. After describing the birth and the miracles of Jesus, the Qur'an suddenly declares, "Then they plotted, and God also plotted, and God is the best of plotters" (Q 3:54).[8]

The basic problem with this verse is simple: Who are "they"? Looking back in previous verses, one finds the disciples of Christ:

> [52]When Jesus sensed their faithlessness, he said, "Who will be my helpers [on the path] toward God?" The Disciples said, "We will be helpers of God. We have faith in God, and you be witness that we have submitted [to Him]. [53]Our Lord, we

believe in what You have sent down, and we follow the apostle, so write us among the witnesses."
(Q 3:52–53)

Could it be that it was Jesus's disciples who plotted? Were they
perhaps deceitful in their pledge of faith? This might seem to be
the obvious answer, but most Muslim interpreters found such
a conclusion impossible, since they assume that the disciples
were faithful followers of Jesus. These interpreters proposed
instead that one go back to the mention of "*their* faithlessness"
at the beginning of verse 52. They argued that "they" in verse
54 refers to the "faithless" Israelites of verse 52 — precisely those
Israelites who were *not* Jesus's disciples. It was those unbelieving Israelites, according to the reading of these interpreters,
who "plotted" against God. But what was their plot?

In order to answer this question, classical Muslim interpreters turned to another famous qur'anic verse, the only place
in the entire Qur'an with a reference to the crucifixion of Jesus.
In Sura 4:157 the Israelites say: "And for their saying, 'We killed
the Messiah, Jesus son of Mary, the apostle of God' — though
they did not kill him nor crucify him, but so it was made to appear to them." The declaration here that the Israelites did not
kill or crucify Jesus seems to be clear. What caused interpreters
headaches is the expression that comes next, rendered here as
"so it was made to appear to them" (Arabic *shubbiha la-hum*).
This was a riddle: What — or who — was made to appear to the
Israelites?

The most common explanation of this ambiguous Arabic
phrase is that the likeness of *Jesus* was made to appear to the
Israelites. *Someone else* was physically transformed to look like
him. It was this person who was crucified in the place of Jesus,
while Jesus himself ascended into heaven, escaping death. The

Israelites looked up on the cross and saw this "substitute," who *appeared to them* as though he were Jesus, and so they thought they were killing the right man. Jesus, however, had slipped through their fingers. Some traditions relate that he rose up to heaven through a hole in the roof of the house where he and the disciples were staying.

The conservative Qur'an commentator Ibn Kathir (d. 1373) describes this series of events in a distinctly anti-Jewish tone: "God saved his Prophet and took him up from among them, and left [the Jews] groping blindly in their confusion, thinking that they had achieved their wish. God, furthermore, caused their hearts to become hard and stubborn against the truth, and afflicted them with humiliation that will not leave them till the 'day of the great call.'"[9]

For his part Zamakhshari offers two possible stories that reflect this interpretation. In the first, when God tells Jesus that his moment to ascend to heaven has come, Jesus asks for a volunteer among his disciples to die in his place: "Jesus said, 'Who would like to have my likeness cast on him, to be killed and crucified, and to enter paradise?' One of them replies, 'I would.' [Jesus's] likeness is cast on him and he is killed and crucified."[10] Certain traditions identify this "volunteer" as the apostle Peter. In any case, this story is a perfect reversal of the Christian idea of Jesus's death. Instead of Jesus dying for his disciples, one of his disciples dies for him.

Yet Zamakhshari also relates a contrary tradition, according to which an enemy of Jesus is the one who is crucified in his place: "[The Jews] went into the house of Jesus and Jesus was raised up while his likeness was cast on the betrayer. They took him and killed him thinking that he was Jesus."[11] This second tradition has become more popular in contemporary Islamic thought. It was even captured in an Iranian film,

The Messiah, which shows Judas Iscariot being transformed by God into Jesus's likeness and—despite his protests—crucified by the Romans.

In any case, all of this brings us back to Q 3:54 (the verse that speaks of God as the "best plotter"). The story of Jesus's crucifixion offered to interpreters a perfect explanation of the divine "plot" referred to in that verse. According to their logic, the Israelites sought to plot against God by killing Jesus. God, however, outwitted them by taking Jesus directly into heaven and changing someone to look like him. That was his "counter-plot." *Tafsir al-Jalalayn* explains: "And they, the disbelievers among the Children of Israel, schemed, against Jesus, by assigning someone to assassinate him; and God schemed, by casting the likeness of Jesus onto the person who intended to kill him, and so they killed him, while Jesus was raised up into heaven; and God is the best of schemers."[12] It is this scenario that lies behind the doctrine that Jesus is still alive in heaven, waiting to descend at the end of time.[13]

What, then, does it mean when the Qur'an says that God is the "best plotter" or "schemer" (*khayru l-makirin*)? Muhammad Asad denies that God could be a "trickster," insisting that this phrase actually means "God *is above* all schemers."[14] Yet the story of Christ's crucifixion is not the only place where we find divine trickery in the Qur'an.

Divine Scheming

Toward the opening of the Qur'an, near the beginning of Sura 2, we read of a people who seek to deceive the believers. These people, when they meet the believers, insist that they believe too. In secret, however, when they return to their "devils" (perhaps an allusion to other gods), they confide, "We are with you; we were only deriding [them]" (Q 2:14). In this way they trick the believers. The Qur'an insists, however, that God knows what they are up to and will get back at them:

> ¹⁷Their parable is that of one who lighted a torch, and when it had lit up all around him, God took away their light, and left them sightless in a manifold darkness. ¹⁸Deaf, dumb, and blind, they will not come back.

God does not simply watch them go astray. He "takes away their light" and keeps them from coming back to the truth, leaving them in darkness. Qur'an 20 speaks of a man who refused to see God's signs in this world. Rising from the dead on the Day of Resurrection, he discovers that he is now blind. "Why have You raised me blind, though I used to see?" he asks (Q 20:125). God responds, "Our signs came to you, but you forgot them, and so you will be forgotten today" (Q 20:126).

With such passages we begin to have a vision of the dynamic relationship between God and humans in the Qur'an. Allah is not a passive observer of humanity; he is intimately involved in the rise and fall of human fortunes. As Toshihiko Izutsu writes, "God in the Koranic Weltanschauung [worldview] does not subsist in His glorious self-sufficing solitude and stand aloof from mankind as does the God of Greek philosophy, but deeply involves Himself in human affairs."¹⁵

God's involvement is seen in a passage of Sura 3 where the Qur'an insists that although God is not injured, or "hurt," by the unbelievers, he has a special way of dealing with them:

> ¹⁷⁷Those who have bought unfaith for faith will not hurt God in the least, and there is a painful punish-

ment for them. [178]Let the faithless not suppose that
the respite We grant them is good for their souls:
We give them respite only that they may increase
in sin, and there is a humiliating punishment for
them.

In other words, God *intentionally* restrains himself from punishing unbelievers. His goal in doing so, however, is not to
show mercy. He does this precisely so that the faithless will fall
deeper into their faithlessness. Thereby they will sin even more
and accordingly merit divine punishment even more.

Something similar is found in Sura 44. Here the unbelievers actually see divine punishment coming upon them and
repent, but only for a while:

> [10]So *watch out* for the day when the sky brings on a
> manifest smoke [11]enveloping the people. [They will
> cry out:] "This is a painful punishment. [12]Our Lord!
> Remove this punishment from us. We have indeed
> believed!" [13]What will the admonition avail them,
> when a manifest apostle had already come to them,
> [14]but they turned away from him and said, "A tu-
> tored madman"?
>
> [15]Indeed, We will withdraw the punishment
> a little; but you will revert [to your earlier ways].
> [16]The day We shall strike with the most terrible
> striking, We will indeed take vengeance [on them].

The repentance of this people who see smoke in the sky will
lead God to relent for a while. In the end, however, he will
strike them with an even greater punishment.[16]

This idea did not pass the classical Muslim interpreters

by—they called it *istidraj* and used it to explain why good things might happen to unbelievers. In fact, for many classical scholars, *istidraj* exceeded God's withholding of punishment. They speculated that at times God actually gives good things to unbelievers in order that they may *not* realize the error of their ways and *not* repent.

The doctrine of *istidraj* seems to be fundamentally what philosophers call a "theodicy." A theodicy usually explains why bad things happen to good people—why, for example, an innocent child is afflicted with a disease or why a tidal wave destroys a coastal village. Here it is the other way around—the notion of *istidraj* is used to explain why good things happen to bad people. The answer is that God is setting these bad people up for their punishment.

That God would do good things for bad people in a way that may seem quizzical is exemplified in the story of the mysterious servant of God (known in Islamic tradition as Khidr) in Sura 18. At one point (v. 77) this "servant" repairs the dilapidated wall of an inhospitable people. Only later do we learn (v. 82) that beneath the wall was a treasure belonging to orphans that the "servant of God" meant to keep hidden from the bad people of the town.[17] Allah used his trickery for the benefit of the vulnerable.

Elsewhere the Qur'an relates how he gave good things to unbelievers and then struck them down when they least expected it:

> So when they forgot what they had been admonished of, We opened for them the gates of all [good] things. When they became proud of what they were given, We seized them suddenly, whereat they became despondent. (Q 6:44; cf. 6:108, 7:94–95)[18]

In a fascinating passage of Sura 10, Moses turns to God and says the following:

> [88]Moses said, "Our Lord! You have given Pharaoh and his elite glamour and wealth in the life of this world, our Lord, that they may lead [people] astray from Your way! Our Lord! Blot out their wealth and harden their hearts so that they do not believe until they sight the painful punishment."

One understands from Moses's speech that God intentionally propped up Pharaoh and his followers *in order that* they might lead others astray. Moses apparently feels that enough is enough. He wants two things from God: that he strip Pharaoh and his clique of their money, and that he harden their hearts (so that they can be punished as unbelievers).

In Sura 89, after reminding its audience of the way God has destroyed earlier peoples, the Qur'an says simply, "Your Lord is indeed in ambush" (Q 89:14). The notion of a divine "ambush" is also suggested by the language of Q 11:121–22, where the divine voice of the Qur'an instructs Muhammad as follows:

> *Say* to those who do not have faith, "Act according to your ability; we too are acting. And wait! We too are waiting."

This dramatic language helps bring home the unpredictability of the qur'anic God. One does not know when he might strike or how he might act. In fact, the Qur'an uses a rich range of vocabulary related to this theme. In Q 3:54 the term used to refer to God's plotting is *makr*, which appears in a number of other passages (Q 7:99, 8:30, 13:42, 27:50).

The philosophically minded scholar Fakhr al-Din al-Razi (d. 1209) knew the definition of *makr* as "an act of deception aiming at causing evil" and insisted, "It is not possible to attribute deception to God."[19] He came up with the explanation that God's *makr* is different, that is, by *makr*, the Qur'an means only that God punishes those who are guilty of evil. But others disagreed. The Spanish Muslim al-Qurtubi (d. 1273) reports that the Prophet Muhammad used to pray, "O God, scheme for me, and do not scheme against me!"[20]

A similar sentiment is found in a story told by the Qur'an interpreter Sahl al-Tustari (d. 896), according to which the qur'anic prophet named Luqman (not known in the Bible) once counseled his son, "'Have hope in God without feeling secure from His ruse (*makr*) and fear God without despairing of his mercy.' [His son] responded [by asking], 'How can I do that when I only have one heart?' He replied: 'O my son, the believer has two hearts, one with which he carries hope in God and the other with which he fears Him.'"[21]

Makr is not the only term used for divine trickery. Elsewhere in the Qur'an (7:182–83, 68:45, 86:15–16) Allah is associated with *kayd*, sometimes rendered as "devising." In Q 7:183 God's giving a respite to the unbelievers is described as a sort of *kayd*: "And I will grant them respite, for My devising (*kaydi*) is indeed sure." This same term is associated also with the stratagems of unbelievers and opponents of the prophets: it is used for pagans (7:195), the brothers of Joseph (12:5), sneaky women in the Joseph story (12:28), and other unbelievers (20: 64, 52:46, 77:39).

Other terms used to describe Allah's trickery include

khida' (4:142; elsewhere attributed to the unbelievers: 2:9, 8:62) and the Arabic verb *aghwa*. In Q 11:34 Noah declares to his opponents that God could lead them astray (*yughwiya-kum*). Tellingly, Satan accuses God (perhaps rightly) of lead-ing him astray on two occasions. In Q 7:16 Satan declares to God, "You have led me astray! (*aghwaytani*)." In Q 15:39 Satan says that *because* God has led him astray, he will lead others astray: "He said 'O Lord, because you have led me astray (*agh-waytani*), I will surely glamorize [evil] for them on the earth, and I will surely lead all of them astray (*la-ughwiyannahum*).'" Muhammad Asad—clearly uncomfortable with the idea of a God who deceives—translates these two occurrences identi-cally as "thou hast thwarted me."

Closely related to those qur'anic passages that speak of both God and Satan "leading astray" are those that speak of how God and Satan "adorn" or "decorate" (Arabic *zayyana*) bad works to make them look good. In a number of passages Satan is responsible for this sort of deception. In Sura 6:43 the divine voice of the Qur'an asks why the unbelievers did not turn to God and then gives the answer:

> Then why did they not entreat when Our punish-ment overtook them! But their hearts had hard-ened and Satan had made what they had been doing seem decorous (*zayyana*) to them.

In other words, Satan played a trick on them, and so they con-tinued in their hard-heartedness.

But God can play tricks on people too: in Qur'an 27:4 God declares, "As for those who do not believe in the Hereafter, We have made their deeds seem decorous (*zayyanna*) to them, and so they are bewildered." God beautifies the evil deeds and unbelief of the unbelievers, and he beautifies the faith of the believers so they remain faithful (Q 49:7). The difference, in other words, is that God leads unbelievers astray, while Satan leads believers astray.

Finally, the Qur'an also associates God with the root *dalla,* meaning "to lead astray" or more precisely to "lead into error." This verb appears in a verse of Sura 6 marked by dramatic imagery:

> Those who deny Our signs are deaf and dumb, in
> a manifold darkness. God leads into error (*yudlil*)
> whomever He wishes, and whomever He wishes He
> puts him on a straight path. (Q 6:39; cf. 14:4)

Those whom God leads into error have "no path," the Qur'an says in another place (Q 42:46).[22] In sum, if the God of the Qur'an guides the believers, he misleads the unbelievers. He does not simply leave them to wander around in darkness, searching for the right road. He actively sets them farther down the wrong road so that they are forever lost.

Ash'aris Vindicated

In his critique of the Mu'tazilite understanding of God, Khalid Blankinship accuses the Mu'tazilites of limiting God's possibility of showing mercy. He argues that the "mechanistic image of a deity constrained by His own laws" meant that God would be "incapable of true mercy."[23] Blankinship, however, misses the other side of the coin. By insisting that God always judged according to justice, the Mu'tazila also made God incapable of vengeance. For the Mu'tazila, God acts in order to reward or punish people precisely as they deserve. He does not act to settle scores.

Yet the evidence of the Qur'an — on this count, at least — is undoubtedly on the side of the Ash'aris. The God of the Qur'an is capable of both guidance and leading astray. In Sura 32:22 the Qur'an insists that those who don't listen to the prophets will endure God's vengeance:

> Who is a greater wrongdoer than him who is re-minded of his Lord's signs, whereat he disregards them? We shall indeed take vengeance upon the guilty.

This same sentiment is expressed differently in Sura 43. Here God assures the Prophet that divine vengeance will eventually overtake those who don't listen to him (even if the Prophet is "taken" — that is, dies — first): "We will indeed take vengeance on them, whether We take you away or show *you* what We have promised them, for indeed We hold them in Our power" (Q 43:41–42). Notably, in both of these passages God's vengeance is carried out for the sake of Muhammad. From a believer's perspective, nothing could be more natural. Muhammad, after all, was God's chosen one, the last and greatest of the prophets.

One lesson, finally, is clear. The God of the Qur'an is in charge of humans. He is master of their lives and master of their deaths. To some, this can even imply that God is arbitrary. The mystic Farid al-Din 'Attar (d. 1221) cites the opinion of someone who said of God, "He's a potter who first makes pots with great skill and then smashes them himself."[24] 'Attar calls this man a "fool."

God Will Mock Them

What is noteworthy for our purposes are the vivid colors with which the Qur'an's author presents Allah. Allah exhibits personal emotions. We see this personality vividly in Sura 2:

> ¹⁴When they meet the faithful, they say, "We believe," but when they are alone with their devils, they say, "We are with you; we were only deriding [them]."
>
> ¹⁵It is Allah who derides them [*allahu yastahzi'u bihim*], and leaves them bewildered in their rebellion.

I've quoted this passage according to the 2011 translation of Qarai, but it is instructive to see how the clause *allahu yastahzi'u bihim* appears in a number of other translations:

Pickthall (1930): Allah (Himself) doth mock them.
Yusuf Ali (1934): Allah will throw back their
     mockery on them.
Arberry (1955): God shall mock them.
Asad (1980): God will requite them for their
     mockery.
Hilali and Khan (1996): Allah mocks at them.

The word that Qarai translates as "derides" (Arabic *yastahzi'u*) can also be understood as "mock" (one classical Arabic dictionary translates, "He mocked at, scoffed at, laughed at, derided, or ridiculed him").[25] Muhammad Pickthall accordingly renders the clause "Allah (Himself) doth mock them." Yet the notion of God's mocking, or deriding, seems inappropriate to some. Muhammad Asad eliminates it entirely and has "God will requite them for their mockery." Similarly, the Indian translator Yusuf Ali seems to resist the simple meaning of this clause and translates, "Allah will throw back their mockery on them."

The translations of Asad and Yusuf Ali reflect rationalist notions of God's transcendence. From their perspective, God is above "mocking" someone, even unbelievers. God's "mockery" of the unbelievers in Q 2:15 is only a tit-for-tat response to unbelievers who "mock" believers by pretending to believe in God (hence the translations of Asad and Yusuf Ali).[26]

Some passages, however, seem to give examples of God's mockery. In Q 9:34 God tells Muhammad, "Give [the faithless] the *good* tidings (*bashshirhum*) of a painful punishment."[27] Is there a tone of sarcasm here? What, after all, could be "good" about a painful punishment? In Q 44:49, God says to a damned soul in hell, "You are indeed the [self-styled] mighty and noble!" Yet what would be "mighty" or "noble" about a soul tortured in the flames of hell?

In Q 3:119, meanwhile, God instructs the Prophet to taunt the People of the Book:

> When they meet you, they say, "We believe," but when they are alone, they bite their fingertips at you out of rage. Say, "Die of your rage!" God indeed knows well what is in the breasts.

Allah's biting rhetoric toward the unbelievers is found again in Sura 7 where the Qur'an compares unbelievers to panting dogs:

> So his parable is that of a dog: if you make for it, it lolls out its tongue, and if you let it alone, it lolls

out its tongue. Such is the parable of the people who
impugn Our signs. (Q 7:176)

Still another passage has more dramatic, even troubling,
imagery. In Sura 22 the Qur'an (in a verse that is difficult to
understand and hotly debated) seems to challenge the unbelievers by proposing that they hang themselves: "Whoever
thinks that God will not help him in this world and the Hereafter, let him stretch a rope to the ceiling and hang himself, and
see if his artifice would remove his rage" (Q 22:15).[28] The God
of the Qur'an is not actually encouraging unbelievers to commit suicide, but perhaps he is, in a way, mocking them for their
unbelief. The Qur'an's portrayal of a God who mocks unbelievers is not new, however. Psalm 2:4 declares, "He who sits in the
heavens laughs, / the Lord has them in derision" (cf. Ps 59:8).

The Sealing of Hearts

As we have seen, the Qur'an's God not only mocks unbelievers
but actively plots against them. This is famously articulated in
those passages in which he "seals hearts."

This expression is found twelve times in the Qur'an:
Q 2:7; 6:46; 7:100, 101; 9:87; 10:74; 16:108; 30:59; 40:35; 45:23;
47:16; and 63:3. In one place (Q 5:13) the Qur'an insists that
God "hardens" hearts, a phrase that seems to be close to those
biblical passages in Exodus that speak of God's hardening the
heart of Pharaoh.[29] Looking back at that episode, Paul writes
in his letter to the Romans (9:17–18) that God can still harden
hearts:

[17]For the scripture says to Pharaoh, "I have raised
you up for the very purpose of showing my power

in you, so that my name may be proclaimed in all
the earth."
¹⁸So then he has mercy upon whomever he
wills, and he hardens the heart of whomever he
wills.

The concluding declaration here—which emphasizes God's
sovereign right to guide and lead astray as he wills—could almost be taken from the Qur'an.

The language of "hearts" also appears in other ways in
the Qur'an. Allah causes hypocrisy to enter the hearts of those
who disregard him (Q 9:76-77); he increases the sickness in
the hearts of those who seek to deceive him (Q 2:10); and he
refuses to purify the hearts of those whom he has led astray
(Q 5:41).

What are we to make of all of this? The creed attributed to
Ash'ari refers to the sealing of hearts as one example of God's
power: "God does have the power to make the unbelievers
sound and to show favour to them so that they become believers, but He willed not to make the unbelievers sound and
not to show favour to them so that they became believers;
(on the contrary) He willed that they should be unbelievers
as He knew (they would be), and He abandoned them, sent
them astray and put a seal on their hearts."[30] One might ask:
If the God of the Qur'an is merciful, why would he lead further astray those who are already lost instead of guiding them
home? The Qur'an simply never answers this question. But
perhaps this is the wrong question to ask of a scripture.

Some Muslim interpreters, however, insisted on trying
to solve the theological enigmas in the Qur'an. This is the case
with Zamakhshari. Commenting on Q 2:7 ("God has set a seal
on their hearts and their hearing, and there is a blindfold on

their sight, and there is a great punishment for them"), he suggests the following:

- Perhaps "sealing" here refers only to an innate disposition of unbelief.
- Perhaps "sealing" is used figuratively—the way people say "the mountain torrent has flown away with someone" when a person has died or "the condor has flown away with someone" when a person is absent for a long time.
- Perhaps it is Satan or unbelievers themselves who have "sealed" their hearts. Zamakhshari explains: "Since it is God who has granted to them the ability and the possibility (to do so), the sealing (of the heart) is ascribed to Him."
- Perhaps these unbelievers would never believe by their own free choice but only by God's coercion, and God's refusal to coerce them is called (figuratively) "sealing."
- Perhaps this expression is simply a response to the unbelievers who themselves declare that God had sealed their hearts and hearing. As Zamakhshari notes, elsewhere in the Qur'an unbelievers declare something to this effect about themselves (notably Q 41:5).[31]

On Q 5:41, which speaks of "the ones whose hearts God did not desire to purify," Zamakhshari explains that God simply knows which hearts cannot be purified: "God knows that his benevolence would remain without gain or effect."[32]

Not everyone was happy with Zamakhshari's efforts to rationalize the Qur'an's language. In his gloss on Zamakhshari's commentary, a scholar named Ibn al-Munayyir (d. 1284) from the Egyptian coastal city of Alexandria responds to the Mu'tazilite's creative interpretations. As concerns Q 5:41, Ibn al-Munayyir comments that there is a simple way of understanding this verse: "This verse is to be understood in accordance with the doctrines of the people of the *sunna*, who say that God (himself) wills it when people succumb to temptation, and that he (is the one who) does not wish to purify their hearts from the impurity of temptation and the filth of unbelief."[33] Ibn al-Munayyir thus meant to correct Zamakhshari's Mu'tazilite "excesses" and restore a plain reading of the Qur'an, even if this led to the conclusion that God wills for some people to sin.

Allah Is the "Guardian of the Faithful"

In Sura 3, the Qur'an summarizes its argument against Jews and Christians by insisting that its own followers are close to Abraham: "Indeed the nearest of all people to Abraham are those who follow him and this prophet and those who have faith, and God is the guardian of the faithful" (Q 3:68).

The point about Abraham is interesting, since it seems in part to be a response to Jewish and Christian claims to have a special connection to Abraham. Yet an even more interesting point about this verse for our purposes is the way in which the Qur'an describes Allah as "guardian of the faithful." The Arabic word rendered "guardian" here is *wali*, a term that Yusuf Ali translates as "protector." A *wali* in Arabic is someone who takes another person under protection, who preserves that person from a threat and defends him or her from enemies. In ancient Islam new converts were taken into the community by finding a *wali* among one of the members of an Arab tribe. In

Islamic law the *wali* is a person who is legally responsible for a child. The *wali al-dam* (the *wali* of "blood") is the "avenger of blood" or "executor of a blood feud."[34]

The point of declaring Allah the "guardian of the faithful" is to identify him as the guardian, or the protector, of the believers but *not* of the unbelievers. This chapter has taught us even more than this. Allah is the opponent, even the enemy, of the unbelievers. He leads them astray, sets ambushes for them, and seals their hearts. God is capable of deception and trickery in doing so. This notion of a vengeful God may seem startling, but it is not entirely new.

IV
A Personal God

9

God of the Bible and the Qur'an

But the plan of salvation also includes those who acknowledge the Creator. In the first place amongst these there are the Muslims, who, professing to hold the faith of Abraham, along with us adore the one and merciful God, who on the last day will judge mankind.

—Lumen gentium, *Second Vatican Council*

In recent years Christians and Muslims have not always respected one another's scriptures. The American pastor Terry Jones attempted to hold an "International Burn a Koran Day" in 2010 on the anniversary of the attacks of September 11, 2001. Although he eventually backed down, the announcement of his event led to protests, some violent, in Pakistan and Afghanistan. Other Christians have gone through with their threats and burned the Qur'an, sometimes posting videos on YouTube to make sure that their action would be visible to the world.

The approach of Muslims to the Bible varies widely. Years ago I was in a cab in Beirut, Lebanon, and noticed a Qur'an that the driver kept on the dashboard (a common practice for Muslim cabbies for whom the Qur'an can be seen almost as a talisman). When he learned that I was a Christian, he invited me to open the glove compartment. There I discovered a copy of the Arabic New Testament. The cabbie told me, "I just want you to know that I consider your book too to be the word of God." Around that time a priest in Beirut recounted to me how one day a Muslim from the neighborhood brought him a Bible that he had found in a trash dumpster, commenting, "That is not where a holy book belongs."

Not everywhere in the Islamic world is the Bible so respected. For instance, it is illegal to take a Bible into Saudi Arabia. Security agents at international airports in the country search through incoming bags for drugs and alcohol, but also for Bibles. If they find one, they may throw it in the trash.

Such hostility appears to be ironic when one takes a closer look at these two scriptures. The Bible and the Qur'an share many of the same characters. Adam, Noah, Abraham, Moses, David, Jesus, and Mary are all central figures in the Qur'an, though qur'anic stories about these figures sometimes differ from what is found in the Bible. In the Qur'an, for example, Noah has a son who does not get in the ark, Moses is the adopted son of Pharaoh's wife (not of Pharaoh's daughter), and Jesus appears to escape the crucifixion, as we have seen. Nevertheless, it is remarkable that the two scriptures share so many characters.

We might even add "God" to this list of characters. As the epigraph to this chapter shows, both Muslims and Christians believe in a God who is creator, one, merciful, and judge. Indeed, the image of God is in many (although not all) ways similar in the Bible and the Qur'an. This is true even when it comes to the central theme of this book: the mercy and vengeance of God. The problem of the relationship between divine mercy and divine vengeance existed long before Muhammad began to preach in Mecca; it was central already to the Bible.

Mercy and Vengeance in the Old Testament

The best place to look in the Bible for divine mercy and divine vengeance may be the story of the Israelites' wanderings in the desert after their exodus from Egypt but before their entry into the promised land. Their situation is dramatic. They have witnessed God's mighty signs in Egypt (including the ten plagues and the splitting of the sea in two), but they are wandering through the desert with no sure source of food and water. Time and again they complain about their fate. They repeatedly lament that in Egypt—although they were slaves—at least they had food:

> ²And the whole congregation of the people of Israel murmured against Moses and Aaron in the wilderness, ³and said to them, "Would that we had died by the hand of the Lord in the land of Egypt, when we sat by the fleshpots and ate bread to the full; for you have brought us out into this wilderness to kill this whole assembly with hunger." (Exod 16:2–3)

At this point God does not respond to the "murmuring" of Israel in anger. He responds with compassion, sending down manna from heaven so that they might eat and be satisfied. And yet in the very next chapter the people are unhappy again, this time because they are thirsty. Again, they long to be back in Egypt and ask Moses, "Why did you bring us up out of Egypt, to kill us and our children and our cattle with thirst?" (Exod 17:3). And again God does not grow angry; he gives Moses the power to bring forth water from a rock.

In other cases, however, God does get angry, very angry, with the Israelites. Later during their wanderings, as they are passing around the land of Edom, they complain yet again, as they are now bored with the manna, "this worthless food" (Num 21:5). By this time, God has had enough. He sends snakes among the people that bite and kill many of them. So the people repent, and Moses intervenes on their behalf. In response, God offers them a way to save those who have been bitten—a serpent, a sort of talisman, is put on a pole, and those who look at it are healed.[1]

In this last example, at least, God's mercy appears to be conditional. He is merciful to those who repent and obey. This is not the only place where God's mercy is conditional in the Old Testament. In Ezekiel 18 we read that the sins of the wicked will be wiped away, but only if they repent:

> [21]But if a wicked man turns away from all his sins which he has committed and keeps all my statutes and does what is lawful and right, he shall surely live; he shall not die. [22]None of the transgressions which he has committed shall be remembered against him; for the righteousness which he has done he shall live. [23]Have I any pleasure in the death of the wicked, says the Lord God, and not rather that he should turn from his way and live?

In this passage we learn that God longs for the wicked to repent and be saved. However, he is not prepared to show mercy to those who refuse to repent of their sins. He is particularly stern with those who worship gods other than the God of Israel.

God's "jealousy" in this Old Testament passage might be compared with God's disdain in the Qur'an of those guilty of *shirk*—attributing something, or someone, other than him with divinity. As we have seen, the sin of associating something else with Allah is the only sin that the Qur'an describes as unforgivable.

God's jealousy is also seen in the Book of Jeremiah. At one point the prophet Jeremiah seeks to intercede for his people, who have been guilty of worshipping false gods. His pleading, however, is in vain. This sin is too much for God to take. "Send them out of my sight, and let them go!" (Jer 15:1), he says. Later in that passage we discover the extent of his anger when God says, "I will make you serve your enemies in a land which you do not know, for in my anger a fire is kindled which shall burn for ever" (Jer 15:14; a prediction of the Babylonian captivity). The God of the Old Testament, like the God of the Qur'an, is capable of fits of anger.

The Old Testament, however, is distinguished by a concern for the people of Israel. Much of it is marked by the special relationship between God and his people. In a beautiful passage of Isaiah (quoted by Jesus in the synagogue of Nazareth in Luke 4:17–18), the prophet declares the marvelous ways in which God will show compassion for Israel, but he also speaks of a "day of vengeance" against the oppressors:

> ¹The Spirit of the Lord God is upon me,
>   because the Lord has anointed me
> to bring good tidings to the afflicted;
>   he has sent me to bind up the brokenhearted,

to proclaim liberty to the captives,
>   and the opening of the prison to those who are
>   bound;
> ²to proclaim the year of the Lord's favor,
>   and the day of vengeance of our God;
>   to comfort all who mourn. (Isa 61:1–2)

Again in Deuteronomy 32 God speaks of his compassion for his people of Israel but of vengeance upon their enemies:

> ³⁵Vengeance (*naqam*) is mine, and recompense,
>   for the time when their foot shall slip;
> for the day of their calamity is at hand,
>   and their doom comes swiftly.
> ³⁶For the Lord will vindicate his people
>   and have compassion on his servants,
> when he sees that their power is gone,
>   and there is none remaining, bond or free.
> ³⁷Then he will say, "Where are their gods,
>   the rock in which they took refuge,
> ³⁸who ate the fat of their sacrifices,
>   and drank the wine of their drink offering?
> Let them rise up and help you,
>   let them be your protection!

> ³⁹See now that I, even I, am he,
>   and there is no god beside me;
> I kill and I make alive;
>   I wound and I heal;
>   and there is none that can deliver out of my
>   hand."

Of particular interest for our purposes is the Hebrew term, *naqam*, that this passage uses to describe God's vengeance. This term is formed from the same Semitic root (*nqm*) that is used to form the qur'anic word *intiqam*, also meaning vengeance (Hebrew and Arabic are both Semitic languages). Put otherwise, not only do both the Qur'an and the Bible speak of divine vengeance, but use the same word root to describe it.

Moreover, if we look at the passage above closely, we notice that the commonalities with the Qur'an go still further. The divine voice in Deuteronomy declares "there is no god beside me" (v. 39), just as the Qur'an declares "there is no god except Him" (e.g., Q 2:163, 255; 3:2, 18). God in Deuteronomy also says, "I kill and I make alive" (v. 39), while the Qur'an states, "There is no god except Him. He gives life and brings death" (Q 7:158). In Deuteronomy God mocks the false gods of the gentiles by proclaiming, "Where are their gods, the rock in which they took refuge, who ate the fat of their sacrifices, and drank the wine of their drink offering? Let them rise up and help you, let them be your protection!" (Deut 32:37–38). A similar rhetorical question is found in the Qur'an, when God addresses the polytheists condemned to hell:

> [73]Then they will be told, "Where are those whom you used to take as 'partners' [74]besides God?" They will say, "They have forsaken us. Indeed, we did not invoke anything before." That is how God leads the faithless astray. (Q 40:73–74)

Like the author of Deuteronomy the author of the Qur'an taunts the unbelievers for the powerlessness of their gods. In both passages the message is the same: there is only one true

God. What is particularly interesting is the similarity of the *rhetorical form:* in both the Bible and the Qur'an, God addresses the unbelievers directly and challenges them, even ridicules them, pointing out the uselessness of their gods.

As for divine mercy, two different Hebrew terms appear in the Old Testament. First is *hesed,* which God shows to his people. In Ps 23:6 we read, "Surely goodness and mercy (*hesed*) shall follow me / all the days of my life." Humans are also to show *hesed.* In Hos 12:6 we read, "So you, by the help of your God, return, / hold fast to love (*hesed*) and justice, / and wait continually for your God."

Tellingly, however, in the Old Testament we also find the Semitic root *rhm* used for mercy. In Deuteronomy we read, "None of the devoted things shall cleave to your hand; that the Lord may turn from the fierceness of his anger, and show you mercy (*rahamim*), and have compassion on you (*werihamka*), and multiply you, as he swore to your fathers" (Deut 13:17). In 2 Samuel David declares that he trusts in the mercy of God, whereas he does not trust man to be merciful: "Then David said to Gad, 'I am in great distress; let us fall into the hand of the Lord, for his mercy (*rahamo*) is great; but let me not fall into the hand of man'" (2 Sam 24:14). Unlike *hesed,* the root *rhm* in the Old Testament is used for a mercy that can come only from God. This is the same root that is used twice in the Qur'an when it speaks about God as *al-rahman al-rahim* ("the Compassionate, the Merciful").

This root is found again in the biblical story of Jonah, a prophet who complains that God is too merciful. After witnessing how God withholds his punishment from the city of Nineveh (the capital city of Israel's nemesis, Assyria), he complains to the Lord:

> I pray thee, Lord, is not this what I said when I
> was yet in my country? That is why I made haste
> to flee to Tarshish; for I knew that thou art a gra-
> cious God and merciful (*rahum*), slow to anger, and
> abounding in steadfast love, and repentest of evil.
> (Jonah 4:2)

Jonah here gives the answer as to why he fled *away* from the
city that God was sending him to (he was planning to escape
to the far-off city of Tarshish). Jonah wasn't afraid of the long
journey, or of getting stoned in the streets of Nineveh. He
wasn't afraid of his mission failing. He was afraid of his mission succeeding. He knew that if he preached to the inhabitants of Nineveh and they repented, God would forgive them.
He wanted them to be punished, not forgiven.

On this note it might be worth adding that later rabbis
had a tendency to emphasize divine mercy over divine vengeance. One interesting place where this tendency shows itself
is in a discussion over Num 23:19, a verse that begins by declaring, "God is not man, that he should lie," but ends (at least
according to one way of reading it) with the statement, "He
speaks but he does not act." A tradition in a rabbinic commentary explains that when God declares good for the world,
the first part of the verse obtains (i.e., God doesn't back down
from a good promise), but when he declares evil, the end of the
verse obtains (he may threaten people but relent in the end).[2]

New Testament Perspectives

From a Christian perspective the story of Jonah prefigures the
story of Jesus. As Jonah was sent from Israel to Nineveh on a

mission of mercy, so Jesus was sent from heaven to earth on a mission of mercy. In Jesus's ministry we see that he has a special concern for sinners.

In the Gospel of Luke Jesus passes through the town of Jericho, and a man named Zacchaeus climbs a tree in order to see over the crowd and get a glimpse of him. Zacchaeus was a tax collector and therefore more or less the most hated man in Jericho (tax collectors were reviled because they cooperated with the Roman occupiers). Jesus, however, decides to visit Zacchaeus (something that provokes shock among the people in the crowds, who begin to murmur against him). This act of unmerited kindness leads Zacchaeus to repent of his sins. Jesus explains: "Today salvation has come to this house, since he also is a son of Abraham. For the Son of man came to seek and to save the lost" (Luke 19:9–10). One thinks of the verse from Ezekiel at the end of the passage quoted above: "Have I any pleasure in the death of the wicked, says the Lord God, and not rather that he should turn from his way and live?" (Ezek 18:23).

In another New Testament passage we find the Pharisees murmuring against Jesus for eating with tax collectors and sinners. Jesus responds by declaring, in a different way, the same message that we find in the story of Zacchaeus (and by quoting Hos 6:6): "Those who are well have no need of a physician, but those who are sick. Go and learn what this means, 'I desire mercy (Greek *eleos*), and not sacrifice.' For I came not to call the righteous, but sinners" (Matt 9:12–13).

Indeed, in some ways this is the fundamental message of the New Testament. When a paralytic is laid before Jesus in Mark 2, Jesus does not heal him at first. Instead, he looks at him and says, "My son, your sins are forgiven" (Mark 2:5). All of this has implications for theology. From a Christian perspective, the ministry of Christ reveals the fundamentally merciful nature of God.

This lesson is taught in the story of the prodigal son from the Gospel of Luke. In this story a man leaves home and squanders all of his money on "loose living." When he has nothing left to eat, he returns to his father in repentance. To the son's surprise, his father does not reprimand him but "saw him and had compassion, and ran and embraced him and kissed him" (Luke 15:20).

More startling are the words of Jesus on the cross. It is one thing to forgive sinners who are repentant such as the prodigal son, but on the cross Jesus prays for the forgiveness of those who have unjustly, and viciously, sought his death, and who never repented (and who were pagans to boot). Still Jesus calls out, "Father, forgive them; for they know not what they do" (Luke 23:34).[3]

Yet from a Christian perspective it is not fundamentally what Jesus *says* that fully reveals the mercy of God, but rather what he does. The death of Jesus on the cross is seen from the perspective of New Testament authors as a blood sacrifice (like that of the Passover lamb), which offers redemption to *sinners*. Paul writes in his letter to Titus, "He saved us, not because of deeds done by us in righteousness, but in virtue of his own mercy" (3:5).

Indeed, the crucifixion from a Christian perspective is where divine mercy and divine justice come together. In the crucifixion, God exacts a punishment for sins according to his justice, but he takes that punishment upon himself according to his mercy. This idea that the sacrifice of Christ embodies both justice and mercy is expressed by Thomas Aquinas (d. 1274). Responding to the idea raised by a Muslim opponent that God could simply wipe away sins with no "satisfaction" or simply have prevented humans from ever sinning, Aquinas writes:

> That would first be contrary to the order of justice, and secondary to the order of human nature, by which man has free will and can choose good or evil. God's Providence does not destroy the nature and order of things, but preserves them. So God's wisdom was most evident in his preserving the order of justice and of nature, and at the same time mercifully providing man a saving remedy in the incarnation and death of his Son.[4]

Yet even with their consciousness of Christ's merciful sacrifice, Christian authors still found a way to speak about the vengeance of God. In Matthew 25 we find a passage in which Jesus predicts his return at the end of time as the "Son of Man," when he will divide humans between the good "sheep" on his right hand and the evil "goats" on his left hand. Preachers and social justice advocates like to quote this passage because it emphasizes the importance of service and compassion for our fellow humans (Jesus congratulates the "sheep" with the following words, "I was hungry and you gave me food, I was thirsty and you gave me drink, I was a stranger and you welcomed me" [Matt 25:35]). However, it is often missed that this passage shows the vengeful face of the divine when Jesus curses those who failed to show compassion. To those on his left hand he declares, "Depart from me, you cursed, into the eternal fire prepared for the devil and his angels" (Matt 25:41).

In his letter to the Romans Paul quotes a line from Deuteronomy 32 (v. 35; cited above) in order to make the point that believers should not take out vengeance on each other:

"Beloved, never avenge yourselves, but leave it to the wrath of God; for it is written, 'Vengeance is mine, I will repay, says the Lord'" (Rom 12:19). Paul finds a new application for this line in Deuteronomy: believers are not to think that they can punish one another and thereby be instruments of God's wrath. There will be punishment, but that is God's job.

This sentiment seems to emerge also in some passages of the Qur'an. For example, after alluding to the problem of the "faithless" among those who surrounded Jesus, the God of the Qur'an does not instruct him to fight them or violently to oppose them. Instead, God assures Jesus that he will take care of things: "Then to Me will be your return, whereat I will judge between you concerning that about which you used to differ" (Q 3:55b).

In his book *Allah* Miroslav Volf emphasizes that when it comes to questions of mercy and vengeance, the Qur'an and the Bible are not as far apart as they might seem.[5] Certain passages in the Bible apparently (like the Qur'an) make God's mercy contingent on human actions. In Exod 20:5–6 God declares that he will punish those who "hate" him (even to the third generation) but act with faithful love (*hesed*) to those who love him and keep his commandments. While many Gospel passages emphasize God's love for sinners and unbelievers, at least one passage in John seems to make God's love conditional: "If you keep my commandments, you will abide in my love" (John 15:10).

And as we have already seen, Paul speaks of the "wrath of God" in Romans 12. He does this earlier in Romans as well: "For the wrath of God is revealed from heaven against all ungodliness and wickedness of men who by their wickedness suppress the truth" (Rom 1:18). Noting such passages, Volf concludes, "So we don't have a God of spineless sentimental love on the Christian side and the God of stern and unbending law on the Muslim side."[6] Justice and mercy are present in both the Christian and Islamic visions of God.

Divine Scheming (Again)

This may be the case, but what about the language in the Qur'an of divine trickery, or God's sealing the hearts of the unbelievers? In Q 3:54 the Qur'an speaks of how God "schemed" and calls him "the best of schemers." Does this hold also for the Bible? Is the God of the Bible also a "trickster"?

The Old Testament prophet Jeremiah seems to accuse God of something approaching trickery. When God announces that he is sending a disaster upon Israel ("from the north"), Jeremiah wonders where all God's promises of peace and tranquility have gone: "Ah, Lord God, surely thou hast utterly deceived this people and Jerusalem, saying, 'It shall be well with you'; whereas the sword has reached their very life" (Jer 4:10).

In another remarkable Old Testament passage (found in 1 Kings 22 and 2 Chronicles 18), God places a "lying spirit" into the mouth of the prophets in order to trick the unfaithful king Ahab into going into a battle that will be his doom. The passage begins with God presiding in his heavenly court and asking who will execute his scheme against Ahab:

> [20]And the Lord said, "Who will entice Ahab, that he may go up and fall at Ramothgilead?" And one said one thing, and another said another. [21]Then a spirit came forward and stood before the Lord, saying, "I will entice him." [22]And the Lord said to him, "By what means?" And he said, "I will go forth, and will

be a lying spirit in the mouth of all his prophets."
And he said, "You are to entice him, and you shall
succeed; go forth and do so." (1 Kgs 22:20–22; cf.
2 Chr 18:19–21)

What of the story of God's hardening the heart of Pharaoh in the Book of Exodus? This story has an obvious parallel with the notion of God sealing hearts—a prominent theme
in the Qur'an (Q 2:7, 6:46, 7:100–101, 9:87, 10:74, 16:108, 30:
59, 40:35, 45:23, 47:16, 63:3). Even before Moses returns to
Egypt from Midian, God announces his plan to harden Pharaoh's heart: "And the Lord said to Moses, 'When you go back
to Egypt, see that you do before Pharaoh all the miracles which
I have put in your power; but I will harden his heart, so that he
will not let the people go'" (Exod 4:21). Back in Egypt Moses
and Aaron perform miraculous signs before Pharaoh, and
time and again God strikes the Egyptians with plagues. Pharaoh, however, repeatedly refuses to let the Israelites go.

The reason for this, on most occasions (e.g., Exod 7:13,
22; 8:15, 19, 32; 9:7), is that Pharaoh's heart is hardened. On
several occasions, however, we discover that God is responsible for his hard heart (Exod 9:12; cf. 10:1, 20, 27; 11:10). When
locusts come down upon Egypt, Pharaoh has had enough: he
calls in Moses and Aaron and confesses that he has sinned
against God. In response, Moses prays to God and God blows
away the locusts with a "strong west wind." However, this was
not to be the last plague: God hardens the heart of Pharaoh
so that "he did not let the children of Israel go" (Exod 10:20).

Later in Exodus we seem to learn the reason why God
chose to harden the heart of Pharaoh. After all of the plagues
have come and gone, and Pharaoh has finally let the Israelites leave their captivity in Egypt, God hardens Pharaoh's heart

one more time. He does this so Pharaoh will pursue the Israel-
ites and, as a consequence, be destroyed along with his army.
This provides an illustration of the glory and might of Israel's
God: "And I will harden Pharaoh's heart, and he will pursue
them and I will get glory over Pharaoh and all his host; and the
Egyptians shall know that I am the Lord" (14:4; cf. Exod 14:17).

This unfolding of events in Egypt might be thought of as
a divine scheme. God planned all of this before he sends Moses
(and Aaron) to confront Pharaoh. Pharaoh is a pawn in God's
plot. His role is to show the glory of Israel's God. A similar
notion appears in the Qur'an, but the plot starts still earlier.
The Qur'an explains that when Pharaoh's relatives picked up
the infant Moses from the basket where his mother had left
him, it was not a random act. God was behind it in order that
"[Moses] be an enemy and a cause of grief to them" (Q 28:8).

Like Muslims (remember Zamakhshari), Christian interpreters also resisted the implication that God would be
responsible for Pharaoh's stubbornness. The third-century
church father Origen in this regard quotes Rom 9:18 (a verse
that reads as though it came out of the Qur'an) where Paul declares, "So then he has mercy upon whomever he wills, and
he hardens the heart of whomever he wills." To Origen, both
God's mercy and God's "hardening" are one action. God in-
tends mercy, but if humans are not receptive to that mercy,
then their hearts will be hardened. Origen compares this to the
rain, which nourishes good soil but has no effect on bad soil.[7]

In the previous chapter we cited the crucifixion as a case
of divine scheming in the Qur'an. Here we might do the same
for the New Testament. There are some suggestions in the New
Testament that the devil played an active role in the killing of
Jesus. The Gospel of John speaks of Satan "entering into" Judas
(John 13:27) when Jesus singles Judas out among the disciples

by handing him a morsel of bread. Judas then goes out and betrays Jesus.

Yet Satan does not have the last word. Indeed, one way to look at the crucifixion is as a sort of "scheme" that fools the devil. Origen seems to arrive at this conclusion while reflecting on the Gospel passage which declares that Jesus will give his life as a "ransom" (see Matt 20:28 and Mark 10:45) for many: "To whom did he give his life a ransom for many? Assuredly not to God, could it then be to the Evil One? For [the Evil One] was holding fast until the ransom should be given to him, even the life of Jesus; being deceived with the idea that he could have dominion over it."[8] One can see here how deception worked in Origen's understanding of the crucifixion. The devil thought that he would receive the life of Jesus in exchange for the lives of Jesus's followers. Little did he know that Jesus would not remain dead.

The notion of God's "tricking" the devil has been put forward variously. For instance, it is portrayed vividly in the 1950 children's fantasy novel *The Lion, the Witch and the Wardrobe* by C. S. Lewis (and the 2005 movie of the same name). In it, the figure who represents Satan (the White Witch) makes a deal with the figure who represents Jesus (the lion Aslan). Aslan will give his life on behalf of a sinner (the "traitor" Edmund). What the White Witch doesn't know, however, is that Aslan will rise again. His death fulfills what Lewis calls a "deeper magic" and breaks entirely the hold that the White Witch has had upon the creatures of her realm. The "table" that represents the former dispensation in which the Witch ruled is broken, and Aslan rises from the dead.

A similar scenario seems to inform Mel Gibson's 2004 film *The Passion of the Christ.* In one of the final scenes, after Jesus has died on the cross, one sees the figure of the devil

looking upwards and screaming in wrath and agony. The devil
has been defeated—or perhaps tricked—by the resurrection
of Christ.

Divine Pathos

Thus already in the Bible we find the idea of God's vengeance,
and even of God's ability to scheme. The Qur'an does not in-
vent these ideas, although it does seem to make them more
central to its understanding of God. Conversely, one aspect of
God's personality that is more central to the Bible is God's tendency to be saddened by human sin.

In a passage from Hosea we find a vivid depiction of
God's disappointment with the way in which Israel was unfaithful to him by rushing to other gods:

> When Israel was a child, I loved him,
>   and out of Egypt I called my son.
> The more I called them,
>   the more they went from me;
> they kept sacrificing to the Ba'als,
>   and burning incense to idols. (Hos 11:1–2)[9]

Here, God remembers, almost wistfully, how he took care of
Israel when Israel (meaning the entire people, not the man for-
merly named Jacob) was only a child. The remarkable point
about this passage, however (and this has been noted by David
Marshall),[10] is that God does not respond to the infidelity of
Israel with anger. As this chapter of Hosea continues, God expresses only tenderness. God thinks his way through the problem of Israel's infidelity and determines that he cannot destroy
the people whom he was accompanied through the years, say-

ing, "How can I hand you over, O Israel! / . . . / My heart re-coils within me, / my compassion grows warm and tender" (Hos 11:8).

Johan Bouman finds a similar tension involving God's anger with—and yet enduring love for—Israel in the Book of Ezekiel.[11] In Ezekiel 20 God describes how Israel repeatedly was unfaithful to him, and how he repeatedly withheld his wrath. In Ezek 20:17 God declares (after noting how the "heart" of the Israelites went after idols), "Nevertheless my eye spared them, and I did not destroy them or make a full end of them in the wilderness." After recalling the unfaithfulness of Israel in the past, God then instructs Ezekiel to speak to the Israelites of his own time and to ask them—as a whole—if they will now be faithful: "Wherefore say to the house of Israel, Thus says the Lord God: Will you defile yourselves after the manner of your fathers and go astray after their detestable things?" (Ezek 20: 30). More poignant still is Isaiah 54:8, where God (who speaks of Israel as his wife in v. 5) declares, "In overflowing wrath for a moment I hid my face from you, but with everlasting love I will have compassion on you."

Later Jewish writings emphasize that God is concerned not only for Israel but for the entire world. In the Babylonian Talmud, a collection of rabbinic traditions that date from after the destruction of the Jerusalem temple in AD 70 but before the composition of the Qur'an in the early seventh century, we find an opinion expressed that seems to contradict those bibli-cal passages which emphasize God's particular favor for Israel. For example, a rabbi named Johanan is remembered as say-ing, "These [the gentiles] are my handiwork, and so are these [the Jews]; how shall I destroy the former on account of the latter?"[12]

Elsewhere in that same section (or "tractate") of the Tal-

mud we find an even more startling expression of God's compassion. We learn that God cares not only for the righteous, but
also for the wicked. "The Holy One, blessed be He, does not rejoice in the downfall of the wicked," the passage begins. It continues by noting how the angels who surround the throne of
God yearned to sing a song of praise when the Egyptians were
cast into the sea after their pursuit of Israel. God, however,
quieted them: "In that Hour the ministering angels wished to
utter the song before the Holy One, blessed be He, but He rebuked them, saying: 'My handiwork [the Egyptians] is drowning in the sea; would ye utter song before me!?'"[13] This fascinating perspective seems to offer almost a "psychological"
insight into God. On the one hand, God executes his judgment
on the wicked Egyptians; yet on the other, he takes no pleasure
in their destruction. God has destroyed the very work of his
hands. That does not please him; it grieves him.

Marshall points to the scene of Jesus weeping over Jerusalem in Luke's Gospel as an example of pathos like that in
the passage from Hosea cited above.[14] Indeed, in this passage
we see Christ not joyful, or satisfied, by the judgment that is
coming to Jerusalem, but in something like a state of emotional torment:

> And when he drew near and saw the city he wept
> over it, saying, "Would that even today you knew
> the things that make for peace! But now they are hid
> from your eyes. For the days shall come upon you,
> when your enemies will cast up a bank about you
> and surround you, and hem you in on every side,
> and dash you to the ground, you and your children
> within you, and they will not leave one stone upon

another in you; because you did not know the time
of your visitation." (Luke 19:41–44; cf. 13:34–35)

In the Gospel of Matthew we find a related scene in which
Jesus declares:

O Jerusalem, Jerusalem, killing the prophets and
stoning those who are sent to you! How often
would I have gathered your children together as a
hen gathers her brood under her wings, and you
would not! (Matt 23:37)

Christ in this passage seems to speak from his divine nature,
declaring how he longed to "gather" the children of Jerusalem
together "as a hen gathers her brood." In both passages there
is a sense of tragedy: Christ knows that judgment is coming
upon the city. He does not gloat or rejoice over the coming destruction of the unrighteous. He laments their doom.

God's ambivalence in these traditions, from both the
New and the Old Testaments, is not found in the "punishment
stories" of the Qur'an, or in its reflections on hell. An interesting example of this is in Sura 29: "They ask you to hasten the
punishment, and indeed hell will besiege the faithless on the
day when the punishment envelopes them from above them
and from under their feet, and He will say, 'Taste what you
used to do!'" (Q 29:54–55).

A similar contrast is found with the accounts of Noah in
the Bible and the Qur'an. As Marshall points out (and as mentioned in Chapter 7), the biblical account leading up to the
flood explains that God was "grieved" at human wickedness
(Gen 6:6).[15] The biblical story of Noah ends with a covenant

between God and Noah in which God promises never to destroy humanity (Gen 8:21–22). By contrast, the qur'anic story
of Noah, in Sura 11, ends with God's promise to destroy future
nations that will go astray:

> It was said, "O Noah! Disembark in peace from Us
> and with [Our] blessings upon you and upon na-
> tions [to descend] from those who are with you, and
> nations whom We shall provide for, then a painful
> punishment from Us shall befall them." (Q 11:48)

There are few signs in the Qur'an that God has compassion for
unbelievers. It is true that in 11:75 the Qur'an calls Abraham
"most forbearing, plaintive [and] penitent" after he argues on
behalf of Lot's sinful people. But God, while recognizing merit
in Abraham's character, does not show himself "forbearing"
toward that people or saddened by their unbelief. Indeed, God
reprimands Abraham for questioning his decree: "O Abraham,
let this matter alone! Your Lord's edict has already come" (Q 11:
76). Why would the God of the Qur'an feel anger but not feel
sadness? Perhaps, as we have already suggested, the emotion
of sadness does not become a lord.

Although our gaze in this book is firmly on the Qur'an
and not Islamic tradition, it is nevertheless worth pointing out
that some hadith offer a different perspective. In one, Muhammad speaks of God's love for repentance in language that mir-
rors the Gospel parable of the lost sheep. He does not simply
speak of God's dispensing mercy, but indeed of his "pleasure"
at the opportunity to be merciful:

> By God, God is more pleased by the repentance of
> His servant than one of you if he found a lost ani-

mal in the desert. When he draws near to Me by the span of his hand, I draw near him by the length of a cubit. When he draws near Me by the length of a cubit, I draw near him by the length of a fathom. When he draws near Me walking, I draw near to him rushing.[16]

Mercy and Judgment in Jewish Tradition

We have seen that the image of God in the Bible corresponds in many ways (although not every way) with the image of God in the Qur'an. And yet Jewish and Christian thinkers continued to reflect on God in new ways during the many centuries between the writings of the Bible and the writing of the Qur'an. For example, the writings of the Jewish rabbis in the Mishnah and the Talmud show a consistent concern with the relationship of the mercy and the justice of God.

Bouman insists that almost any mention of God's justice in rabbinic writings is followed by a mention of his mercy.[17] In fact, in the Babylonian Talmud we find the opinion that the "World is judged with goodness."[18] On occasion the rabbis simply refer to God as "the merciful one." In Aramaic— the language of the Talmud—this is *rahmana*.[19] We might compare the way the Qur'an refers to God as *al-rahman* ("the Compassionate").[20]

Yet the rabbis in no way denied that God is also judge. Another tradition in the Babylonian Talmud emphasizes the justice of God and maintains that God tolerates no unrighteousness:

The born are to die, the dead to be brought to life, and the living to be judged. [It is, therefore, for

them] to know and to make known, so that it become known, that He is God, He the fashioner,
He the creator, He the discerner, He the judge, He
the witness, He the complainant, and that He is of
a certainty to judge, blessed be He, before whom
there is no unrighteousness.[21]

As they elaborated this relationship between divine mercy and
divine justice, certain rabbis connected the aspect of mercy
(*rahamim* in Hebrew) with one divine name, Yahweh, and the
aspect of vengeance, or judgment (*din* in Hebrew), with another divine name, Elohim.

This division may in some ways be based on the text of
the Old Testament. Passages that use the divine name Yahweh
for God (associated in critical biblical scholarship with the
"Yahwist" source) tend to emphasize the nearness or imma-
nence of God. When God walks in the garden of Eden or smells
the pleasing sacrifice of Noah, the text uses "Yahweh" (a name
rendered "the Lord" in the Revised Standard Version). Passages that use the divine name "Elohim" (associated in critical
biblical scholarship with the "Priestly" source, among others)
tend to emphasize the otherness, or the transcendence, of God.
When God creates the world in six days, or puts Abraham to
the test, the Bible uses Elohim (rendered "God" in the Revised
Standard Version).

Rabbinic writings, however, find in these names indica-
tions of more than the "nearness" or "transcendence" of God.
They find reflections of mercy and judgment. The rabbinic
commentary on Genesis known as *Genesis Rabbah* makes this
distinction explicit. In the commentary on the opening words
of Gen 8:1 ("But God [Elohim] remembered Noah"), we find
the following tradition:

> Woe to the wicked who turn the Attribute of Mercy
> into the Attribute of Judgment. Wherever the Tetra-
> grammaton [Yahweh] is employed it connotes the
> Attribute of Mercy, as in the verse, "The Lord, the
> Lord God, merciful and gracious" [Exod 34:6]. . . .
> Happy are the righteous who turn the Attribute of
> Judgment into the Attribute of Mercy. Wherever
> Elohim is employed it connotes the Attribute of
> Judgment: Thus "Thou shalt not revile Elohim"
> [Exod 22:28].[22]

Thus the rabbis insisted that God's "two names" are connected
to two different elements of the divine "personality" and reflect
the mercy and judgment that coexist in his nature. God is not
merciful or just. He is both.

Mercy and Judgment in Eastern Christian Tradition

As the rabbis were developing the traditions that would ultimately lead to the Aramaic-language Talmud, the many Christians of the Middle East were writing poems and homilies in
Syriac, their own version of the Aramaic language. Syriac literature in the centuries before the origins of the Qur'an includes
contributions from the three main Christian communities: the
East Syrians (also known, inaccurately, as "Nestorians"), the
Chalcedonians (or "Melkites"), and the West Syrians (or "Jacobites").

In considering how Christians dealt with the problem of
mercy and justice, it makes sense to focus on the Syriac tradition in particular. Syriac is a Semitic language like Arabic and
was widespread in the Middle East on the eve of Islam. In cer-

tain regions Arabic speakers lived alongside Syriac speakers. Indeed, many Christian Arabs would have been exposed to Syriac. In divine liturgy they likely heard the Bible proclaimed in Syriac and then translated on the spot into Arabic. They also likely heard Arabic versions of hymns and poetic works translated (perhaps spontaneously) from Syriac church fathers such as Ephrem (d. 373).

The writings of Ephrem—known in Syriac tradition as the "Harp of the Spirit"—were widespread through all three of the Christian communities.[23] Tellingly, for Ephrem the heart of Christ's mission was mercy. Christ was a spiritual doctor who came to heal the spiritually sick. Ephrem's convictions regarding the mercy of God in Christ are prominent in a poem he wrote on the "sinful" woman of Luke 7 who anoints Christ (a poem that in fact alludes to a number of Gospel episodes):

> Listen and take heart, my beloved,
> how God is compassionate:
> He forgave the Sinful Woman her sins
> And supported her in her grief;
> He opened the eyes of the man blind from the womb
>   [John 9:6]
> And the pupils of his eyes beheld the light;
> To the paralytic He granted recovery—
> He stood up and carried his bed as he walked!
>   [Matt 9:2]
> —while to us, He has given us Pearls,
> His holy Body and blood.
> He carried His medicines secretly
> But was healing with them openly;
> He went about the land of Judah
> Like a doctor carrying his medicines.

> Simeon invited Him to a meal [Luke 7:36, 40],
> To eat food in his house.
> The Sinful Woman rejoiced when she heard
> That He was in Simeon's house, reclining and being
>   entertained.
> Her thoughts gathered, like the sea,
> And her love seethed like the waves.
> She saw how the Sea of Mercy
> Had contained Himself in a single place,
> So she decided to go and drown
> All her wickedness in His waves.[24]

For Ephrem, Christ manifested, time and again, the compassion of God. "Like a doctor carrying his medicines" Jesus came not for the whole and the righteous, but for the sick and the sinners. For Ephrem the beauty of Christ is that he loved humans *first*. He did not wait for them to repent but loved them in their sin, in their spiritual sickness.

All of this is moving, but it cannot be denied that the Syriac tradition also includes some dire warnings about the vengeance of God and indeed in some ways anticipates the language of the Qur'an in this regard. This can be seen in a homily on the great flood in the time of Noah written in the century before Islam by the West Syrian Syriac father Jacob of Serugh (d. 521). Jacob, known by his own nickname the "Flute of the Spirit," speaks in his homily of those who refused to listen to the preaching of Noah:

> Not even with the sound teaching they were
>   reproached.
> Their heart was covered, likewise their eyes along with
>   their ears,

for by their own will, the doors of their intellect were
closed.[25]

This language is not entirely unlike that of the Qur'an where it
speaks of God's sealing the hearts, eyes, and ears of unbelievers (Q 2:7). Jacob writes of the unbelievers, "by their own will,"
closing their hearts, eyes, and intellect.

Elsewhere Jacob seems to get closer to the language of the
Qur'an when he speaks of divine vengeance. In another homily
(one of a collection known as "Homilies Against the Jews") we
find him commenting on the anger of God against the Jews for
crucifying Jesus (Jacob holds them responsible). Jacob speaks
of how God "avenged" Jesus by punishing the Jews:

> The avenger of Jesus, whom you crucified, is Adonai.
> He put His hand on you and humiliated you throughout
> all the earth;
> You rose up against His son and His anger went up, like
> smoke;
> He stopped the Spirit from dwelling again among your
> tribes.[26]

Thus we might conclude that the Qur'an's idea of divine vengeance does not come out of nowhere. If there were Christians
in the Qur'an's original audience, they would not have found
the message of vengeance unfamiliar.

Evaluating the Biblical Image of God

Yet not everyone would like to join the biblical and qur'anic
images of God too closely. The Pakistani Muslim scholar
Fazlur Rahman finds the biblical image of God as "father" to

be fundamentally problematic. In his work *Major Themes of the Qur'an* Rahman criticizes this image on several occasions, without ever explicitly naming Judaism or Christianity. At one point he writes, "But such religious ideologies as have put their whole emphasis on God's love and self-sacrifice for the sake of His children have done little service to the moral maturity of man."[27] Rahman stops short of explicitly accusing Jews or Christians of being "morally immature," but the message is clear enough.

For Rahman the problem with the biblical image of God (here he seems to be thinking in particular of the Christian image of God) is that it lets humans off the hook. By not emphasizing divine judgment and focusing on divine mercy, Christians have no reason to amend their own moral behavior. By thinking of themselves as "children of God," Christians never "grow up."

A bit later in that same work Rahman's language is more abrasive. Alluding to the Qur'an's critique of Judaism and Christianity, he writes: "This picture of a doting father and a spoilt child is hit directly by the Qur'anic verses that prohibit child-play and frivolity on God's part, as well as those verses . . . that criticize Jews and Christians for laying proprietary claims upon God."[28] There are two different issues here in Rahman's polemic. The first is a characterization—or perhaps a caricature—of biblical theology and anthropology (by which humans are "spoilt children"). The second is an idea advanced by the Qur'an (see Q 2:135 and 5:18): Jews and Christians insist that they are the only ones whom God loves. Still, in both cases Rahman means to criticize the father-child relationship that is so important to the Bible.

A second Pakistani scholar, Daud Rahbar, has a kinder estimation of the biblical image of God. Instead of speaking of a "doting father," Rahbar speaks of the Bible's emphasis on God's love for humanity. This he contrasts with the Qur'an's emphasis on justice: "In the Bible this central notion is God's Fatherhood and His love for mankind. . . . In the Qur'an the corresponding central notion is God's strict justice."[29]

In the present book, however, we have seen that it is simplistic to say that the God of the Qur'an is a God of "justice." Instead, we have seen that the principal characteristics of God are two: mercy and vengeance. What is more, the Qur'an does not seek to reconcile these two qualities. It means to assert both of them and thereby to keep God's ultimate nature a mystery. As we move toward a conclusion, it is time to address that mystery directly.

10

Rereading the Qur'an

With dust my heart is thick, that should be clear,
A glass to mirror forth the Great King's face;
One ray of light from out Thy dwelling-place
To pierce my night, oh God! And draw me near.

—*Hafez,* Divan, *XXIV*

In 1947 an Egyptian Muslim thinker named Muhammad Ahmad Khalafallah (d. 1991) completed a dissertation in Cairo with a thesis that would hardly seem radical to most students of the Qur'an in the West. He argued that the Qur'an includes many aspects of storytelling. By his own account, Khalafallah's motivation in advancing this argument was to defend the Qur'an. He was writing against "atheists, Orientalists, and missionaries."[1] Some Muslims in Egypt, however, were outraged by his claims. The Qur'an is not a bunch of stories, they insisted (caricaturing his argument), but rather the true, revealed word of God. The outrage grew to the point that Khalafallah was never allowed to defend his thesis, and his reputation (along with that of his doctoral supervisor) was forever tarnished.

A worse fate awaited a later Egyptian scholar, Nasr Hamid Abu Zayd (d. 2010). He argued that the Qur'an can be understood in some places to be metaphorically, and not literally, true. For this he was initially criticized and eventually (on June 14, 1995) declared an apostate in an Egyptian court. Forcibly divorced from his wife (since a non-Muslim man cannot be married to a Muslim woman), he fled with her to Holland.[2]

What both Khalafallah and Abu Zayd were addressing (to the dismay of some of their coreligionists) is the quality of qur'anic speech. They both held that the Qur'an needs to be understood in light of its particular rhetorical and linguistic qualities. I argue something similar here.

In the previous chapter we discovered the biblical roots of the Qur'an's twin affirmation of God's vengeance and God's mercy. We have not yet, however, solved the paradox of this twin affirmation. How can it be that Allah is vengeful and capable of plots and stratagems and yet also merciful, gentle, and forgiving? The reason why we have not solved this paradox is simple: it cannot be solved.

The Qur'an means intentionally to keep God's nature a mystery. The Qur'an is not a theological guidebook that describes God in a precise and coherent manner. It is closer to a sermon, an exhortation, or an argument meant to persuade humans to believe. At times, the Qur'an emphasizes the gentleness or mercy of God; at other times, it emphasizes his vengefulness and even his capacity to trick or deceive humans. But the Qur'an never tries to put all of this together into a coherent theological construction.

Another way of putting this is that the Qur'an is more interested in humans and their response to its message than it is interested in God. This may seem surprising. After all, the Qur'an speaks constantly about God; the word "Allah" appears about twenty-seven hundred times in the text. And yet the *way* the Qur'an invokes God tells us something about the qur'anic author's ultimate concern. Fazlur Rahman puts it this way: "The Qur'an is a document that is squarely aimed at man."[3]

The Qur'an as an Argument

The French Dominican scholar of Islam Jacques Jomier has gone still further. He insists that the key to understanding the Qur'an is simply to appreciate its process of argumentation. The Qur'an, in his opinion, proceeds with an almost constant series of arguments, "exposing, questioning, calling one to reflect." He adds: "The Qur'an itself is the echo of discussions which took place at the time of Islam's appearance. It reports objections, responds to them, exhorts, blames, and sometimes speaks ironically."[4]

This makes the Qur'an fundamentally different from the great majority of the Bible. For the most part the Bible is made up of historical narratives, poetic or wisdom literature, and prophetic discourses. Only in certain sections, for example in the divine discourse in the Book of Job or in a number of Paul's epistles, do biblical authors develop systematic arguments.

The Qur'an, by contrast, is almost ceaselessly involved in an argument. Indeed, one of the terms that the Qur'an uses to refer to itself is *maw'iza,* meaning "admonition" or "awakening."[5] The Qur'an is simply not concerned with abstract discussions regarding the origin of evil or philosophical reflections on the path to avoiding suffering or living a flourishing life. The Qur'an is concerned above all with vindicating its own divine origin and with persuading its audience to submit to God and obey the Prophet, to join the community of believers and oppose the community of unbelievers.

Many of the Qur'an's arguments involve setting up binary options. As Jomier puts it, the Qur'an constantly offers a series of choices: "There is God or there is not God, there is the blind and the seeing, truth and falsehood, the believer and the unbeliever, the good to do and the evil to avoid, paradise and hell."[6]

The Qur'an's strategies of argumentation have been explored still further by Rosalind Gwynne. In her book *Logic, Rhetoric, and Legal Reasoning in the Qur'an,* Gwynne identifies a number of logical strategies that the qur'anic author uses to advance his argument. She writes that these sorts of arguments "all turn ultimately on the ontological difference between good and evil, faith and disbelief, virtue and sin."[7] Gwynne notes that in the Qur'an God doesn't simply debate unbelievers; he also encourages the Prophet Muhammad (Q 16:125) and all of the believers (Q 29:46) to debate (Arabic *jadala*) them.[8]

As a graduate student I studied under the guidance of a Muslim imam in Lebanon. Twice a week we met to read the Qur'an and qur'anic commentary. During those lessons, however, my instructor frequently departed from the subject matter in order to criticize Christian teaching in an attempt to persuade me to convert to Islam. These attempts grew tiresome, and one day I asked him, "Shaykh, why do you keep on arguing against Christianity? Aren't we simply here to read the Qur'an?" He responded, "But the Qur'an itself instructs me to do so," and he quoted the opening of Q 29:46: "Do not argue with the People of the Book except in a manner which is best, except such of them as are wrongdoers."

This Muslim imam saw his zeal for "debating" or "arguing" as a response to this qur'anic injunction. In some ways, however, he was simply following the example of God. Allah is the great debater in the Qur'an. The divine voice in the qur'anic text is constantly addressing its opponents and confronting their positions. If one opens the Qur'an at the beginning, it won't take long to come across the first argument. After the opening prayer (Sura 1, *al-Fatihah*), the opening section of Sura 2 includes the following:

> [8]Among the people are those who say, "We have faith in God and the Last Day," but they have no faith. [9]They seek to deceive God and those who have faith, yet they deceive no one but themselves, but they are not aware. [10]There is a sickness in their hearts; then God increased their sickness, and there is a painful punishment for them because of the lies they used to tell.

Here the Qur'an, arguing against some unnamed group that it accuses of hypocrisy, does not use the techniques of comparison or contrast which interest Gwynne, but rather a type of argument that is closer to defamation: it explains the apparent deviance of this group not as a difference of opinion but as a result of a "sickness" in their hearts (one that God has increased). The force of this argument is evident: the audience is presented with a choice of siding with those who are "sick" or of submitting fully to God.

The Qur'an is so interested in advancing arguments, with disputation, that in certain cases this concern seems to shape its formulation of doctrine. For example, and as we have already seen, the Qur'an teaches that at the moment of punishment, or when unbelievers lie on their deathbeds, it will be too late to convert and believe. This doctrine seems to be implicit in the way the Qur'an speaks of the death of Pharaoh. In Sura 10 the Qur'an reports that Pharaoh came to believe at the end of his life but suggests that his belief did not save his soul:

> [90]We carried the Children of Israel across the sea, whereat Pharaoh and his troops pursued them, out of defiance and aggression. When overtaken by drowning, he called out, "I do believe that there is no god except Him in whom the Children of Israel believe, and I am one of those who submit [to Him]!" [91][He was told,] "What! Now? When you have been disobedient heretofore and were among the agents of corruption?! [92]So today We shall deliver you in your body so that you may be a sign for those who come after you." Many of the people are indeed oblivious to Our signs.

Although the Qur'an does not say so explicitly, the implication of this passage (from the way God speaks to Pharaoh in v. 91) is that Pharaoh was still damned even though he believed and confessed his belief out loud. God "delivered him in his body" (a detail that may follow from a Jewish tradition, although some Muslim apologists connect it to the "mummification" of Egypt's Pharaohs),[9] but his soul was damned.

A story that Muslim commentators told about this passage explains that the angel Gabriel actively prevented Pharaoh from receiving mercy: "Gabriel thrust mud from the sea into his mouth, lest [God's] mercy embrace him."[10] There is, however, no need to imagine an angel shoving mud into the mouth of Pharaoh. The Qur'an's point is simply that at the moment of death it is too late to repent and believe. This doctrine, the rejection of conversion at the last moment, is explicit in Sura 4:

> ¹⁸But [acceptance of] repentance is not for those who go on committing misdeeds: when death approaches any of them, he says, "I repent now." Nor is it for those who die while they are faithless. For such We have prepared a painful punishment.

A statement in Q 39 is similar: "Turn penitently to Him and submit to Him before the punishment overtakes you, whereupon you will not be helped" (Q 39:54). Why, we might ask, would the Qur'an develop this notion that it is too late to repent and believe when one is in the throes of death? Why wouldn't God accept repentance at the last moment if he is truly merciful and just?

The answer seems to be that the author of the Qur'an wants the audience to convert and believe *now,* not to postpone conversion and think that they can go on disbelieving and then save themselves on their deathbeds.

The Gospel of Luke tells the story of a rich man who is punished in the flames of hell for his neglect of the poor beggar Lazarus, who used to sit at the rich man's gate. From his place of punishment, the rich man sees Lazarus in the "bosom of Abraham" and calls out, "Father Abraham, have mercy on me, and send Lazarus to dip the tip of his finger in water and cool my tongue; for I am in agony in these flames" (Luke 16: 24). It is too late for him to receive mercy, however: Abraham responds, "Child, remember that during your lifetime you received your good things, and Lazarus in like manner evil things; but now he is comforted here, and you are in agony" (Luke 16:25). The point of the story of the rich man is to encourage people to have mercy on the poor now, before one is damned to hell and it will be too late. The Qur'an takes this a step further, insisting that it will *already* be too late at the moment of death. The message is thus more urgent.

Khalafallah and the "Literary Truth" of the Qur'an

The work of Khalafallah might help us further illustrate this point. Khalafallah wrote his dissertation at what is now the University of Cairo (at the time it was known as King Fuad I University, after the name of the first king of independent Egypt) under the guidance of a well-known Egyptian scholar of the Qur'an, Amin al-Khuli.[11] The title of his dissertation, *Min asrar al-i'jaz,* "On the Secrets of [the Qur'an's] Inimitability," suggests that his initial intent for the work was apologetic. Khalafallah indeed meant to defend the traditional Islamic doctrine that the Qur'an is a perfect book (a doctrine known in Arabic as *i'jaz*), but he did so by arguing that its perfection is often connected to the way that it tells stories. In the end, however, he found himself accused of blasphemy.

In order to understand Khalafallah's project one needs to see that he was worried by those who held that the Qur'an is not historically accurate. How could it be, for example, that prophets in the Qur'an who lived years apart, and in different lands, all resemble each other? On occasion, prophets separated from each other by hundreds or thousands of years (and who presumably spoke different languages, not only Arabic) say precisely the same things. This does not seem to reflect historical reality.

Moreover, different versions of the same account in the Qur'an sometimes differ in their details: For example, the

Qur'an in some cases blames Satan for the downfall of Adam and Eve (Q 2:36, 7:20), but in other cases it blames Adam (Q 20:121). In certain passages Pharaoh is drowned (Q 17:103, 28:40, 43:55), but in one passage (Q 10:92) he is not. In Sura 19 only one angel gives the annunciation to Mary (Q 19:17–21), but in Sura 3 (Q 3:45) more than one angel does so. In several passages the Qur'an speaks of the world being created in six days (e.g., Q 10:3), but in another passage (Q 41:9–12) God creates the world in eight days. Thus Khalafallah was worried about two sorts of problems: qur'anic narratives that seem to contradict history, and qur'anic narratives that seem to contradict each other.

In order to respond to these problems Khalafallah contends that the Qur'an is not always concerned with articulating a strict historical truth. Instead, it is concerned with articulating a message that will lead its audience to accept Muhammad as a true prophet of God. Khalafallah explains that different passages were revealed on different occasions and for different reasons. It is only natural, then, that they should differ in their details. The Qur'an's author—who from Khalafallah's perspective is God himself—shaped his message according to the particular expectations, and the psychology, of the audience at any given moment.

Khalafallah illustrates this "rhetorical shaping" with reference to the qur'anic account of the Companions of the Cave (mentioned in Chapter 3) in Sura 18. This account relates how some young men took refuge from hostile unbelievers in a cave where they fell asleep for 309 years (Q 18:25). They are "woken up" only at a time when the people of the town are no longer hostile. The account, which is connected to a Christian legend known as the Seven Sleepers of Ephesus, is meant to act as a sign that the Qur'an's promises of the resurrection of the

body are to be believed (18:21). If God can wake up the "companions" after hundreds of years, he can resurrect dead bodies
on the Day of Judgment no matter how much time has passed.

In his discussion of this account, Khalafallah argues
that it is told not to relate "historical truth" (*al-haqiqa al-
ta'rikhiyya*).[12] He turns to the traditional report that the story
was revealed by God only after the pagans of Mecca, having
been prompted by the Jews in the city of Medina, tried to confound Muhammad by asking him to provide knowledge about
it. To Khalafallah, this report is the key to understanding the
entire narrative: God's point in revealing this story was not to
explain what *really* happened to the Companions of the Cave,
but to confound the pagans. So what would God do in this
situation? Would he reveal the "historical truth" about the
Companions of the Cave (if indeed it was historical) or rather
the story according to the way it was known in Muhammad's
place and time? For Khalafallah such cases show that God was
not always interested in history. In certain cases he was interested in stories above all in order to vindicate his prophet.

Accordingly, when Khalafallah finally published his dissertation in 1951, he gave it a new title: *Al-Fann al-qasasi fi al-
Qur'an al-karim*, "Narrative Art in the Noble Qur'an" or "The
Art of Story-Telling in the Noble Qur'an." This title reflects the
importance to Khalafallah of the idea of a "story"—in Arabic,
qissa.[13] As he points out, the Qur'an in places seems to refer
to its own revelation as a *qissa*, as in the opening of the Companions of the Cave account, "We tell to you their story (*qissa*)
in truth" (Q 18:13).[14] Yet to Khalafallah a *qissa* is more than
a story. In order to define the term he turns to the medieval
Muslim exegete Fakhr al-Din al-Razi (d. 1209), who describes
qasas (plural of *qissa*) as "a collection of statements comprising

whatever leads one to religion and guides one to the truth and commands one to seek salvation."[15]

Another example that Khalafallah gives of the Qur'an's distinctive "narrative art" is the case of the (nonbiblical) prophet Hud and his unbelieving people, known as 'Ad, in Q 54. In this Sura, as Khalafallah notes, the Qur'an does not offer any details of the life and mission of Hud. Nothing is told of his deeds or words among the people of 'Ad except "'Ad impugned [Hud]" (v. 18). On the other hand, the Qur'an offers some vivid details in its description of the punishment of 'Ad:

> [19]Indeed, We unleashed upon them an icy gale on an incessantly ill-fated day, [20]knocking down people as if they were trunks of uprooted palm trees. [21]So how were My punishment and warnings?! (Q 54: 19–21)

Khalafallah comments: "[The Qur'an] does not mention their houses or dwellings. It does not mention for us the debate and discussion that happened between Hud and his people. It leaves all of that out and rushes to describe the punishment. It presents this with a brilliant literary description using expressions which move one to sympathy."[16]

The point of the Qur'an in the way it tells the story of Hud, according to Khalafallah, is not to teach a historical lesson about an ancient people, but rather to make an impression on the Prophet Muhammad's audience: "The Qur'an has done all of this for a simple reason . . . to transmit into the hearts of the contemporaries of the Prophet fear of divine punishment. It seeks to pass on to them images which will make that fear strong and violent."[17]

In Khalafallah's opinion such passages also show the Qur'an's particular interest in touching human *emotion* more than the human intellect. The way in which the Qur'an tells such stories of punishment, and the way in which it describes the Day of Judgment, or heaven and hell, shows that it is directed toward the "emotional capacity" of its audience and not its "capacity of intellectual reflection."[18] Elsewhere Khalafallah summarizes his perspective: "The Qur'an takes narrative materials which include historical events and occurrences, but it presents them in a narrative manner and it conveys them in an *emotional* manner."[19] Here it is important to mention again that the Qur'an not only describes itself as a *qissa*, "story" (Q 3:62, 12:3), but also as a sermon or an admonition (Arabic *maw'iza*).

Thus for Khalafallah the Qur'an is not a history book. Its "stories" are crafted in a way to guide people to the truth. In his dissertation Khalafallah makes this point explicitly. He writes that instead of "historical truth," the prophet stories of the Qur'an are about "literary truth" (Arabic *haqiqa adabiyya*). Tellingly, this expression would disappear in the published version of his work, after the controversy surrounding the dissertation.[20] It was no doubt too controversial.

Indeed, all of this was too much for Khalafallah's religious colleagues in Egypt. Even though his goal with his dissertation was essentially Islamic apologetics, the idea that the Qur'an was less than a perfectly accurate historical document left him in hot water. A number of critical articles about the dissertation were published in the Egyptian newspaper *Al-Risala* condemning Khalafallah. Meanwhile, professors from the powerful religious institution Al-Azhar University also intervened, claiming a right to comment on all work dealing with Islam in Egypt. An article published in the official publication of Al-

Azhar in late 1947 twists the views of Khalafallah, insisting that
he believes that the Qur'an "is the word of Muhammad, the
skillful weaver of tales, and not the word of God, transcending
all analogy and contingency." This, the article concludes, make
the work a "supreme crime of atheism and ignorance."[21]

It is worth adding, perhaps, that these accusations were
made against Khalafallah in the days of the relative freedom in
Egypt of King Farouk (r. 1936–1952), and at a state university.
Even then, however, stepping past the border lines of ortho-
doxy had consequences. Khalafallah was finally relieved of his
teaching position at Fuad University so that he would not have
a pernicious effect on its students. His advisor Amin al-Khuli
also faced attacks for his role in forming Khalafallah's heterodox opinions. In 1952 Khalafallah would write a new thesis
on a Muslim scholar (Abu al-Faraj al-Isbahani), but he would
never achieve a significant status among Egyptian intellectuals.

In order to explain the opposition to Khalafallah's ideas,
the French Catholic intellectual Jacques Jomier (who was living
in Egypt at the time) wrote the following: "The traditional perspectives of Islam are extremely clear. If a document contains
elements of style which are overly characteristic of an historical epoch or an individual, the divine origin of this document
is excluded. No middle term can be recognized between two
things: either the author is God, or the author is man."[22]

For Khalafallah the author of the Qur'an was certainly God; however, he held that the Qur'an is not a newspaper article or a news report that tries to tell the facts as they
happened. It is a literary work that shapes the stories of the
prophets with its audience in mind.

Khalafallah's perspective on the narrative aspect of the
Qur'an aligns with the basic argument that I have been developing in this book, although I have not been writing from

the perspective of a Muslim believer, and I'm not interested in supporting the dogma that the Qur'an is an "inimitable" book. I have been arguing that the Qur'an leaves the reader with certain paradoxes about God (for example, that he is both vengeful and merciful) because its interest is not in describing God, but in converting humanity. It leaves God's nature a mystery.

While Khalafallah does not put things in this way, he does argue that the Qur'an's message is shaped by a concern for the psychology of its audience. As Jomier puts it, "Khalafallah concludes that the Qur'an's role of spiritual direction influenced the style and the eloquence of the text."[23] Khalafallah notes to this end that the stories which appear in the Qur'an do not feature detailed descriptions of all of the characters involved. The Prophet himself is the star, and other characters appear and disappear around him. Khalafallah comments accordingly: "The events are only depicted to move souls and affect emotions. Opinions are mentioned in order to move one's heart to remain in inner places of the mind."[24]

Jomier (who indeed seems to have been influenced by Khalafallah) also notes this element of qur'anic narrative: "Everything is centered on the essential as in the theater when the spotlights are focused on one person and everything else disappears in shadow. We are far away from the complexity of reality but the lesson sinks in more deeply in memory and emotion."[25]

Fear of God

If Khalafallah and Jomier argue that the Qur'an shapes its stories about prophets in order to have an effect on its audience, we might add that the Qur'an shapes its descriptions of God in the same way. Khalafallah writes, "The Qur'an chooses literary, narrative materials in order to fulfill its objective and carry out its intention and it avoids statements, characters and details other than that."[26] This is true for the prophets, and this is true for God.

The Qur'an's portrayal of God, and in particular its threats against sinners and unbelievers, deeply affected Muslim piety. The Qur'an condemns those who treat the life of this world as though it is a plaything, or mere amusement or diversion. Qur'an 7:51 explains that the consequence for doing this could be damnation: "As for those who took their religion for diversion and play and whom the life of the world had deceived, today We will forget them as they forgot the encounter of this day of theirs, and used to impugn Our signs." The problem with living life as though it were pure diversion is that doing so involves forgetting the "encounter"—forgetting the Day of Judgment. People who live life this way, one might say, put their guard down.

Qur'an 6:31–32 contrasts those who treat life as a diversion and those who are "Godwary":

> [31]They are certainly losers who deny the encounter with God. When the Hour overtakes them suddenly, they will say, "Alas for us, for what we neglected in it!" And they will bear their burdens on their backs. Behold, evil is what they bear! [32]The life of the world is nothing but play and diversion, and the abode of the Hereafter is surely better for those who are Godwary. Will you not exercise your reason?

The term rendered here as "Godwary" is related to the Arabic noun taqwa, which is central to the entire qur'anic system of spirituality. It is sometimes rendered as "fear of God." Muhammad Asad translates it as "God-consciousness"—a translation that conjures images of Sufis who are on the path toward spiritual enlightenment. However, passages such as 6:31–32 make it clear that to have *taqwa* involves consciousness of the threat of divine punishment—a consciousness that will lead believers to live serious and sober lives in obedience to God and thereby to "protect" themselves.

Taqwa in the Qur'an is ultimately a pious disposition of self-preservation. In Q 39:24 the Qur'an speaks of "someone who *fends off* with his face the terrible punishment." For this reason Toshihiko Izutsu speaks of *taqwa* as "a protective shield of pious obedience."[27] God is not only the source of blessing and grace; he is also the source of threat. One should live in thanksgiving for God's blessings but also in fear of the possibility that this same God might condemn one to hell. According to this qur'anic spiritual vision, one should not live with rejoicing as though the battle for salvation is won. It is not yet won. It may still be lost.

In Sura 7 we find one of the many passages that describe the confrontation of Moses and Pharaoh. Here, the ministers of Pharaoh embrace the message of Moses (Pharaoh himself remains stubborn and hard-hearted), announcing their belief in the miracles that Moses performed and then piously (in unison, apparently) calling out to God, "Our Lord! Pour patience upon us, and grant us to die in submission to you (*muslimin*)" (Q 7:126). In other words, the very possibility of dying in submission to God (or, literally, as a Muslim) seems to be in the hands of God. He could lead one astray, and the pious should live with consciousness of that possibility.

In this regard it is perhaps worth pointing out the opinion of the theologian Ash'ari that it is not possible even to say

"I am a Muslim" without adding "if God wills" (*inshallah*).[28] Other Muslim scholars, for example al-Maturidi, disagreed, but Ash'ari's perspective has not gone away. A similar notion recently was tweeted by a Muslim scholar on Twitter. He wrote that he asked three scholars about the best prayer, and they all replied, "Pray that when you die, you go as a believer."[29]

Izutsu emphasizes the role that divine threat plays in encouraging piety. After introducing the notion of *taqwa* he writes: "The pivotal point of all this is the eschatological concept of the Day of Judgment, with God Himself presiding over everything as the stern, strict and righteous judge, before whom men stand only in silence with bowed heads. The image of this decisive day should be held up constantly before the eyes of men in such a way that it might lead them to absolute earnestness, instead of levity and carelessness, in life."[30] It is the notion of *taqwa* that should lead to this "earnestness." Elsewhere the Qur'an uses a stronger term than *taqwa*, namely *khawf*, which simply means "fear." In Q 6:15 God instructs Muhammad to say, "I fear the punishment of a tremendous day." Qur'an 11:103 praises those "who fear the punishment of the Hereafter."

In Q 3:175 God tells the Qur'an's audience that they should not fear the followers of Satan—instead, they should fear God: "That is only Satan frightening [you] of his followers! So fear them not, and fear Me, should you be faithful."

Particularly revealing, however, is one verse that doesn't simply speak of humans' fear (*khawf*) but of God's *intentionally* causing humans to fear. In Sura 39 the Qur'an offers a description of what will happen to those who are damned in hell, and then—remarkably—explains why God has bothered to describe hell in such frightful terms: "There will be canopies of fire above [the damned], and canopies beneath them. With that God frightens His servants. So, My servants, be wary of Me!" (Q 39:16). Muhammad Asad translates the key phrase in more dramatic language: "In this way does God imbue his servants with fear."[31]

The Qur'an's efforts to "imbue" humans with fear profoundly affected later Muslim mystics. In his work *God Is Beautiful* Navid Kermani describes the experiences of Muslims who meditated on the Day of Judgment and the threat of damnation. Some Muslims, Kermani writes, are said to have been so affected from hearing passages in the Qur'an that they died on the spot. Kermani explains that these instantaneous deaths were usually caused from hearing threats of hellfire: "This much is plain: death is caused not by an excess of bliss, but by verses whose content is perceived as threatening."[32]

Elsewhere Kermani tells the story of a Muslim named 'Ali Zayn al-'Abidin (a figure known to Shi'ites as one of the twelve imams who succeeded the Prophet Muhammad). He notes a tradition that 'Ali would turn pale while doing his ritual washing before prayer. When someone noticed his condition and asked what was wrong, he responded, "Do you know before Whom I am about to stand [in prayer]?"[33] In another passage Kermani quotes a tradition according to which the Prophet Muhammad himself once said, "If you knew what I know, you would laugh little and weep much."[34] In another tradition Muhammad declares, "The man who cries because of the fear of God will not enter hell until milk returns into udders."[35]

Thus the fear of divine judgment in Islamic tradition is an ancient and venerable tradition. It is not those who lack faith who are afraid of God's judgment. It is precisely those who do have faith who fear, because they know that Allah is not only a God of compassion, but also a God of vengeance.

A saying from the Book of Proverbs became the title of

a late Renaissance Latin choral piece, "initium sapientiae timor Domini"—"The fear of the Lord is the beginning of wisdom."[36] This saying could fit well into the Qur'an.

In God's Image?

On the other hand, certain currents within Islam, especially among mystics or Sufis, conceived of an intimate relationship between God and humans. Indeed, some Muslim mystics have dared to declare that they have achieved something like union with God. One famous mystic named al-Hallaj is said to have achieved this state and to have said, "I am Truth!" He was accused of blasphemy and killed in 922. Still, it is worth emphasizing that many Muslims experience spiritual intimacy with God through their prayer lives.

The idea that humans are created in the image of God—the theological doctrine of *imago Dei*—is missing from the Qur'an. The closest that the Qur'an gets to this idea is a declaration in Sura 2 in which God announces to the angels that he is creating man to be a "vicegerent," or "successor" (Q 2:30). It seems, however, that the idea of humans bearing God's image would undermine the Qur'an's understanding of God's otherness.

On the other hand, the biblical tradition of *imago Dei* seems to have entered into the tradition, where it is found in two different sorts of hadith. First, it appears in certain hadith which simply relate that "God created Adam in his image." For example, a hadith in Bukhari says, "God . . . created Adam in his image. His height was 60 cubits"[37] (about 90 feet). Second, it appears in other hadith that are about good conduct (Arabic *adab*) when one is in a fistfight. In a hadith reported by Muslim, Muhammad says, "When one of you fights his brother, let him avoid the face, for God created Adam in his image."[38] This hadith is rather jarring, as it seems to suggest that because the human face resembles God, and out of a pious respect for God's looks, one should punch an opponent somewhere besides the face.

Tellingly, there was an effort by certain anti-anthropomorphic scholars to offer an interpretation of this hadith that would allow one to avoid the conclusion that Adam was created in the image of God. According to this interpretation, supported by a scholar from Baghdad known as Abu Thawr (d. 854), what the hadith means when it says "God created Adam in His image" is that "God created Adam in his [lowercase "h"] image," that is, in Adam's own image. I heard this interpretation at a conference of Muslim-Christian relations in England some years ago from a scholar who wanted to insist that Muslims do not believe in the doctrine of *imago Dei*.

In any case, although this is a grammatically plausible reading of the hadith, it does not seem a logical reading— especially if one takes into consideration the version of the hadith involving hitting someone in the face (which would make sense only if the "image" at stake is the image of God). What we are left with is a hadith that is at least as anthropomorphic as Gen 1:26, where God says, "Let us make man in our image" (inasmuch as it suggests that the human face really looks like the face of God).[39]

In this book I have tried to make the case that the God of the Qur'an *is* anthropomorphic but in a different sort of way; he is not anthropomorphic because he looks like a human. It is true that certain passages of the Qur'an refer to God's hand (such as Q 3:73, 5:64, 23:88), face (Q 55:27), and eyes (Q 11:37, 23:27, 52:48, 54:14); and a number of passages seem to refer to God "sitting on" or "settling into" the divine throne (Q 7:54,

13:2, 20:5, 25:59, 32:4, 57:4) or blowing into mud to create Adam (Q 15:28–29, 38:71–72) or blowing into Mary or Jesus (Q 21:91, 66:12).

Yet the more important point is that in the Qur'an God is anthropomorphic in his character, not in his physical appearance. The God of the Qur'an is a personal God who responds to human actions with pleasure or anger. He grows pleased with those who submit and grows angry with those who refuse to submit.

Arthur Arberry writes: "In Islam, God does not reveal himself. Being transcendent, He can never become the object of knowledge . . . God reveals guidance only."[40] Arberry is right that the God of the Qur'an is transcendent, even mysterious, inasmuch as the Qur'an never resolves how he is at once merciful and vengeful. But Allah is certainly not transcendent in the sense of being aloof or unconcerned with the affairs of humans. He is intimately, or one might say personally, involved with them all.

Epilogue
The Qur'an on Peaceful Coexistence

R ecent years have seen a spread of blasphemy laws around the Islamic world. In Pakistan, blasphemy against the Qur'an or the Prophet Muhammad is a capital crime. In 2010 a Pakistani Christian named Asia Bibi was sentenced to death by hanging for (allegedly) insulting the Prophet Muhammad and the Qur'an during a dispute with her Muslim neighbors as they picked berries together. Mobs formed (spurred on by radical imams calling believers over mosque loudspeakers to "defend" the Prophet) and Asia was beaten in front of her family. In the years that followed vigilante groups killed both Shahbaz Bhatti, a Christian government minister, and Salman Taseer, a Muslim governor of the Punjab, who spoke in defense of Asia. In October 2018 the Supreme Court of Pakistan acquitted Asia, leading to waves of massive protests across the country. Signs carried by protestors announced that the love of the Prophet, and the love of Allah, compelled them to demand Asia's death. One widely photographed banner stated, "Hang the blasphemer, cursed Asia."

Pakistan is not the only country where rage over blasphemy has spread, and Christians are not the only victims of that rage. On March 19, 2015, a twenty-seven-year-old Muslim woman named Farkhunda was beaten to death by a mob in Kabul, Afghanistan, when she was accused of burning the Qur'an. Most of those in Afghanistan who took up her defense did so by insisting that she did not actually burn the Qur'an — that is, they attempted to prove her innocent of the crime. Very few actually questioned whether burning the Qur'an should be a crime deserving death at all.

In May 2017 the Christian governor of Jakarta, Indonesia, Basuki "Ahok" Tjahaja Purnama, was sentenced to two years in prison for questioning the traditional interpretation of Q 5:51, which reads, according to the translation of Qarai, "Do not take the Jews and the Christians for allies: they are allies of each other." The word rendered here as "allies" (Arabic *awliya'*) can also be understand as "leaders," and that is how it is rendered in a widespread Indonesian translation of the Qur'an: "Do not take Christians and Jews and make them your leaders." Ahok's crime was his public challenge of this translation. In Indonesia Q 5:51 has subsequently become a symbol of a certain kind of Islamic enthusiasm. An artist for Marvel comics named Ardian Syaf drew a picture of one of the X-Men with "QS 5:51" on his costume to celebrate the verse (his contract was eventually terminated by Marvel).

So some (but not all) Muslims took up the defense of their Prophet and their God over purported blasphemy in Pakistan, Afghanistan, and Indonesia by demanding the punishment of the "blasphemers." But would God want them to do so? Does God need humans to defend him? Can't God do the punishing himself?

The irony of blasphemy laws, or vigilante killings inspired

by accusations of blasphemy, is that the Qur'an seems to make the point time and again that it is God's role to take vengeance on those who insult the prophets. Humans are not to usurp God's divine right of vengeance. It is God who destroys unbelieving peoples and God who punishes unbelievers in hell. On certain occasions God seems to insist explicitly on vengeance as his special right. In Q 7:87, after describing a series of divine punishments brought down upon sinful people, the Qur'an offers some counsel on what believers should do when they are faced with unbelievers. Its advice is simple: be patient. The Qur'an explains: "If a group of you have believed in what I have been sent with, and a group have not believed, be patient until God judges between us, and He is the best of judges." In other words, humans are not meant to take out vengeance on behalf of God. Vengeance is God's job.

It would be wrong to conclude that if Allah can be vengeful, so too Muslims are called to be the same. In fact, precisely the contrary is the case: *because* God is vengeful, humans need not take vengeance. Believers are called to be patient, to endure sinners and even unbelievers, and trust that God will sort things out in the end. They must not presume to judge or punish unbelief in the place of God.

This sentiment is played out in a well-known tradition preserved in the collection of hadith by the ninth-century Muslim scholar Ahmad b. Hanbal (d. 855) that involves two faithful companions of the Prophet Muhammad, Abu Bakr and Umar, who would later become the first and second caliphs, respectively (they were both also fathers-in-law of the Prophet). In the biography of the Prophet, Abu Bakr and Umar have distinct personalities. Abu Bakr is calm, prudent, even avuncular. He is patient in the face of both sinful Muslims and non-Muslims. Umar is tempestuous, quick to fly into a rage against sinners, and outraged by any hint of heresy or impiety. In Ahmad's tradition, Muhammad compares their personalities to that of earlier qur'anic prophets:

> Your likeness, O Abu Bakr, is that of Abraham who said, "But whoso follows me, he verily, is of me. And whoso disobeys me, still You are indeed Oft-forgiving, Most Merciful" [Q 14:36]. And your likeness, O Abu Bakr, is that of Jesus who said, "If you punish them, they are Your slaves, and if You forgive them, verily, You, only You, and the all-Mighty, the All-Wise" [Q 5:118]. And your likeness, O Umar, is that of Noah who said: "My Lord! Leave not one of the disbelievers on the earth!" [Q 71: 26]. And indeed your likeness, O Umar, is that of Moses, who said, "My Lord, harden their hearts, so that they will not believe until they see the painful torment" [Q 10:88].[1]

This tradition might be thought of as offering two possible Muslim dispositions toward unbelievers. Muslims, in Muhammad's day and still today, may follow the path of Abu Bakr. They may wish, or even pray, that God will be merciful to non-Muslims, forgiving them in this world and the next. We have seen in the course of this book that a reasonable theological argument can be made for the salvation of non-Muslims. Abu Bakr personifies this argument.

Alternatively, Muslims may follow the path of Umar. They might be outraged by the (perceived) stubbornness, ingratitude, and faithlessness of non-Muslims. They may wish, or even pray, that God will punish them in this world (as Noah does) or the next (as Moses does). This attitude (although it is not the sort of thing that non-Muslims would welcome) is their theological prerogative.

In other words, Muslims might be "Abu Bakr" Muslims or "Umar" Muslims. This tradition, however, does not afford the possibility of violence against non-Muslims. There is no third option. In this tradition Abu Bakr and Umar alike recognize that it is God's right to forgive or punish infidels. Abu Bakr Muslims hope and pray that God will forgive infidels, and Umar Muslims hope and pray that God will punish them. Either way, the decision to forgive or punish is God's, and no Muslim has the right to take that away from him.

On February 4, 2019, Pope Francis and the grand imam of al-Azhar in Egypt, Ahmed el-Tayeb, signed "A Document on Human Fraternity," which seems to extend this point. The document declares: "The pluralism and the diversity of religions, colour, sex, race and language are willed by God in His wisdom, through which He created human beings."[2] This declaration caused controversy, especially among Catholic observers, who asked: How could God will more than one religion; does he mean to contradict himself?

In the context of the document, however, it appears that the point of this statement is to advance an argument about religious liberty. The very next line reads: "This divine wisdom is the source from which the right to freedom of belief and the freedom to be different derives." The sentiment in this controversial document is that God not only allows for diversity (including diversity of beliefs), he wills it. This follows from the opening line of Q 49:13: "We created you from a male and a female and made you nations and tribes that you may be well acquainted with one another." The word for "nations" here is *umam,* the same word used (in the singular) by Muslims for the Islamic religious community (*umma*). Thus one might say, from the Qur'an's perspective at least, that God desires for humans to encounter difference and to tolerate difference, even religious difference. Humans are to coexist. It is God's role to forgive or punish.

So what choice will God make? The answer is a mystery. The Qur'an insists that it is God's will to do as he pleases and no one can, or will, know what that is. Not even Muhammad claimed to know what God would do with unbelievers. In Q 17:54 God tells him:

> Your Lord knows you best. He will have mercy on
> you if He wishes, or punish you, if He wishes, and
> We did not send you to watch over them.

Still, significant elements of Islamic tradition emphasize God's forgiveness. We have seen this in our study in Chapter 6 on the thought of Ibn Taymiyya, who today is often thought of as the progenitor of contemporary Islamic fundamentalism, as a polemical firebrand. However, when Ibn Taymiyya thinks through the scenario of the Day of Judgment, he is shaped by those traditions that emphasize God's mercy. This leads him, and others, to conclude that hellfire must be principally therapeutic. Those who are sent to hell are not damned forever. They are to be punished—in accordance with divine justice—but once they have suffered the requisite amount, an amount consistent with the gravity of their sins, they will be released from hell and admitted to paradise.

Islamic traditions on divine mercy are often focused on the scenario of Judgment Day. In a hadith reported on the authority of Salman al-Farisi, a Persian convert to Islam and one of Muhammad's companions, we learn the following: "Verily, there are one hundred (parts of) mercy for Allah, and it is one

part of this mercy by virtue of which there is mutual love between the people and ninety-nine reserved for the Day of Resurrection."[3] If this tradition emphasizes God's mercy on the
Day of Judgment, the Qur'an emphasizes divine mercy and
divine vengeance in equal parts. The Qur'an wants its audience to love God for his mercy and fear him for his vengeance:
"Do those who devise evil schemes feel secure that God will
not make the earth swallow them, or the punishment will not
overtake them whence they are not aware?" (Q 16:45). As for
those who escape this life without suffering divine vengeance,
their eternal fate is subject to the inscrutable decree of God:

> To God belongs whatever is in the heavens and the
> earth. Whether you disclose what is in your hearts
> or hide it, God will bring you to account for it. Then
> He will forgive whomever He wishes and punish
> whomever He wishes, and God has power over all
> things. (Q 2:284)

Indeed, at the very heart of the Qur'an's strategy to win the
submission of its audience is its depiction of a God who is fundamentally mysterious and unpredictable. The audience is left
knowing that God's will is inscrutable. They are left with no
choice but to submit, and they can never feel complacent. In
Sura 6 the Qur'an offers a scene of unbelievers on the Day of
Judgment who complain of their condemnation. As though
aware of verses like 2:284 (quoted above), they protest, "Had
God wished we would not have ascribed any partner [to Him],
nor our fathers, nor would we have forbidden anything!"
(Q 6:107). God, however, is not swayed by their argument.
There will be no excuses on that day.

In the course of this book we have also had the occasion

to consider this portrayal of a mysterious, all-powerful, personal God in the light of the Qur'an's biblical subtext. The goal of doing so is not to compare "Allah" favorably or unfavorably to "Yahweh" or "Christ." Instead, the goal is to show that the Qur'an's theological language is developed in conversation with, and at times in response to, early Jewish and Christian ways of thinking about God. It seems to me that the Qur'an does not mean to separate its God from the God of the Bible. Allah in the Qur'an is the God of Adam, Noah, Abraham, Moses, Jesus, and Mary as much as he is the God of Muhammad (and the other Arab prophets mentioned in the text). So the Qur'an does not mean to present a new or different God from the God of the Bible. It does, however, advance a particular understanding of that God. The "qur'anic difference" regarding God is sometimes thought to involve a concern with divine transcendence or otherness (especially in contrast with Christianity in light of its teaching of the incarnation). In this book, however, we have seen how intimately involved the God of the Qur'an is with the affairs of humans. He schemes for them and against them. He is capable of saving them (sending thousands of angels to help the believers in battle) and of tricking them by making their evil deeds seem good.

It is indeed God's sovereignty more than his transcendence that is emphasized by the Qur'an. It follows from this emphasis on sovereignty that God insists as well on his unique right to judge and punish. Thus, diversity and difference on earth—for example the presence of Muslims and non-Muslims—are not pretexts for believers to persecute unbelievers. The Qur'an is quite clear about this point. Difference is a test:

> Had God wished He would have made you one
> community, but [His purposes required] that He

should test you with respect to what He has given
you. So take the lead in all good works. To God
shall be the return of you all, whereat He will inform you concerning that about which you used to
differ. (Q 5:48b)

The turn of phrase in this passage "take the lead in all good
works" might be rendered "race with another in good works"
(Muhammad Pickthall translates it, "Vie one with another in
good works").[4] This, I might humbly suggest in conclusion, is
the call of the Qur'an to all of us, Muslims and non-Muslims
alike.

Notes

For all mentions of Qarai see Reynolds, *Qur'an and the Bible*. For a discussion see Conventions.

Introduction

1. U. F. Abd-Allah, "Mercy: The Stamp of Creation," Nawawi Foundation, 2004, https://www.theoasisinitiative.org/nawawi-mercy.

2. Ibid., 6.

3. In fact, Muslim scholars have long debated whether the *basmala* is to be thought of as part of the qur'anic revelation (that is, the words given to the Prophet Muhammad by the angel Gabriel) or an introductory formula that precedes the revelation. In the standard 1924 Cairo edition of the Qur'an (upon which all modern English translations are based), it is counted as part of the revelation for Sura 1 but not for the other Suras where it appears.

4. Western scholars of the Qur'an have often identified the use of *al-rahman* as a name for God with a particular period of Muhammad's proclamation, namely, the "second Meccan" period. On the association of *al-rahman* with this period, see Nöldeke et al., *History of the Qur'an*, 99 (this is the English translation of *Geschichte des Qorâns*, a work originally published in German in three volumes over several decades in the late nineteenth and early twentieth centuries).

5. Modified translation of Qarai. Or again, in a verse that seems to argue against polytheists who attribute children to God: "*Say, 'They say, "the Compassionate (al-rahman) has taken offspring." Immaculate is He! Rather they are [His] honoured servants'*" (Q 21:26). Modified translation of Qarai.

6. On this, see Neuwirth, "Raḥma," 31.

7. The title of the letter is taken from Q 3:64, "*Say, 'O People of the Book!*

Come to a common word between us and you: that we will worship no one but God, that we will not ascribe any partner to Him, and that some of us will not take some others as lords besides God.'"

8. See "The ACW Letter: A Common Word Between Us and You," A Common Word, http://www.acommonword.com/the-acw-document/.

9. Khorchide, *Islam ist Barmherzigkeit.*

10. Lawrence, *Who Is Allah?*, 15.

11. Rahman, *Major Themes*, 1.

12. Muhammad Pickthall, *The Meaning of the Glorious Qur'an* (London: Knopf, 1930; rpt. Kuala Lumpur: Islamic Book Trust, AH 1422/AD 2001, incorporating 248 "corrections" made by Iqbal Husain Ansari of Karachi); Abdullah Yusuf Ali, *The Holy Quran: Text, Translation and Commentary* (Lahore: Muhammad Ashraf, 1938); Arthur Arberry, *The Koran Interpreted* (London: Allen & Unwin, 1955; rpt. New York: Simon & Schuster, 1996); Asad, *Message of the Qur'an;* Taqi al-Din Hilali and Muhsin Khan, *Interpretation of the Meanings of the Noble Qur'an in the English Language* (Riyadh: Maktaba Dar-Us-Salam, 1993); Ali Quli Qarai, in Reynolds, *The Qur'an and the Bible.*

13. Qur'an 5:98 declares to the audience, "Know that God is severe in retribution, and that God is all-forgiving, all-merciful."

14. The Arabic here is *dhu rahmatin wasi'a* and could be understood to mean "dispenser of wide mercy," but most translators agree with Qarai's rendering. Arberry translates "of mercy all-embracing," and Muhammad Asad translates "Limitless is your Sustainer in His grace."

15. To Izutsu these two aspects of God correspond with two dispositions that the Qur'an demands of humanity: "Correspondingly, there occurs, on the human side, the basic contrast between 'thankfulness' on the one hand, and the 'god-fearing' attitude, on the other" (*God and Man in the Koran*, 77).

16. This is a reference to the German work known as *Die Geschichte des Qorâns* (T. Nöldeke), the first volume of which was published in 1860 (see note 4 above).

17. See Marshall, *God, Muhammad and the Unbelievers*, 171.

18. A. Hirsi Ali, "Why Islam Needs a Reformation," *Wall Street Journal*, March 20, 2015.

19. Incidentally, my decision not to rely on a chronological reading of the Qur'an agrees with that of the Pakistani scholar Fazlur Rahman (whom I criticize on other matters in this book). Toward the end of his chapter on "God" in *Major Themes of the Qur'an*, Rahman writes, "If this kind of analysis shows anything, it is that the Qur'an must be so studied that its concrete unity will emerge in its fullness" (15).

20. The way in which Islamic theology often departs from the Qur'an

is also emphasized by Izutsu (*God and Man in the Koran*) in his chapter "Koranic Key-Terms in History," 36–72 (esp. 46–48).

21. Rahbar, *God of Justice*, 222, 227.

22. *Lumen gentium*, 16, available at http://www.vatican.va/archive/hist _councils/ii_vatican_council/documents/vat-ii_const_19641121_lumen -gentium_en.html.

23. It is not clear to what address of Pope Francis Hawkins is referring. Pope Francis, however, has on several occasions affirmed that Muslims and Christians worship the same God, often by paraphrasing *Lumen gentium*. This affirmation is found, for example, in his apostolic exhortation *Evangelii gaudium*, paragraph 252, available at https://w2.vatican.va/content /francesco/en/apost_exhortations/documents/papa-francesco_esortazione -ap_20131124_evangelii-gaudium.html.

24. N. Qureshi, "Do Muslims and Christians Worship the Same God?," RZIM, December 27, 2015, http://rzim.org/global-blog/do-muslims-and -christians-worship-the-same-god/. For an alternative position by an evangelical Christian, see Volf, *Allah*.

25. This verse is often seen as the Qur'an's response to Num 11:23, in which God asks Moses, "Is the Lord's hand shortened?"

26. Izutsu, *God and Man in the Koran*, 101.

27. In another passage the Qur'an goes on to say that when Allah brings these sailors back safely home, they return to their pagan ways: "When they board the ship, they invoke God putting exclusive faith in Him, but when He delivers them to land, behold, they ascribe partners [to Him], being ungrateful for what We have given them! So let them enjoy. Soon they will know!" (Q 29:65–66).

28. Reynolds, *The Qur'an and the Bible*.

29. It is perhaps noteworthy that books on "themes" of the Qur'an by both Abu l-Hasan 'Ali Nadwi and Faruq Sherif are both missing the topic of "God." See Nadwi, *Guidance from the Holy Qur'an*, and Faruq Sherif, *A Guide to the Contents of the Qur'an* (London: Ithaca, 1985).

1

The Qur'an and the Bible

1. The original edition of Régis Blachère's French translation of the Qur'an was organized in a "chronological" order. So too is the French translation of Sami Aldeeb Abu Sahlieh, *Le Coran: texte arabe et traduction française*, 2nd ed. (Ochettaz: Aldeeb, 2016); also available in Arabic and English versions: *Al-Qur'an al-karim bi-l-tasalsul al-ta'rikhi* (Ochettaz: Aldeeb, 2015); and *The*

Koran: Arabic Text with the English Translation: In Chronological Order According to the Azhar with Reference to Variations, Abrogations and Jewish and Christian Writings (CreateSpace, 2016). Arthur Jeffery, *The Koran: Selected Suras* (Mineola, NY: Dover, 1958), organizes the Suras that he translates into a four-part division (Early Meccan, Middle Meccan, Late Meccan, Medinan) canonized by Nöldeke et al., *History of the Qur'an.*

2. A classic example of this perspective concerns Q 96. According to Islamic tradition the first revelation given to the Prophet consisted of the first five verses of that Sura. The rest of the Sura (vv. 6–19) was revealed at a later date, *after* portions of other Suras (including parts of 68 and 74) were revealed.

3. On this point, see further E. Stefanidis, "The Qur'an Made Linear: A Study of the *Geschichte des Qorâns'* Chronological Reordering," *JQS* 10 (2008): 1–22, esp. 10–11.

4. The carbon dating performed on a number of different manuscripts written in the earliest known (*hijazi*) script has yielded a wide range of dates, most of which are quite early (some of which precede even the traditional dates of Muhammad's life). See further G. S. Reynolds, "Variant Readings: The Birmingham Qur'an in the Context of Debate on Islamic Origins," *Times Literary Supplement,* August 5, 2015. For more on the interpretation of Qur'an manuscripts (and the controversies surrounding their interpretation), see Keith Small, *Textual Criticism and Qur'an Manuscripts* (Lanham, MD: Lexington, 2012), and more recently Asma Hilali, *The Sanaa Palimpsest: The Transmission of the Qur'an in the First Centuries AH* (London: Institute of Ismaili Studies, 2017). The early results of the carbon dating seem to be confirmed by the inability of early qur'anic commentators (beginning in the late eighth century) to understand certain aspects of the Qur'an. Those commentators develop stories to explain qur'anic passages that provide enough narrative material for storytelling, but when they are faced with passages that do not, they are often left guessing. They do not understand, for example, the "mysterious" letters that are found at the beginning of twenty-nine Suras, or the identity of the Sabi'un, a group named in Q 2:62 and 5:69 that is among those groups promised salvation. Their inability to identify such things implies that the Qur'an was a text that was already "ancient," and the meaning of the text was not transmitted with the text itself.

5. On this, see my introduction in G. S. Reynolds, ed., *Qur'an in Its Historical Context* (London: Routledge, 2008), 1–26.

6. The most important project to that end, organized by the Free University of Berlin, is known as Corpus Coranicum. For the moment the Corpus project is developing a database of ancient Qur'an manuscripts (as part of a

larger database including information on variant readings and texts related to the Qur'an). See http://corpuscoranicum.de/.

7. Bible citations are from the Revised Standard Version.

8. The problem with such stories is not that they don't fit the context of the qur'anic passage, but that they fit it so well. In other words, they seem to have been created to do just that (this sort of report is known in Islamic exegetical tradition as *ta'yin al-mubham,* the "clarification of ambiguity"). Such stories seem to be the stuff of storytellers.

9. The Qur'an refers at greater length to the story of Jonah in Sura 37: 139–48, but there, too, it does not provide all of the details.

10. In another passage on Jonah, in Q 21, the emphasis is on the way in which God saved Jonah from distress. A different lesson is taught: "So We answered his prayer and delivered him from the agony, and thus do We deliver the faithful" (Q 21:88).

11. The most obvious exception is the first Sura of the Qur'an, *al-Fatihah,* which is clearly framed as a prayer *to* God and not divine speech. Despite this, it is still considered by Islamic tradition to be part of the revelation. There are also individual verses, such as 6:114, that also seem to be in the voice of the believer. Still other passages (such as Suras 113 and 114) are made into divine speech by the presence of the word *qul* ("Say!"), an imperative which implies that God has commanded the Prophet to speak the following words.

12. Nicolai Sinai, "The Qur'an," in *Routledge Handbook on Early Islam,* ed. Herbert Berg (London: Routledge, 2017), 10. See also Sinai, *The Qur'an,* ch. 1.

13. Sinai, "The Qur'an," 11.

14. Mehdi Azaiez, *Le contre-discours du Coran* (Berlin: de Gruyter, 2015).

15. For example: "Were *you* to see when they are brought to a halt by the Fire, whereupon they will say, 'Alas, were we to be sent back [into the world], we would not deny the signs of our Lord, and we would be among the faithful!'" (Q 6:27).

16. Many different scholars have observed that the term *nabiy* appears principally in passages that the tradition labels as "Medinan" and therefore might be thought of as a "borrowing" from the Jewish community of that city. There are, however, exceptions (e.g., Q 6:112) and, more importantly, the very framing of the Qur'an itself as a divine message given to one man for the sake of his people bespeaks a biblical idea of prophecy. In other words, there is no reason to think of Muhammad "discovering" the biblical idea of a prophet only in Medina.

17. Islamic tradition relates that the pagan cult of Mecca included "soothsayers" (Arabic *kuhhan*), and some scholars have imagined that Muhammad framed his proclamation in the language of these soothsayers.

18. Notably Qarai's translation (which I have modified) renders this phrase "*This* is the Book" and thereby reflects the traditional idea that the Qur'an is speaking about the Qur'an.

19. For this phrase I am indebted to Michael Pregill, "Exegesis," in Berg, ed., *Routledge Handbook on Early Islam*, 98.

20. On this, see especially D. Madigan, *The Qur'an's Self-Image: Writing and Authority in Islam's Scripture* (Princeton: Princeton University Press, 2001).

21. Anne-Sylvie Boisliveau, *Le Coran par lui-même: Vocabulaire et argumentation du discours coranique autoréférentiel* (Leiden: Brill, 2015).

22. It is interesting that the Qur'an has the unbelievers rejecting Muhammad's proclamations as something "old" or "ancient." If the unbelievers in this Sura were pagans, as Islamic tradition tells us, they should have found Muhammad's preaching to be something "new" and "innovative." This is yet another sign that the original context of the Qur'an involved many more Jews and Christians than the tradition lets on.

23. Nöldeke writes, "The more one becomes acquainted with the best biographies of Muhammad, as well as with the uncorrupted source for our knowledge of his mind, the Koran, the more one becomes convinced that Muhammad sincerely believed in the truth of his mission to replace the false idolatry of the Arabs with a higher, soul-saving religion" (*History of the Qur'an*, 2).

24. Ibid.

25. Ibid., 4.

26. Nöldeke writes, "It would be a miracle if prophets were without blemish and sin, particularly in the case of Muhammad, who was at the same time a military leader and a statesman" (ibid.).

27. Still, Nöldeke concludes his discussion on Muhammad's sincerity with a note of admiration. For Nöldeke, Muhammad was still someone who "never lost faith in his divine mission" (ibid.).

28. Karl-Friedrich Pohlmann, in a relatively recent work in German, attempts to explain the Qur'an in this way. See K.-F. Pohlmann, *Die Entstehung des Korans. Neue Erkenntnisse aus Sicht der historisch-kritischen Bibelwissenschaft* (Darmstadt: Wissenschaftliche Buchgesellschaft, 2012).

29. F. Donner, "The Qur'an in Recent Scholarship," in Reynolds, ed., *Qur'an in Its Historical Context*, 29–50, 34.

30. *Zabur* may be related to the Hebrew term for a Psalm (*mizmor*), although this is not certain. There are certain passages in the Qur'an—e.g., 16:44; 23:53; 26:196; 35:52; 54:43, 52—where the plural of *zabur, zubur,* appears with a meaning closer to "scriptures."

31. Elsewhere (Q 53:36–37) the Qur'an also speaks of the "sheets" (*suhuf*), perhaps scriptures, of Moses and Abraham.

32. On the question of when the Bible was first translated into Arabic, see Sidney Griffith, *The Bible in Arabic: The Scriptures of the "People of the Book" in the Language of Islam* (Princeton: Princeton University Press, 2013), esp. 41–51.

33. Thus 20:113: "Thus We have sent it down as an Arabic Qur'an and We have paraphrased the warnings in it variously, so that they may be Godwary, or it may prompt them to remembrance" (see also 16:103; 26:192–95; 39: 27–28; 41:2–4, 44; 42:7; 46:12).

34. Q 21:47, 31:16; cf. Matt 13:31–32, Mark 4:30–32, Luke 13:18–19.

35. Q 2:88, 4:155; Deut 30:6; Jer 4:4, 9:24–25; Acts 7:51–53; Rom 2:28–29; Phil 3:3; Col 2:11.

36. Q 16:77; cf. 1 Cor 15:51–52.

37. Perhaps the closest thing to a quotation in the Qur'an is 5:32 ("That is why We decreed for the Children of Israel that whoever kills a soul without [its being guilty of] manslaughter or corruption on the earth, is as though he had killed all mankind, and whoever saves a life is as though he had saved all mankind"). This, however, is not a quotation of the Bible but rather of the Jewish text known as the Mishnah (m. Sanh. 4:5).

38. Islamic tradition insists that the Prophet was anyway illiterate. This doctrine is often justified by pointing to the way the Qur'an describes its Prophet with the Arabic term *ummi* (7:157–58) and interpreting this term as "illiterate." However, this term also appears in the plural (3:20, 75; 62:2) to describe the Prophet's entire people. Instead of "illiterate" it seems to mean "gentile" in the sense of someone who has not yet heard the word of God. The interest in Islamic tradition in defining this term as "illiterate" is connected to apologetics: if Muhammad were illiterate (so the argument goes), then he could not have gotten his information on earlier prophetic stories by reading the books of Jews and Christians.

39. The term that is later used to mean "corruption of scripture"—*tahrif*—is taken from this turn of phrase.

40. Al-Bukhari, *Sahih*, 52, "K. al-Shahadat," #2685.

41. For example, the early historian al-Ya'qubi (d. 897) or the qur'anic commentator al-Biqa'i (d. 1480).

2

God and the Prophets

Epigraph: Al-Bukhari, *Sahih*, 97, "K. al-Tawhid," #7453.

1. "Therefore I tell you, every sin and blasphemy will be forgiven men, but the blasphemy against the Spirit will not be forgiven" (Matt 12:31).

2. Al-Bukhari, *Sahih,* 97, "K. al-Tawhid," #7436.

3. On this tradition, preserved in an account of the night journey on the authority of Ibn 'Abbas, see F. S. Colby, *Narrating Muhammad's Night Journey* (Albany, NY: SUNY Press, 2008), 34.

4. See al-Bayhaqi, *Allah's Names and Attributes,* trans. G. F. Haddad (Damascus: As-Sunnah Foundation, 1998), 73.

5. Muhammad ibn 'Alawi, *Islamic Doctrines and Beliefs,* vol. 1, *The Prophets in Barzakh,* trans. G. F. Haddad (Damascus: As-Sunna Foundation, 1999), 138.

6. Some classical Muslim scholars, including most Mu'tazilites, allowed for a name to be assigned to God that God does not use for himself in the Qur'an. Others, including most of the Ash'arites (excluding notably al-Baqillani), disagreed (although they allowed also for names for God attested in the hadith). See Gimaret, *Noms divins,* 39–42. In certain cases some Muslim theologians refused to call God with names that, on the contrary, *are* used from him in the Qur'an since, they argued, the meaning of such a term had changed through time (this is the case, for example, with *wakil,* which is used for God in Q 3:173). See ibid., 41. Gimaret establishes the four principal lists of "ninety-nine names" that developed through time and shows that these four lists have only forty-four names in common. A fifth list, with other variations and attributed to the traditionalist Sufyan b. 'Uyayna (d. 811), is based uniquely on names found in the Qur'an. See ibid., 55–62, 69–71.

7. See al-Bukhari, *Sahih,* 54, "K. al-Shurut," #2736; 80, "K. al-Da'awat," #6410; 97, "K. al-Tawhid," #7392; Muslim, *Sahih,* 48, "K. al-Dhikr," #2677b.

8. On this, see Gimaret, *Noms divins,* 53.

9. Another one of those passages is Q 3:85, which declares: "Should anyone follow a religion other than *islam,* it shall never be accepted from him, and he will be among the losers in the Hereafter." This verse can be read, and today it often is, to mean that the only acceptable religion is Islam (with a capital *I*). This sort of reading could lead one to become an exclusivist: to conclude that only by following Islam will one find a heavenly reward. The original sense of this verse, however, is more likely found with the *meaning* of the Arabic word *islam,* that is, "submission"—which is to say that the only acceptable way of being religious is to submit to God. One might also compare Q 3:19: "Indeed, with God religion is *islam,* and those who were given the Book did not differ except after knowledge had come to them, out of envy among themselves. And whoever denies God's signs [should know that] God is swift at reckoning."

10. In fact, the meaning of the term is complicated, since it seems to be related to the word *hanpa* in Aramaic/Syriac, which means "pagan" or "gen-

tile." The Qur'an may be using this term with the idea that Abraham is a "gentile" monotheist, in other words, that he became a believer in God alone and not through divine revelation—that is, independently, through an observation of natural signs.

11. The notion that this was a "great" sacrifice signaled to most Muslim commentators that the Qur'an must be speaking about more than a ram given to Abraham; they often connect it to the animal sacrifice in the annual Islamic pilgrimage in Mecca (the hajj). One of the central rites of the pilgrimage is to butcher an animal. This is done in imitation of that "great" sacrifice Abraham once made. In any case, we can appreciate the way in which this story highlights the importance of obedience to God. The sacrifice was a "test," according to Q 37:106, a test that Abraham (and his son) passed.

12. One might compare the following passage from the epistle of James: "Come now, you who say, 'Today or tomorrow we will go into such and such a town and spend a year there and trade and get gain'; whereas you do not know about tomorrow. What is your life? For you are a mist that appears for a little time and then vanishes. Instead you ought to say, 'If the Lord wills, we shall live and we shall do this or that'" (4:13–15).

13. To Marshall, the concentration of punishment stories in the Meccan period reflects a phase of Muhammad's developing convictions: In Mecca, Muhammad was convinced that his job was only to communicate the message (balagh) given to him. Eventually, God would punish those who refused to listen to that message. In Medina, Muhammad came to see himself as the agent of that punishment through his wars against the unbelievers. See Marshall, God, Muhammad and the Unbelievers, 156. Marshall holds, however, that while Muhammad's attitude toward the unbelievers changes over time in the Qur'an, that of God does not: "The main thrust of God's attitude to unbelievers remains constant" (ibid., 88).

14. C. Gilliot, "Réflexions sur les raisons qui peuvent conduire à se convertir à l'Islam," Lumière et Vie 276 (October–December 2007): 99–106, 105.

15. In this light we can understand the reason why the Qur'an so often refers to him as a "warner," nadhir (a term that appears forty-four times in the Qur'an).

16. Marshall, God, Muhammad and the Unbelievers, 156.

17. Volf, Allah, 155.

18. "'A Common Word' Christian Response," Yale Center for Faith and Culture at Yale Divinity School, http://faith.yale.edu/common-word/common-word-christian-response.

3
Heaven and Hell

1. Mir, "Concept of Divine Mercy," 48.

2. P. Casanova, *Mohammed et la fin du monde* (Paris: Geuthner, 1911–1924).

3. S. Shoemaker, *The Death of a Prophet* (Philadelphia: University of Pennsylvania Press, 2012).

4. Muslim, *Sahih*, 54, "K. al-Fitan wa-Ashrat al-Sa'a," #2953c. For the English translation and Arabic text, see *Sahih Muslim*, trans. al-Khattab (Riyadh: Dar-us-Salam, 2007), 7:359.

5. In the Qur'an, however, the term *barzakh* is used differently, referring to a barrier that divides the heavenly and earthly realms or divides different waters. See Q 23:99–100, 25:53, 55:20.

6. This verse is related to an anecdote found in the *Paraleipomena of Jeremiah* (a Jewish text, also known as 4 Baruch, from the second century AD) by which Abimelech (see Jer 38:7–13) is made to fall asleep just before the destruction of Jerusalem by the Babylonians and is awoken sixty-six years later, when Jerusalem lies in ruins.

7. The dog in the Companions of the Cave account was known also in earlier Christian legend. The idea that a dog accompanied the "sleeping" believers reflects the Christian metaphor of believers as "sheep," Christ as a "good shepherd" (John 10:11, 14), and the devil as a "wolf." The dog is meant to be a sheepdog that protects the faithful flock. On this, see further, Reynolds, *Emergence of Islam*, 131–33.

8. In addition to Q 50:20, see Q 6:73, 18:99, 20:102, 23:101, 27:87, 36:51, 39:68, 69:13, 74:8, and 78:18. Compare the following passages of the New Testament: Matt 24:31, 1 Cor 15:51–52, and 1 Thess 4:16.

9. Notably, the doctrine seems to have been taught in the period of the Qur'an's origins by a Syriac theologian known as Babai (d. 628). See G. S. Reynolds, *The Qur'an and Its Biblical Subtext* (London: Routledge, 2010), 165.

10. This argument in the Qur'an, that the resurrection of the dead is like the effect of rain on dry earth, might be related to a Jewish tradition that God will resurrect the dead with dew. For example, see b. Shabbat 88b.

11. In Q 50:15 we find God himself declaring, "Have We been exhausted by the first creation? No, they are in doubt about a new creation" (cf. 53:47).

12. The notion of counterdiscourse in the Qur'an has been studied and clarified by the French scholar Mehdi Azaiez, *Le contre-discours coranique* (Berlin: de Gruyter, 2015).

13. I am referring here to Muhammad Aḥmad Khalafallah (d. 1991), author of *Al-Fann al-qasasi fi al-Qur'an al-karim* [The Narrative Art of the

Qur'an]. As we discuss in Chapter 10, Khalafallah used the expression "literary truth" for the Qur'an in the original version of his thesis but edited this expression out in the published version of his book. See Jomier, "Quelques positions," 63.

14. The abyss (*al-hawiya*, Q 101:9), the blazing fire (*al-jahim*, Q 44:47), the scorching fire (*al-saqar*, Q 74:26), the raging fire (*al-laza*, Q 70:15), the crusher (*al-hutama*, Q 104:4–6), the inferno (*al-sa'ir*, Q 22:4), and Gehenna (*jahannam*, Q 3:12, etc.).

15. John Chrysostom, *Homilies on Matthew*, 43[44].4.

16. Q 9:72, 13:23, 16:31, 18:31, 19:61, 20:76, 35:33, 38:50, 40:8, 61:12, 98:8.

17. Ephrem, *Hymns on Paradise*, trans. S. Brock (Crestwood, NY: St. Vladimir's Seminary Press, 1998), 1:4.

18. Ibid., 9:1a.

19. Ghamidi, *Islam*, 190.

20. See also 2:25, 3:15, 4:57, 37:48–49, 38:52, 44:54, 52:20, 55:56–61, 55:70–76, and 78:33.

21. I am referring to the work of Christoph Luxenberg, *Die syroaramäische Lesart des Koran: Ein Beitrag zur Entschlüsselung der Koransprache* (2000), published in English as *The Syro-Aramaic Reading of the Koran: A Contribution to the Decoding of the Language of the Koran* (Berlin: Schiler, 2007). Luxenberg's book, principally because of his argument that the "maidens" or "virgins" of paradise are actually grapes, received enormous media attention after its publication (appearing even on the front page of the *New York Times*).

22. Bukhari, *Sahih,* 56, "K. al-Jihad," #2796.

23. Islam Question & Answer, "Will Men in Paradise Have Intercourse with al-hoor aliyn?," August 30, 2000, https://islamqa.info/en/10053.

24. Muslim, *Sahih,* 1, "K. al-Iman," #181a; English translation, 1:288.

25. Hermanson, "Eschatology," 320.

26. Al-Zamakhshari, *Al-Kashshaf,* 4:462.

4

Divine Mercy

1. Bukhari, *Sahih,* 78, "K. al-Adab," #5999.

2. Abu l-Kalam Azad, *Tarjuman al-Qur'an,* in Baljon, *Modern Muslim Koran Interpretation,* 59.

3. Mir, "Concept of Divine Mercy," 43.

4. On this, see Marshall, "Mercy," 80–82.

5. Khalil argues that this "discredits the notion that the emphasis on

divine mercy is simply a *modern* hermeneutic phenomenon" (*Islam and the Fate of Others*, 21).

6. Rahman, *Major Themes*, 6. In his emphasis on divine mercy, Rahman was evidently responding to what he felt was an antagonistic portrayal of Allah in earlier Western scholarship. He writes: "Many a Western scholar (through a combination of ignorance and prejudice) has depicted the Qur'anic God as a concentrate of pure power, even as brute power—indeed, as a capricious tyrant" (ibid., 1).

7. Ibid., 6.

8. Mir, "Concept of Divine Mercy," 46.

9. On this see, for example, Ibn Kathir (d. 1373), who reports the following opinion in his Qur'an commentary: "[*Al-Rahman*] carries a broader scope of meanings pertaining to the mercy of Allah with His creation in both lives. Meanwhile [*al-rahim*] is exclusively for the believers" (*Tafsir* 1:67). There is no clear basis for this distinction in the Qur'an.

10. See Gimaret, *Noms divins*, 381.

11. Very often these terms appear as rhyme words at the end of verses, but this hardly invalidates their importance. As Bouman argues (*Gott und Mensch*, 151–53), all of this marks a deep concern of the Qur'an with the divine attribute of mercy.

12. See Izutsu, *God and Man in the Koran*, 230.

13. On each occasion it is a biblical character who uses this turn of phrase: Moses—asking forgiveness after the golden calf episode (Q 7:151; but notably only for Aaron and himself, not for the Israelites as a whole)—Jacob (12:64), Joseph (12:92), and Job (21:83). See Jomier, *Dieu et l'homme*, 49.

14. A. Ambros, with S. Procházka, *A Concise Dictionary of Koranic Arabic* (Wiesbaden: Reichert, 2004), 205. See also Jomier, "Nom divin," 363–64.

15. See also Q 36:11, 23; 50:33; 67:20.

16. This is not the only name that Arabian monotheists used for God. The French archaeologist Christian Robin has carefully catalogued names for God used by Jews in the South Arabian kingdom of Himyar in the fifth and sixth centuries. In addition to *rahmanan* ("the Compassionate"; the *an* at the end of the word is the definite article used in certain South Arabian languages), they used a name close to Arabic *allah* ('*lahan*) along with *rabb* ("lord")—a term closely related to a name used for God in the Qur'an. A remarkable shift occurs around the year AD 380 in the religious inscriptions of South Arabia (written in the South Arabian language known as Sabaean). Inscriptions earlier than this date speak of pagan deities, and inscriptions after this date are almost without exception monotheistic. For some time the inscriptions of South Arabia are mostly of a general monotheistic sort (a few

are explicitly Jewish), but beginning around AD 525–530, when the Jewish king Joseph (known as Dhu Nuwas in Islamic tradition) was killed, certain inscriptions have Christian formulas, reflecting the domination of Christian kings up through AD 575 with the death of the king Abraha. After this date very few inscriptions are found in South Arabia (reflecting a general civilizational decline there). See C. Robin "Le judaïsme de Himyar," *Arabia* 1 (2003): 71–172, esp. 98.

Muhammad ("the praised one"), the name given to Islam's prophet, may be used for God in a Jewish inscription dating from AD 523 found near the South Arabian city of Najran. On this, see C. Robin, "Himyar et Israël," *Comptes-rendus des séances de l'Académie des Inscriptions et Belles-Lettres* 148 (2004): 831–908, 876. However, Robin notes an alternative possibility that this name could be read *mahmud*.

17. "O Merciful One (*h rhm*) and O One who causes death (*h ymyt*), and O *Rḍw* [a term related to Arabic *ruda*] may the people be established [in this place]." This inscription is connected to the Qur'an not only by the reference to the god invoked as the "merciful one," but also by the description of this god as one who "causes death." The Qur'an regularly speaks of Allah as one who causes death (*yumit*; see, e.g., Q 2:258, 3:156, 7:158, 9:116) and life. The citation is from Ahmad al-Jallad, *An Outline of the Grammar of the Safaitic Inscriptions* (Leiden: Brill, 2015), 241. My attention to this inscription was sparked by the chapter by Ilkka Lindstedt, "Pre-Islamic Arabia and Early Islam," in *Routledge Handbook on Early Islam,* ed. Herbert Berg (Abingdon: Routledge, 2018).

18. Robin ("Le judaïsme de Himyar," 114) notes one intriguing inscription that seems to anticipate the Qur'an by referring to God as *rhmnn mtrhmn* ("*rahmanan* the merciful," an expression related to *al-rahman al-rahim*). South Arabian monotheistic inscriptions also include various paraphrases: "master of heaven," "lord of heaven and earth," "lord of the living and the dead," which are close to qur'anic turns of phrase for God. On this, see ibid., 117. More recently an article has been published in Arabic on an inscription in the South Arabian script known as *zabur* (all inscriptions in this script are generally thought to be pre-Islamic), which seems likewise to have a version of the *basmala* invocation. See M. al-Hajj et al., "*Naqsh jabal dhabub: naqsh jadid bi-khatt al-zabur*," *Majallat al-'Ibar* 1 (2018): 12–43.

Nöldeke has argued that Muhammad began to use *al-rahman* at a specific moment, what he calls the "2nd Meccan" period. He argues further that this name is particularly associated with this period: it appears only once in (what Nöldeke sees as) earlier Suras. Nöldeke writes that there is only one earlier use of this divine name, namely Q 55 (which is titled *al-Rahman*), v. 1; only a few in Suras from the "3rd Meccan" period (Q 13:30 and 41:2); and none at all from the Medinan period. Nöldeke accordingly wonders why Muhammad stopped using this name. He speculates: "It could possibly have been his intention to avoid being suspected of worshipping two deities" (Nöldeke et al., *History*, 99). For his part Jacques Jomier concludes that the pagans of Mecca believed in a god named *allah* (along with other gods), but they did not recognize *al-rahman*. The goal of Muhammad, he holds, was to persuade his audience that *al-rahman* and *allah* are two names of the same God. Both theories are speculative. Jomier refers to, among other verses, 25:60: "When they are told: 'Prostrate yourselves before *al-rahman*,' they say, 'What is '*al-rahman*? Shall we prostrate ourselves before whatever you bid us?' And it increases their aversion" (cf. also 13:30, 17:110, 21:36). Jomier, "Nom divin," 366.

19. David Marshall argues that the mention of mercy in Q 6:12 is best understood in the light of the preceding verse, Q 6:11, in which the Qur'an alludes to the punishment that God has unleashed on the unbelievers: "*Say,* 'Travel over the land, and then observe how was the fate of the deniers.'" It is meaningful, Marshall concludes, that the declaration of God's mercy in Q 6:12 is "surrounded by menacing references to God's judgement" (Marshall, "Mercy," 81).

20. The end of the verse is repeated verbatim at the end of v. 20: "Those who have ruined their souls will not have faith."

21. Modified translation of Qarai.

22. See Marshall, "Mercy," 79.

23. The two dimensions of creation are joined in Q 10:31: "*Say,* 'Who provides for you out of the sky and the earth? Who controls [your] hearing and sight, and who brings forth the living from the dead and brings forth the dead from the living, and who directs the command?' They will say, 'God.' *Say,* 'Will you not then be wary [of Him]?'"

24. Translated from the collection of the scholar Abu Hayyan al-Tawhidi (d. after 1010) by Khalidi, *The Muslim Jesus*, 145. For the original Arabic, see Tawhidi, *al-Basa'ir wa-l-dhakha'ir*, ed. Ibrahim al-Kaylani (Damascus: Maktabat Atlas, 1965–1977), 2:423.

25. Izutsu, *God and Man in the Koran*, 231.

26. Or again, "Then He proportioned him and breathed into him of His Spirit, and made for you hearing, sight, and hearts. Little do you thank" (Q 32:9; cf. 23:78).

27. Rahman writes, "For this reason, God's mercy reaches its logical zenith in 'sending Messengers,' 'revealing Books,' and showing man 'the Way'" (*Major Themes*, 9).

28. This is a quotation from the Saudi Muhammad al-Munajjid, "The

Mercy of Allah Towards His Slaves," Islam Question & Answer, June 17, 2007, https://islamqa.info/en/20468.

29. The Baghdadi Mu'tazili school held that God *chooses* to help humans—that is, provide them with *lutf*—out of his generosity.

30. 'Abd al-Jabbar, who dedicates an entire volume (vol. 13) of his encyclopedic theological work *al-Mughni* to the question, defines *lutf* as "anything that moves a man to choose obedience or makes it easier for him to choose so." M. McDermott, *The Theology of al-Shaikh al-Mufid* (Beirut: Dar al-Mashriq, 1978), 76.

31. O. Leaman, "Lutf," *Encyclopaedia of Islam*, 2nd ed. (Leiden: Brill, 1960–2006), 5:833b. The Mu'tazili perspective is generally followed also by Shi'ites such as al-Hilli (d. 1325).

32. 'Abd al-Jabbar, *Mutashabih al-Qur'an*, ed. 'Adnan Zarzur (Cairo: Dar al-Turath, 1969), 2:734.

33. Nadwi, *Guidance from the Holy Qur'an*, 13, 14. The idea of prophecy as a sort of mercy is suggested, as Johan Bouman has pointed out, by Q 28: 43, "Certainly We gave Moses the Book, after We had destroyed the former generations, as [a set of] eye-openers, guidance and mercy for mankind, so that they may take admonition." Here we have the sense that Allah realized, after dealing with generations of humans who did not heed the message of the prophets (and whom Allah consequently destroyed), that humans needed something more. He accordingly sent a scripture to Moses so that future generations might pay attention, repent, and be saved. See Bouman, *Gott und Mensch*, 168.

34. For what follows I am indebted to the excellent article of U. Rubin, "Repentance and Penitence," *Encyclopaedia of the Qur'ān*, ed. Jane Dammen McAuliffe, 6 vols. (Leiden: Brill, 2001–2006), 4:426–30.

35. Muslim, *Sahih*, 50, "K. al-Tawba," #2748a. See also #2748b, c.

36. Ibn Majah, *Sunan*, "K. al-Zuhd," 37:4394. Cf. al-Tirmidhi, *Jami'*, "K. al-Da'awat," 48:168.

37. Bouman writes appropriately, "God waits for humans to first fulfill certain specific conditions, before forgiveness will be shared" (*Gott und Mensch*, 174).

38. On this, see ibid., 178.

39. Marshall, "Mercy," 184. God in the Qur'an (e.g., 3:155) is called *halim*, a term often translated as "gentle" but which in the Qur'an seems to have a more ominous aspect. Izutsu comments: "God forgives sins committed by men and is gentle, but it is not a simple gentleness; it is a gentleness based on power, forbearance based on calm wisdom, which is possible only because it is coupled with an infinite power. It suggests, therefore, that there is always

in the background the possibility of a dreadful and drastic punishment" (*God and Man in the Koran,* 208).

40. One might compare Q 4:105–7, a passage where the Qur'an warns its audience against praying for "traitors" (*kha'inin*).

41. The number "seventy" appears in two other places in the Qur'an: Q 69: 32 and Q 7:155. The former speaks of a chain in hell that is "seventy cubits" long; the latter is a reference to the seventy elders whom Moses selects in Num 11:25. It is thus possible that the Qur'an's author simply liked the number and that the connection of Q 9:80 with Matthew 18 is coincidental. However, inasmuch as both Q 9:80 and Matt 18:21–22 are concerned with forgiveness, I find it more likely that the two are connected.

42. The example of Noah in Sura 71 of the Qur'an suggests that it is permissible to pray for the destruction of the unbelievers: "And Noah said, 'My Lord! Do not leave on the earth any inhabitant from among the faithless. If You leave them, they will lead astray Your servants, and will beget none except vicious ingrates. My Lord! Forgive me and my parents, and whoever enters my house in faith, and the faithful men and women, and do not increase the wrongdoers in anything but ruin'" (Q 71:26–28).

43. In Sura 19 Abraham declares to his father: "Peace be to you! I shall plead with my Lord to forgive you. He is indeed gracious to me. I dissociate myself from you and whatever you invoke besides God. I will supplicate my Lord. Hopefully, I will not be unblessed in supplicating my Lord" (Q 19: 47–48; cf. Q 14:41, 60:4). In Sura 26 the Qur'an quotes his prayer: "Forgive my father, for he is one of those who are astray" (Q 26:86).

44. The idea of praying for the guidance of unbelievers is sometimes based on a hadith found in the collection of Muslim according to which the Prophet prayed to God for the conversion of an Arab tribe (Daws): "It was said: 'Let Daws be destroyed,' whereupon he (Allah's Messenger) said: 'Allah guide aright the tribe of Daws and direct them to me.'" Muslim, *Sahih,* 44, "K. Fada'il al-Sahaba," #2524. For the English translation and Arabic text, see *Sahih Muslim,* trans. al-Khattab, 6:388.

45. al-Wahidi, *Asbab nuzul al-Qur'an,* trans. Guezzou, 95.

46. The well-known commentator Abu Ja'far al-Tabari (d. 923) explains Q 3:28 with a tradition (attributed to the early companion of the prophet Ibn 'Abbas) which maintains that the only time to be kind to unbelievers is when one is powerless before them and under their mercy (for example, if one is taken as a prisoner of war): "God forbade the people to show kindness towards the rejecters of faith, or take them as friends instead of the people of faith, except if the rejecters of faith had prevailed over them. In this case they can show kindness towards them outwardly, but should dif-

fer with them in matters of faith." Translation from Ayoub, *Qur'an and Its Interpreters*, 76–77. For the Arabic, see Tabari, *Tafsir*, ed. Shakir (Cairo: Dar al-Ma'arif, 1961–1969), 6:313–15.

47. Marshall, "Mercy," 83.

48. Izutsu, *God and Man in the Koran*, 120.

49. Ibid., 134.

50. Izutsu also proposes that we might see creation and prophetic messages as two sorts of signs, or *ayat*. The first is nonverbal, and the second is verbal: "The non-verbal *ayat* have one conspicuous advantage: they can be and *are* actually addressed to mankind at large without any discrimination; moreover they can be given directly without any intermediary, while the verbal type can be given directly only to one particular person, the Prophet, and only indirectly and mediately to mankind" (ibid., 136).

51. Cf. Q 10:57 and 16:64, which are similar. Q 31:3 makes revelation "a guidance and mercy for the virtuous."

52. Al-Mahalli and al-Suyuti, *Tafsir al-Jalalayn*, on Q 1:3 (trans. p. 1).

53. On this, see Izutsu, *God and Man in the Koran*, 213–14.

54. The term is qur'anic: Q 3:154, 5:50, 33:33, 48:26.

55. Izutsu, *God and Man in the Koran*, 140.

56. On guidance in the Qur'an, Izutsu comments eloquently: "[Guidance] was originally a concept relating to the experience of real travelling in the desert. Now in the Koran it is a religious concept relating to the course of human life metaphorically taken as a vast desert that man has to travel across" (ibid., 157).

5
Allah and the Fate of Sinners

1. This is the position, for example, of Abu Hamid al-Ghazali in his work known as the *Ihya'*. On this, see Khalil, *Islam and the Fate of Others*, 45.

2. Khalil writes, "The Qur'an, through its openness, undoubtedly allows for a wide variety of soteriological interpretations" (ibid., 6).

3. For this quotation I am indebted to Khalil (ibid., 41). He is quoting from Ghazali, *Faysal al-tafriqa bayna al-Islam wa-l-zandaqa*, according to Al-Ghazali, *On the Boundaries*, 126.

4. Muslim, *Sahih*, 50, "K. al-Tawba," #6969, 7:125.

5. See al-Dhahabi, *K. al-Kaba'ir*, ed. 'Abd al-Rahman b. Sa'd (Beirut: Dar al-Kutub al-'Ilmiyya, 2006).

6. In recent years many Muslims have labeled Salafi-Jihadis as Kharijites because of their attacks on fellow Muslims. When the Saudi regime made

this charge against Osama bin Laden, he responded by noting that his movement, unlike Kharijites, does not consider sinful Muslims to fall into the
category of unbelief: "We should respond to some of the [Saudi] regime's
allegations, whose repetition has upset people both day and night throughout the past two years. It has accused the *mujahidin* of following the path of
the Kharijites, but they know that we have nothing to do with such a school
of thought. Our messages and conduct attest to this. . . . We believe that no
sin besides that of unbelief makes a believer step outside his faith, even if it is
a serious sin, like murder or drinking alcohol. Even if the culprit died without repenting of his sins, his fate is with God, whether He wishes to forgive
him or to punish him" (*Messages to the World: The Statements of Osama bin
Laden,* ed. B. Lawrence; trans. J. Howarth [London: Verso 2005], 262). That
Ash'ari was concerned to avoid discord (*fitna*) in the Islamic community is
also evident from his position that faithful Muslims should not rebel against
an unrighteous ruler: "They think it proper to pray for the welfare of the
imams of the Muslims, not to rebel against them with the sword, and not to
fight in civil strife" (quoted in Watt, *Islamic Creeds,* 45).

7. See Watt, *Islamic Creeds,* 43.

8. Muslim, *Sahih,* 1, "K. al-Iman," #26a; 1:122.

9. Watt, *Islamic Creeds,* 45.

10. On his website Islam Question & Answer, Muhammad al-Munajjid
responds to a question of whether sinful Muslims will go to paradise by reporting a hadith in which the Prophet says, "Whoever dies not associating
anything with Allah will enter Paradise, and whoever dies associating anything with Allah will enter Hell." While this hadith seems to suggest that all
Muslims will be saved, al-Munajjid then goes on to say that those who do
not pray effectively cease being Muslims and will be damned: "The one who
does not pray at all, either in his house or in the mosque, and does not at-
tend Jumu'ah [Friday] or prayers in congregation, has also rendered his good
deeds invalid and has fallen into kufr [unbelief] by not praying at all." He
defends this position by quoting another hadith (found in the collection of
Nasa'i, "K. al-Salat," #463): "The Messenger of Allah (blessings and peace of
Allah be upon him) said: 'The covenant that stands between us and them—
i.e., the characteristic that separates the Muslims from the disbelievers—is
the prayer. Whoever does not pray has disbelieved.'" "Will Every Muslim
Enter Paradise, Even If He Was a Hypocrite or Did Not Pray or Committed
Shirk?," August 7, 2013, https://islamqa.info/en/147996.

11. Ibrâhîm Salâh al-Hudhud, "Extremists, Modern Heretics," Oasis,
March 21, 2017, http://www.oasiscenter.eu/articles/jihadism-and-violence
/2017/03/21/extremists-modern-heretics.

12. For a discussion of the teaching of ISIS on apostasy, see issue 7 of its magazine *Dabiq* ("From Hypocrisy to Apostasy"), https://clarionproj ect.org/docs/islamic-state-dabiq-magazine-issue-7-from-hypocrisy-to -apostasy.pdf.

13. Hermanson, "Eschatology," 318.

14. Cf. 2:284, 3:129, 5:39, 9:66, 12:56, 17:54, 29:21, 42:8, 48:13–14.

15. Quoted in Watt, *Islamic Creeds*, 30. Watt's translation comes from one of six Hanbali creeds recorded in the medieval work of Ibn Abi Ya'la (d. 1065), *Tabaqat al-Hanabila*. The creed from which I have quoted is attributed to Ibn Hanbal himself.

16. Ibid., 44.

17. Ibid., 52.

18. "A balance of hope and fear is therefore the general Muslim attitude towards one's eternal state, serving as both a deterrent against wrongdoing and an assurance of divine mercy" (Hermanson, "Eschatology," 319).

19. Read literally, this passage could suggest that everyone will actually *enter* hellfire but that the believers will later be rescued. The meaning turns on the Arabic term (in v. 71) *warid*, rendered "come to" above. This term is alternatively understood to mean to "descend into" or to "arrive at the brink."

20. Bukhari, *Sahih*, 10, "K. al-Adhan," #806.

21. Bukhari, *Sahih*, 81, "K. al-Riqaq," #6573; 8:305–8. See also the version in Bukhari, *Sahih* 10, "K. al-Adhan," #806.

22. Quoted in Watt, *Islamic Creeds*, 78, from Ghazali's work *The Revival of the Religious Sciences*. By "monotheists" here, Ghazali means specifically "Muslims," but elsewhere (in *Faysal al-tafriqa bayna al-Islam wa-l-zandaqa*) he entertains the possibility that non-Muslim monotheists too could be saved. I discuss this point in the following chapter.

23. Here I am following the translation of Khalil, *Islam and the Fate of Others*, 40. Bukhari, *Sahih*, 65, "K. al-Tafsir," #4741.

24. Quotation from al-Ghazali, *On the Boundaries*, 125, translation from Khalil, *Islam and the Fate of Others*, 40.

25. A version of this is found, for example, in the *Sunan* of Ibn Majah: "'The Jews split into seventy-one sects, one of which will be in Paradise and seventy in Hell. The Christians split into seventy-two sects, seventy-one of which will be in Hell and one in Paradise. I swear by the One Whose Hand is the soul of Muhammad, my nation will split into seventy-three sects, one of which will be in Paradise and seventy-two in Hell.' It was said: 'O Messenger of Allah, who are they?' He said: 'The main body.'" Ibn Majah 36, "K. al-Fitan," #3992.

26. See Khalil, *Islam and the Fate of Others*, 42. Ghazali develops his argu-

ment further with reference to a variant of this hadith that seems to report the contrary: all sects will be in paradise *except* one. By Ghazali's reading this means that many sects will pass through hell, but only one will be there permanently. Still another version of this hadith names that sect: they are not sinners but rather heretics (Arabic *zanadiqa*). Khalil suggests that by quoting this version Ghazali has in mind the Muslim philosophers and the Isma'ilis, two Muslim groups whom he accuses of unbelief. See ibid., 169 n. 82.

27. Quoted in Watt, *Islamic Creeds*, 52.

28. Q 2:286, 4:111, 6:164, 17:13–15, 29:12, 35:18, 39:7, 53:38–42, 82:19.

29. See Gätje, *Qur'an and Its Exegesis*, 182.

30. Hermanson, "Eschatology," 318. On intercession, see also A. J. Wensinck and D. Gimaret, "Shafa'a," *Encyclopaedia of Islam,* 2nd ed. (Leiden: Brill, 1960–2006), 9:177b–79a.

31. This is an allusion to the account of Moses slaying an Egyptian, which the Qur'an (following Exodus 2) alludes to in several passages: Q 20:40; 26:19–20; 28:15, 33.

32. Bukhari, *Sahih*, 65, "K. al-Tafsir," #4476.

33. Ghamidi (*Islam*, 230), following Amid Ahsan Islahi, sees the intercession of Muhammad as a possible means to salvation for those Muslims who do not repent immediately from their sin but who do repent before their death.

34. Bukhari, *Sahih*, 81, "K. al-Riqaq," #6467.

35. Behind this verse are those biblical passages (Exod 4:22–23; Deut 14:1–2; Jer 31:9; John 1:12–14; Rom 8:16–17, 9:8) that speak of believers as children of God. This verse is also close to a declaration in the Mishnah that the Qur'an seems to refute: "Israelites are beloved as they are called the sons of God" (m. Avot 3:14). Elsewhere the Qur'an denies on principle that God could have sons or daughters (2:116–17, 6:100, 9:30, 10:68, 17:40, passim). On this, see further Reynolds, *Qur'an and the Bible,* 194–95.

36. See also Q 2:284, 3:129, 9:66, 17:54, 29:21, 42:8.

37. Quoted in Watt, *Islamic Creeds*, 44.

38. "They disapprove of disputation and quarrelling about religion, of contention over predestination, and of argument over that in their religion about which the disputatious argue and disagree" (Ash'ari quoted in ibid.).

39. K. Blankinship, "The Early Creed," in Winter, ed., *Cambridge Companion*, 33–54, 49.

40. Ibid., 50.

41. Ibid.

42. Near the opening of the talk Benedict quoted the Byzantine emperor Manuel Palaeologus (who was at the time being held as a prisoner of war by

the Ottoman Turks) in his conversation with a Muslim scholar as follows: "He addresses his interlocutor with a startling brusqueness, a brusqueness that we find unacceptable, on the central question about the relationship between religion and violence in general, saying: 'Show me just what Mohammed brought that was new, and there you will find things only evil and inhuman, such as his command to spread by the sword the faith he preached.'" See "Faith, Reason and the University Memories and Reflections," September 12, 2006, http://w2.vatican.va/content/benedict-xvi/en/speeches/2006/september/documents/hf_ben-xvi_spe_20060912_university-regensburg.html.

43. Ibid.

44. The text of the "Open Letter to His Holiness Pope Benedict XVI" was published in *Islamic Studies* 45 (2006): 604–13, and is widely available online.

6
Allah and the Fate of Unbelievers

Epigraph: See Bukhari, *Sahih*, 63, "K. Manaqib al-ansar," #3885.

1. Hussain Nadim, "Can Mother Teresa, a Non-Muslim, Go to Heaven?," *Express Tribune Blogs*, August 24, 2012, http://blogs.tribune.com.pk/story/13564/can-mother-teresa-a-non-muslim-go-to-heaven/.

2. Hermanson comments: "Yet if God's compassion ensured that sinning Muslims could be saved — at least on non-Mu'tazilite views — through God's forgiveness and the intercession of the Prophet, then there seemed to be a need to extend this compassion to non-Muslim monotheists, particularly where they had never had the opportunity to accept Islam, but had still led lives of virtue" ("Eschatology," 322).

3. The identity of the Sabaeans is unclear. The Qur'an might be referring to the modern-day Mandaeans, a group that was once numerous in the marshes of southern Iraq where they practiced rites marked by baptism. They also became known in the West as "Christians of St. John."

4. This view is found, for example, in W. Rudolph, *Die Abhängigkeit des Qorans von Judentum und Christentum* (Stuttgart: Kohlhammer, 1922), 87. It seems to me more likely that the Qur'an is intentionally exaggerating or distorting Christian doctrine. On this, see Reynolds, "On the Presentation of Christianity," 52–54.

5. Ghamidi, *Islam,* 88.

6. Quoted in Gätje, *Qur'an and Its Exegesis,* 178.

7. Muslim, *Sahih*, 1, "K. al-Iman," #240; English trans. 1:243.

8. On this, see Khalil, *Islam and the Fate of Others,* 32. For the relevant passage in Ghazali's work, see al-Ghazali, *On the Boundaries,* 126–28.

9. Khalil, *Islam and the Fate of Others*, 33. See al-Ghazali, *On the Boundaries*, 126.

10. Khalil, *Islam and the Fate of Others*, 39.

11. This is a poignant scene that shows Muhammad's affection for his uncle, who had protected him at a time when the nascent Islamic community was threatened. See Muslim, *Sahih*, 1, "K. al-Iman" (ch./*bab* 10); English trans. 1:119–22.

12. Dawson McAllister, "What If Someone Never Hears About Jesus?," Christianity Today, http://www.christianitytoday.com/iyf/advice/faithdoubt/what-if-someone-never-hears-about-jesus.html.

13. Al-Ghazali, *On the Boundaries*, 126; quoted in Khalil, *Islam and the Fate of Others*, 41.

14. Translation is that of Khalil, *Islam and the Fate of Others*, 42, from the *Faysal*. Cf. the translation of Jackson in al-Ghazali, *On the Boundaries*, 129.

15. See Khalil, *Islam and the Fate of Others*, 48.

16. Al-Zamakhshari (who quotes the Ibn al-'As tradition) in Gätje, *Qur'an and Its Exegesis*, 183.

17. See ibid. For the Arabic, see al-Zamakhshari, *Al-Kashshaf*, 2:432. Zamakhshari's perspective is connected to the doctrine of the Mu'tazila known as "the promise and the threat," according to which neither grave sinners nor non-Muslims will escape eternal punishment in hell.

18. See the partial English translation of T. Michel, *A Muslim Theologian's Response to Christianity* (Delmar, NY: Caravan, 1984).

19. Ibn Qayyim al-Jawziyya, *Hidayat al-hayara fi ajwibat al-yahud wa-l-nasara* (Cairo: Maktabat al-Qima, 1977).

20. On this, see Khalil, *Islam and the Fate of Others*, 76.

21. Ibn Taymiyya, *Al-Radd 'ala man qala bi-fana' al-janna wa-al-nar*, ed. Muhammad b. 'Abd Allah al-Simhari (Riyadh: Dar al-Balansiyya, 1415/1995).

22. See Hoover, "Islamic Universalism," 183–85.

23. This is an important point for their deliberations on the eternity of hellfire. Ibn Taymiyya insisted that there was no consensus on this question among the first three generations of Muslims (these were the generations known as the Salaf) and therefore it was open to debate. His Sunni opponents insisted that there was a consensus (the technical Arabic term is *ijma'*) among later scholars, but Ibn Taymiyya questioned whether such a thing was even possible. On this, see ibid., 181–201.

24. Ibid., 197.

25. Regarding the development of Ibn Qayyim's thought on this question, see Hoover, "Against Islamic Universalism."

26. For a recent defense of this doctrine, see D. B. Hart, *That All Shall Be Saved* (New Haven: Yale University Press, 2019).

27. See Hoover, "Islamic Universalism," 188. Hoover speaks in this regard of Ibn Taymiyya's "theodicy of optimism" (196). Khalil (*Islam and the Fate of Others,* 100–101) notes how in certain of his writings Ibn Qayyim seems to speak as though he upholds the contrary position—that hell is eternal. Khalil sees this as evidence of a development of doctrine in Ibn Qayyim's mind that led him ultimately to universalism. He writes that Ibn Qayyim "gradually acquired more confidence in the universalist paradigm" (101). Hoover, however, argues convincingly that Ibn Qayyim retreated from universalism at the end of his life, perhaps because of the intervention of al-Subki on this question.

28. See, for example, Muslim, *Sahih,* 50, "K. al-Tawba," #2751; English trans. 7:125.

29. Ibid. One hadith that figured prominently in the thinking of Ibn Taymiyya and Ibn Qayyim al-Jawziyya was the following report of Ibn 'Abbās: "It is not necessary for anyone to judge God with respect to His creatures or to assign them to a garden or a fire." See Hoover, "Islamic Universalism," 186.

30. Al-Zamakhshari, as we have seen, had a different perspective on this phrase. Gätje, *Qur'an and Its Exegesis,* 182. See al-Zamakhshari, *Al-Kashshaf,* 2:430.

31. This tradition is quoted by Ibn Taymiyya in *Response to Whoever Says That the Garden and the Fire Will Pass Away* and by Ibn Qayyim al-Jawziyya in *Shifa' al-'alil* [The Healing of the Sick], ed. al-Sayyid Muhammad al-Sayyid and Sa'id Mahmud (Cairo: Dar al-Hadith, 1414/1994), 554. See Hoover, "Islamic Universalism," 183, 186.

32. A qur'anic verse cited by Ibn Taymiyya and Ibn Qayyim al-Jawziyya seems to suggest the same conclusion. Qur'an 78:23 declares that the inmates of the fire will "reside therein for ages." Commenting on this verse, they both explain that the Qur'an does not say here that unbelievers remain in the fire "forever"—only for "ages" or "long stretches of time" (as Hoover renders the relevant Arabic term, *ahqab*). Long stretches of time are long, and in hell they would certainly feel very long, but they do have an end.

33. See Hoover, "Islamic Universalism," 186.

34. The latter question led to a public dispute between the two scholars; see Hoover, "Against Islamic Universalism," 388.

35. Al-Subki argued that this matter had been determined by the "consensus" of Muslim scholars and therefore could not be questioned; see Hoover, "Islamic Universalism," 187–88.

36. On this, see Hoover, "Against Islamic Universalism," 397–99.

37. See Hoover, "Against Islamic Universalism."

38. This categorization is often attributed to a book by A. Race, *Christians and Religious Pluralism: Patterns in the Christian Theology of Religions* (Maryknoll, NY: Orbis, 1982).

39. On this, see Khalil, *Islam and the Fate of Others*, 6 n. 19. He refers to Rashid Rida, *Tafsir al-Qur'an al-hakim al-shahir bi-tafsir al-Manar* (Beirut: Dar al-Ma'rifa, 1970), 6:73.

40. Q 6:74–83, 19:41–48, 21:51–67, 26:69–104, 37:83–96, 43:26–27, 60:4.

41. This verse is close to a declaration in the Mishnah, "Israelites are beloved as they are called the sons of God" (m. Avot 3:14), and a number of New Testament passages, such as Rom 8:16–17. Elsewhere, the Qur'an denies on principle that God could have sons or daughters (2:116–17, 6:100, 9:30, 10:68, 17:40, passim).

42. K. Blankinship, "The Early Creed," in Winter, ed., *Cambridge Companion*, 33–54, 50.

7
Divine Wrath

1. Muslim, *Sahih*, 4, "K. al-Salat," #222; English trans. 1:597.

2. Translation from Khalidi, *The Muslim Jesus*, 74.

3. Izutsu, *God and Man in the Koran*, 230.

4. Ibid., 95.

5. On God's scheming, or devising, see also Q 3:54, 8:30, 10:21.

6. On the sealing of hearts, see also Q 2:7, 6:46, 7:101, 9:87, 10:74, 16:108, 30:59, 40:35, 45:23, 47:16, 63:3.

7. Q 4:88, 4:143, 7:186, 13:33, 30:29, 39:23, 39:36, 40:33, 42:46.

8. Rahbar, *God of Justice*, 225.

9. Qarai renders the Arabic expression *la yuhibbu* in both verses as "does not like." I have modified this to "does not love." Elsewhere we read that God does not love the "wrongdoers" (*al-zalimun*). For others whom God does not love, see Q 2:190, 205; 4:36, 107; 5:64, 87; 6:141.

10. Volf, *Allah*, 174.

11. Ibid., 182–83. Volf (ibid., 181–83) sums up common Christian and Muslim convictions regarding God's love and mercy as follows: (1) God loves creatures in a compassionate, gift-giving sort of way; (2) God is just; (3) God's justice is an aspect of his love for—or mercy toward—creatures; and (4) human beings are called to love their neighbors as they love themselves. Volf also contends that Muslims could move toward Christians,

among other things, in affirming (1) that God *is* love, (2) that God loves the other, (3) that God loves the ungodly too, and (4) that God commands us to love enemies since he loves all people.

12. For example, Old Testament, Deut 32:6, 1 Chr 29:10, Isa 64:8, Jer 31:9; New Testament, Matt 5:16, Mark 11:25, Luke 6:36, John 1:14, Rom 1:7.

13. Jahiz, "Radd ʿala al-nasara," in *Rasaʾil al-Jahiz*, ed. ʿAbd al-Salam Harun (Cairo: Maktabat al-Khanji, 1964–1979), 3:(301–51), 333.

14. My translation; Qarai renders "have incurred Your wrath."

15. In arguing against the idea that an accurate appreciation of the Qur'an's God could be had by analyzing the divine names in the Qur'an (many of which appear in pairs of opposites), Rahbar comments: "These opposites, when isolated from their real contexts, and so brought together, create the impression that [the] Qur'an's God is One who harms and profits, favours and withholds favour, guides and misguides, loves and hates, shows mercy or demonstrates justice, according as His 'mood' might decide" (*God of Justice*, 12).

16. Cf. Q 2:263, 267; 3:97; 4:131; 14:8; 27:40; 31:12; 39:7; 64:6.

17. Rahbar (who died in 2013) completed his Cambridge University thesis in 1953. In 1959, while in Turkey, he converted to Christianity. Even before his conversion, Rahbar was considered a suspect figure by some Muslims after he presented a paper critical of Islamic tradition at a 1958 colloquium in Lahore, Pakistan. Some details of this controversy are given in "Postscript of the Preface," in Rahbar, *God of Justice*, xix–xxi.

18. Rahbar's conclusions are not far from those of Johan Bouman, who argues (after analyzing Sura 7) that in the Qur'an, "Mercy remains ordered within the known structure of justice" (*Gott und Mensch*, 173). Bouman also writes that in the Qur'an, "justice sets the boundaries for the exercise of mercy, forgiveness and love" (ibid., 178).

19. See, for example, 22:19–22 (hell) / 22:23–24 (heaven); 35:33–35 (heaven) / 35:36–37 (hell); 44:43–50 (hell) / 44:51–57 (heaven); 55:43–44 (hell) / 55:46–78 (heaven); 56:11–40 (heaven) / 56:41–56 (hell).

20. See Rahbar, *God of Justice*, 146–47.

21. Ibid., 147.

22. Ibid., 226.

23. Ibid., 5.

24. K. Blankinship, "The Early Creed," in Winter, ed., *Cambridge Companion*, 33–54, 50.

25. Asad, *Message of the Qur'an*, 837–38 n. 10.

26. For this section I am indebted to an unpublished paper shared with me by Prof. Issam Eido: "Divine Wrath in Qur'anic Texts: Different Approaches for Forming the Enemy."

27. This verse is related to those passages of the Old Testament in which the Israelites regret that Moses has taken them out of Egypt, where they ate well (see Exod 16:3; Num 11:4–6, 33; 21:5).

28. One can detect behind this phrase the biblical metaphor of the uncircumcised heart that is directed against the Israelites in both the Old Testament (Jer 9:26; cf. also Lev 26:41, Deut 10:16) and the New Testament (Acts 7:51; cf. Rom 2:29).

29. Qur'an 58:14 also seems to refer to the Jews when God declares: "Have *you* not regarded those who befriend a people at whom God is wrathful? They neither belong to you, nor to them, and they swear false oaths [that they are with you] and they know" (cf. Q 60:13).

30. Qarai renders *maqt* as "outrage." Ambros defines *maqt* as "a loathing, hatred" (Arne A. Ambros, *A Concise Dictionary of Koranic Arabic* [Wiesbaden: Reichert, 2004], 257).

31. Abu al-Layth al-Samarqandi, *Tanbih al-ghafilin* (Cairo: al-Matba'a al-Yusufiyya, n.d.), 216; quoted and translated by Khalidi, *The Muslim Jesus*, 135.

32. Qur'an 4:47 points to God's transforming the figures of the People of the Sabbath as a warning to the People of the Book (Jews and Christians): "O you who were given the Book! Believe in what We have sent down confirming what is with you, before We blot out the faces and turn them backwards, or curse them as We cursed the People of the Sabbath, and God's command is bound to be fulfilled."

33. "They split up into three parties. One said, 'Let us ascend and dwell there'; the second said, 'Let us ascend and serve idols'; and the third said, 'Let us ascend and wage war [with God].' The party which proposed, 'Let us ascend, and dwell there'—the Lord scattered them; the one that said, 'Let us ascend and wage war' were turned to apes, spirits, devils, and night-demons" (b. Sanh. 109a).

34. Indeed, in one passage the Qur'an downplays the importance of the Sabbath, declaring, "The Sabbath was only prescribed for those who differed about it" (Q 16:124).

35. Al-Tabari, *Tafsir,* 1:332.

36. Bouman writes, "[Allah] is and remains the Lord and king in the entire unfolding of history from creation to the final judgement" (*Gott und Mensch,* 180).

37. Izutsu, *God and Man in the Koran,* 77.

38. Ibid., 199.

39. Marshall, "Mercy."

8

The Avenger

1. Catholic News Service, "Pope Francis Suggests Translation Change to the 'Our Father,'" December 8, 2017, *America: The Jesuit Review,* https://www.americamagazine.org/faith/2017/12/08/pope-francis-suggests-translation-change-our-father.

2. As Gimaret notes, Ibn Taymiyya felt that it was inappropriate to count this name among the lists of God's beautiful names—even if the Qur'an uses this name for God (*Noms divins,* 66).

3. This passage may suggest that not only Pharaoh's army but all of the Egyptians were drowned, in contradiction to the account in Exodus.

4. For example, *'iqab, 'uquba, 'adhab.* On this, see Gimaret, *Noms divins,* 353–54, who refers to the commentators Razi and Tusi.

5. The Arabic word for "table" in the Qur'an—*ma'ida*—is related to the term in the Ethiopic Bible for "table" in Ps 78:19.

6. In fact, this passage is also closely related to the "bread of life" discourse in John 6. There, the crowds following Jesus demand that he perform a sign like that Moses performed in the wilderness. Jesus responds by describing the heavenly food—the Eucharist—that he will provide and that is greater than any earthly food:

> [30]So they said to him, "Then what sign do you do, that we may see, and believe you? What work do you perform? [31]Our fathers ate the manna in the wilderness; as it is written, 'He gave them bread from heaven to eat.'" [32]Jesus then said to them, "Truly, truly, I say to you, it was not Moses who gave you the bread from heaven; my Father gives you the true bread from heaven. [33]For the bread of God is that which comes down from heaven, and gives life to the world." (John 6:30–33)

7. Al-Mahalli and al-Suyuti, *Tafsir al-Jalalayn,* 5:115.

8. My translation.

9. Ibn Kathir, *Tafsir,* 2:143; quoted by Ayoub, *Qur'an and Its Interpreters,* 166.

10. Al-Zamakhshari, *Al-Kashshaf,* 1:587.

11. Ibid.

12. Al-Mahalli and al-Suyuti, *Tafsir al-Jalalayn,* 62.

13. See the discussion in Chapter 3.

14. Asad, *Message of the Qur'an,* 89.

15. Izutsu, *God and Man in the Koran*, 95. Elsewhere, Izutsu describes how Allah oversees all things: "All human affairs even the minutest and apparently most insignificant details of life are put under the strict supervision of Allah" (ibid., 129).

16. "Why has there not been any town except the people of Jonah that might believe, so that its belief might benefit it? When they believed, We removed from them the punishment of disgrace in the life of this world and We provided for them for a time" (Q 10:98). The qur'anic hint that Nineveh was ultimately destroyed might reflect the biblical Book of Nahum, which predicts the ultimate demise of the city.

17. The idea that this account might be thought of under the category of divine trickery was suggested to me by Jacob Kildoo.

18. A hadith connects this qur'anic verse explicitly to the notion of *istidraj*, with Muhammad saying, "If you see God most high giving a servant in this world who is rebellious the things he likes, this is *istidraj*." See 'Ali b. Sultan Muhammad al-Qari, *Mirqat al-mafatih sharh mishkat al-masabih* (Beirut: Dar al-Fikr, 1422/2002), #3257.

19. Quoted in Ayoub, *Qur'an and Its Interpreters*, 166.

20. See ibid., 166.

21. Sahl al-Tustari, *Tafsir*, 138, on Q 24:37.

22. On God's "leading into error," see also Q 4:88, 143; 7:178, 186; 13:33; 17:97; 18:17; 39:23, 36; 40:33; 42:44, 46.

23. K. Blankinship, "The Early Creed," in Winter, ed., *Cambridge Companion*, 33–54, 52.

24. Quotation from the poem known as the *Asrarname*, quoted by H. Ritter, *The Ocean of the Soul*, trans. J. O'Kane (Leiden: Brill, 2013), 43.

25. *An Arabic-English Lexicon*, ed. E. Lane (London: Williams and Norgate, 1863–1893), 2954a.

26. They also mock warnings of the Day of Judgment (Q 6:5; 11:8; 16:34; 26:6; 39:48; 40:83; 45:33; 46:26), the "signs" of God (Q 30:10), or the prophets themselves (Q 15:11, 21:41, 36:30, 43:7).

27. My translation.

28. Qarai's rendering of this verse, which I have quoted here, follows the standard interpretation. *Tafsir al-Jalalayn*, for example, explains this verse as an instruction to the unbeliever to tie a rope to the roof of his house and hang himself. "Let him choke to death because of it," the commentary explains (369). Zamakhshari also mentions this interpretation (which involves reading the word *qata'a*—literally "to cut"—as a reference to choking or hanging). However, he then adds a second interpretation, according to which the Qur'an means instead to challenge unbelievers to stretch out a

rope to heaven (indeed, the word that Qarai renders as "ceiling" literally means "heaven") to see whether they can ascend there. See al-Zamakhshari, *Al-Kashshaf,* 3:148. To this end Asad renders this verse as follows: "If anyone thinks that God will not succour him in this world and in the life to come, let him reach out unto heaven by any [other] means and [thus try to] make headway: and then let him see whether this scheme of his will indeed do away with the cause of his anguish" (*Message of the Qur'an,* 564).

29. In another place it is not clear who exactly is responsible for the hardening of hearts. Qur'an 6:43 says "their hearts were hardened and Satan had made what they had been doing seem decorous to them."

30. Creed of Ash'ari, in Watt, *Islamic Creeds,* 42.

31. On Zamakhshari's discussion, see Gätje, *Qur'an and Its Exegesis,* 222, or the original Arabic, al-Zamakhshari, *Al-Kashshaf,* 1:49–52.

32. Quoted in Gätje, *Qur'an and Its Exegesis,* 154. For the original Arabic, see al-Zamakhshari, *Al-Kashshaf,* 1:634.

33. Ibid. Ibn al-Munayyir's gloss is printed in the apparatus of al-Zamakhshari, *Al-Kashshaf,* 1:634 n. 3.

34. Hans Wehr, *A Dictionary of Modern Written Arabic,* ed. J. Milton Cowan, 4th ed. (Urbana, IL: Spoken Language Services, 1994), 1289.

9
God of the Bible and the Qur'an

1. This act will be interpreted in the New Testament as an anticipation of the way Christ on the cross offers healing. See John 3:14–15.

2. *Genesis Rabbah* 53:1.

3. A similar line (addressed, however, to Jesus) is spoken by Stephen in the account of his martyrdom in the Acts of the Apostles: "And as they were stoning Stephen, he prayed, 'Lord Jesus, receive my spirit.' And he knelt down and cried with a loud voice, 'Lord, do not hold this sin against them'" (Acts 7:59–60).

4. Thomas Aquinas, *Reasons for the Faith,* trans. J. Kenny, *Islamochristiana* 22 (1996): 31–52, 45.

5. See Volf, *Allah,* 157.

6. Ibid.

7. See Origen, *Philocalia,* 29:9–10. For a discussion, see C. M. McGinnis, "The Hardening of Pharaoh's Heart in Christian and Jewish Interpretation," *Journal of Theological Interpretation* 6 (2012): 43–64, 46–47.

8. Origen, *On Matthew,* trans. R. E. Heine (Oxford: Oxford University Press, 2018), 16:8.

9. My attention was drawn to this passage by Marshall, "Mercy."

10. See ibid.

11. See Bouman, *Gott und Mensch*, 154.

12. b. Sanh. 98b, Soncino translation (see www.halakhah.com).

13. b. Sanh. 39b.

14. Marshall, "Mercy."

15. Ibid.

16. Muslim, *Sahih*, 50, "K. al-Tawba," #267.

17. Bouman, *Gott und Mensch*, 155.

18. b. Avot 3:15.

19. See Bouman, *Gott und Mensch*, 159.

20. In Chapter 4 I note the use of the related term *rahmanan* for God in both Jewish and Christian inscriptions of South Arabia.

21. b. Avot 4:22.

22. *Genesis Rabbah* 33:3. See *Genesis Rabbah*, trans. H. Freedman (London: Soncino, 1961), 1:262–63.

23. Ephrem lived before the Council of Chalcedon (451) and the division of Christian communities into "Nestorians," Melkites, and Jacobites.

24. S. Brock, trans., *Treasure-house of Mysteries: Explorations of the Sacred Text Through Poetry in the Syriac Tradition* (Yonkers, NY: St. Vladimir's Seminary, 2012), 186.

25. Jacob of Serugh, *On the Flood*, in *Homiliae Selectae Mar-Jacobi Sarugensis*, ed. P. Bedjan (Paris: Harrassowitz 1905–1910), 4:24. I am grateful to Prof. Abdulmasih Saadi for pointing out this passage to me.

26. Jacob of Serugh, *Homélies contre les juifs*, Patrologia Orientalis 174, ed. and trans. M. Albert (Turnhout: Brepols, 1976), 146.

27. Rahman, *Major Themes*, 9.

28. Ibid., 9–10.

29. Rahbar, *God of Justice*, 223–24.

10
Rereading the Qur'an

Epigraph: *Poems from the Divan of Hafiz*, trans. Gertrude Bell (London: Heinemann, 1897), 95.

1. Jomier, "Quelques positions actuelles," 66. See Khalafallah, *Al-Fann*, 10.

2. For a good summary of Abu Zayd's story, see Fauzi M. Najjar, "Islamic Fundamentalism and the Intellectuals: The Case of Naṣr Ḥāmid Abū Zayd," *British Journal of Middle Eastern Studies* 27, no. 2 (2000): 177–200.

3. Rahman, *Major Themes*, 1.

4. Jomier, *Dieu et l'homme,* 165, 172.

5. See Q 2:66, 275; 3:137; 5:46; 7:145; 10:57; 11:120; 16:125; 24:34.

6. Jomier, *Dieu et l'homme,* 168.

7. Gwynne, *Logic, Rhetoric, and Legal Reasoning,* 130.

8. Ibid., 192.

9. The tradition that Pharaoh alone was saved is in the *Mekhilta de-Rabbi Ishmael, Beshallah 7* (ca. late fourth century AD).

10. Al-Mahalli and al-Suyuti, *Tafsir al-Jalalayn,* on Q 10:90 (p. 224 of the English translation).

11. Al-Khuli (d. 1967) was chair of the department of qur'anic exegesis at the time.

12. Khalafallah, *Al-Fann,* 24 (see also p. 86).

13. It is tempting to compare Khalafallah's notion of the Qur'an as a *qissa,* "story," and a later current in Christian exegesis of the Bible known as narrative theology. The notion of narrative theology as represented by George Lindbeck and Stanley Hauerwas—criticized in the work of Francesca Murphy, *God Is Not a Story* (Oxford: Oxford University Press, 2007)—is that Christian truth can be thought of principally as a story, with its own internal logic, and cannot be judged according to some system of universal rationality. In terms of interpretation of scripture, this often means that the question of principal importance is the way in which the community receives biblical passages, and not their historical context or "objective" truth.

14. Cf. 12:3, an introduction to the Sura known as Joseph: *nahnu naqussu 'alayka ahsana l-qasasi,* "We relate to you the best of stories."

15. Khalafallah, *Al-Fann,* 24.

16. Ibid., 153–54.

17. Ibid., 154.

18. Ibid., 155.

19. Ibid., 156.

20. On this, see Jomier, "Quelques positions actuelles," 63.

21. Jomier, "Quelques positions actuelles," 72.

22. Ibid., 71–72.

23. Ibid., 63.

24. Khalafallah, *Al-Fann,* 341.

25. Jomier, *Dieu et l'homme,* 63.

26. Khalafallah, *Al-Fann,* 154.

27. Izutsu, *God and Man in the Koran,* 238.

28. See Gardet and Anawati, *Introduction,* 61.

29. Sayed M. Modarresi, https://twitter.com/SayedModarresi/status/877 243171708784640.

30. Izutsu, *God and Man in the Koran*, 234.

31. Asad, *Message of the Qur'an*, 798.

32. Kermani, *God Is Beautiful*, 305.

33. Ibid., 314.

34. Ibid., 334. The tradition is preserved in al-Tirmidhi (d. 892), *Al-Jami'*, book 34:9 (nos. 2312, 2313), 4:134.

35. al-Tirmidhi, book 34:8 (no. 2311), 4:133.

36. The saying comes from Prov 9:10; the choral piece is by the Flemish composer Orlande de Lassus (d. 1594).

37. See Bukhari, *Sahih*, 79, "K. al-Isti'dhan," #6227. I have quoted the hadith from C. Melchert, "God Created Adam in His Image," *Journal of Qur'anic Studies* 13 (2011): 113–24, 114. This same hadith is also in the "K. al-Anbiya'" of Bukhari (Kitab 60, #3326).

38. See, for example, Muslim, *Sahih*, 45, "K. al-Birr," #2612; trans. 6:475. See Melchert, "God Created Adam," 115. As Melchert notes, a shorter version of this hadith is reported by Ahmad b. Hanbal. Other versions omit the phrase "God created Adam in His image." Another hadith variant speaks of "insulting" someone's face instead of hitting it (ibid., 116–17).

39. Christopher Melchert wonders whether it could reflect a reaction among certain hadith scholars against Muslim theologians (above all Mu'tazila) who were against any anthropomorphism. Melchert writes, "It is as if heightened concern among Muslim theologians to preserve divine transcendence mirrored a heightened predilection among others, notably Hadith folk, for anthropomorphism" ("God Created Adam," 121).

40. A. J. Arberry, *Revelation and Reason in Islam* (London: George Allen & Unwin, 1958), 11.

Epilogue

1. Ibn Hanbal, *Musnad*, 3:301–3.

2. "A Document on Human Fraternity for World Peace and Living Together," http://w2.vatican.va/content/francesco/en/travels/2019/outside/documents/papa-francesco_20190204_documento-fratellanza-umana.html.

3. Muslim, *Sahih*, 50, "K. al-Tawba," #2753; trans. 7:127.

4. Muhammad Pickthall, *The Meaning of the Glorious Qur'an* (London: Knopf, 1930), 125.

Bibliography

Asad, Muhammad. *The Message of the Qur'an*. Gibraltar: Al-Andalus, 1984.

Ayoub, Mahmoud M. *The Qur'an and Its Interpreters*. Vol. 2. Albany: State University of New York Press, 1992.

Bakker, Direk. *Man in the Qur'an*. Amsterdam: Drukkerij Holland, 1965.

Baljon, J. M. S. *Modern Muslim Koran Interpretation (1880–1960)*. Leiden: Brill, 1961.

Bauer, Karen. "Emotion in the Qur'an: An Overview." *Journal of Qur'anic Studies* 19 (2017): 1–30.

Birkeland, Harris. *The Lord Guideth: Studies in Primitive Islam*. Oslo: Aschehoug, 1956.

Boisliveau, Anne-Sylvie. "Présentation coranique des messages prophétiques anciens: l'attitude de *kufr* dénoncée." Pages 144–56 in *Books and Written Culture of the Islamic World*, edited by A. Rippin and R. Tottoli. Leiden: Brill, 2014.

Bouman, Johan. *Gott und Mensch im Koran: Eine Strukturform religiöser Anthropologie anhand des Beispiels Allah und Muhammad*. Darmstadt: Wissenschaftliche Buchgesellschaft, 1977.

Al-Bukhari. *Sahih*. Sunnah.com, and Arabic-only printed edition. Beirut: Dar al-Kutub al-'Ilmiyya, 1420/1999.

Gardet, Louis, and Georges Anawati. *Introduction à la théologie musulmane: essai de théologie comparée*. Paris: Vrin, 1981.

Gätje, Helmut. *The Qur'an and Its Exegesis: Selected Texts with Classical and Modern Muslim Interpretations*. Translated by A. Welch. London: Routledge, 1976.

Ghamidi, Javed A. *Islam: A Comprehensive Introduction*. Translated by S. Saleem. Lahore: Al-Mawrid, n.d.

Al-Ghazali. *On the Boundaries of Theological Tolerance in Islam: Abu Hamid al-Ghazali's al-Faysal al-Tafriqa.* Translated by S. Jackson. Karachi, Pakistan: Oxford University Press, 2002.

Gimaret, Daniel. *Les noms divins en Islam. Exégèse lexicographique et théologique.* Paris: Cerf, 1988.

Gwynne, Rosalind W. *Logic, Rhetoric, and Legal Reasoning in the Qur'an: God's Arguments.* London: Routledge, 2004.

Ibn Hanbal, Ahmad. *Musnad Imam Ahmad bin Hanbal.* Edited by Huda al-Khattab, translated by Nasiruddin al-Khattab. Riyadh: Darussalam, 2012.

Hermanson, Marcia. "Eschatology." Pages 308–23 in *The Cambridge Companion to Classical Islamic Theology,* edited by T. Winter. Cambridge: Cambridge University Press, 2008.

Hoover, Jon. "Against Islamic Universalism: 'Ali al-Harbi's 1990 Attempt to Prove That Ibn Taymiyya and Ibn Qayyim al-Jawziyya Affirm the Eternity of Hell-Fire." Pages 377–99 in *Neo-Hanbalism Reconsidered: The Impact of Ibn Taymiyya and Ibn Qayyim al-Jawziyya,* edited by G. Tamer and B. Krawietz. Berlin: de Gruyter, 2013.

———. "Islamic Universalism: Ibn Qayyim al-Jawziyya's Salafi Deliberations on the Duration of Hell-Fire." *Muslim World* 99 (2009): 181–201.

Izutsu, Toshihiko. *God and Man in the Koran: Semantics of the Koranic Weltanschauung.* Tokyo: Keio Institute of Cultural and Linguistic Studies, 1964.

Jomier, Jacques. *Dieu et l'homme dans le Coran: L'aspect religieux de la nature humaine joint à l'obéissance au Prophète de l'islam.* Paris: Cerf, 1996.

———. "Le nom divin 'al-Rahman' dans le Coran." Pages 361–81 in *Mélanges Louis Massignon,* vol. 2. Damascus: Institut français de Damas, 1957.

———. "Quelques positions actuelles de l'exégèse coranique en Egypte révélées par une polémique récente (1947–51)." *MIDEO* 1 (1954): 39–72.

Ibn Kathir. *Tafsir.* Beirut: Dar al-Fikr, 1389/1970.

Kermani, Navid. *God Is Beautiful.* Translated by T. Crawford. Maldin, MA: Polity, 2015.

Khalafallah, Muhammad Ahmad. *Al-Fann al-qasasi fi al-Qur'an al-karim.* 4th ed. London: Al-Intishar al-'Arabi, 1999 (1951).

Khalidi, Tarif. *The Muslim Jesus: Sayings and Stories in Islamic Literature.* Cambridge, MA: Harvard University Press, 2001.

Khalil, Mohammad Hassan. *Islam and the Fate of Others: The Salvation Question.* Oxford: Oxford University Press, 2012.

Khorchide, Mouhanad. *Islam ist Barmherzigkeit: Grundzüge einer modernen Religion.* Freiburg: Herder, 2014.

Lawrence, Bruce. *Who Is Allah?* Chapel Hill: University of North Carolina Press, 2015.

Lutpi, Ibrahim. "The Qur'anic 'Sealing of the Heart.'" *Die Welt des Orients* 16 (1985): 126–27.

Al-Mahalli, Jalal al-Din, and Jalal al-Din al-Suyuti. *Tafsir al-Jalalayn.* Edited by Marwan Siwar. Beirut: Dar al-Jil, 1410/1995. English translation by F. Hamza. Louisville, KY: Fons Vitae, 2008.

Ibn Majah. *Sunan.* Edited by Muhammad Hasan Nassar. Beirut: Dar al-Kutub al-'Ilmiyya, 1998.

Marshall, David. *God, Muhammad and the Unbelievers: A Qur'anic Study.* Richmond: Curzon, 1999.

———. "Mercy in Christian and Muslim Perspective." Pages 178–85 in *Rahma: Christian and Muslim Studies in Mercy,* edited by Valentino Cottini, Diego Sarrió-Cucarella, and Felix Körner. Rome: Gregorian, 2018.

Miles, Jack. *God in the Qur'an.* New York: Knopf, 2018.

Mir, Mustansir. "The Concept of Divine Mercy in the Qur'ān." *Islamochristiana* 42 (2016): 43–56.

Muslim. *Sahih.* Sunnah.com, and Arabic/English printed edition. Translated by al-Khattab. Riyadh: Dar-us-Salam, 2007.

Nadwi, Abu l-Hasan 'Ali. *Guidance from the Holy Qur'an.* Translated by Abdur Raheem Kidwai. Markfield: Islamic Foundation, 2005.

Neuwirth, Angelika. "Raḥma: Notions of Mercy and Their Qur'anic Foundations." *Islamochristiana* 42 (2016): 21–41.

Nöldeke, T., F. Schwally, G. Bergstrasser, and O. Pretzl. *The History of the Qur'an.* Edited and translated by W. H. Behn. Leiden: Brill, 2013. Originally published in German, T. Nöldeke, *Geschichte de Qorâns,* 1860.

Origen. *The Philocalia of Origen.* Translated by G. Lewis. Edinburgh: Clark, 1911.

Qutb, Sayyid. *Fi zilal al-Qur'an.* Beirut: Dar al-Shuruq, 1412. English translation: *In the Shade of the Qur'an.* Markfield: Islamic Foundation, 2001.

Rahbar, Daud. *God of Justice: A Study in the Ethical Doctrine of the Qur'an.* Leiden: Brill, 1960.

Rahman, Fazlur. *Major Themes of the Qur'an.* 2nd ed. Chicago: University of Chicago Press, 2009.

Räisänen, Heikki. *The Idea of Divine Hardening: A Comparative Study of the Notion of Divine Hardening, Leading Astray and Inciting to Evil in the Bible and the Qur'an.* Helsinki: Finnish Exegetical Society, 1976.

Reynolds, Gabriel Said. *The Emergence of Islam.* Minneapolis: Fortress, 2012.

———. "On the Presentation of Christianity in the Qur'an and the Many Aspects of Qur'anic Rhetoric." *Al-Bayan* 12 (2014): 42–54.

————. *The Qur'ān and the Bible: Text and Commentary.* New Haven: Yale University Press, 2018.

Sinai, Nicolai. *The Qur'an: A Historical-Critical Introduction.* Edinburgh: Edinburgh University Press, 2017.

Al-Tabari. *Tafsir. Jami' al-bayan fī ta'wil al-Qur'an.* Edited by Muhammad 'Ali Baydun. Beirut: Dar al-Fikr, 1408/1988.

Al-Tirmidhi. *Al-Jami'.* Edited by Bashshar 'Awad Ma'ruf. Beirut: Dar al-Gharb al-Islami, 1998.

Al-Tustari, Sahl. *Tafsir.* Translated by A. and A. Keeler. Louisville, KY: Fons Vitae, 2011.

Urvoy, Dominique, and Marie-Thérèse Urvoy. *L'action psychologique dans le Coran.* Paris: Cerf, 2007.

Volf, Miroslav. *Allah: A Christian Response.* New York: HarperOne, 2011.

Al-Wahidi, Abu al-Hasan. *Asbab nuzul al-Qur'an.* Edited by Kamal Zaghlul. Beirut: Dar al-Kutub al-'Ilmiyya, 1411/1991. English translation by M. Guezzou, *Al-Wahidi's Asbab al-Nuzul.* Louisville, KY: Fons Vitae, 2008.

Watt, W. Montgomery, trans. *Islamic Creeds: A Selection.* Edinburgh: Edinburgh University Press, 1994.

Winter, T., ed. *Cambridge Companion to Classical Islamic Theology.* Cambridge: Cambridge University Press, 2008.

Al-Zamakhshari, Muhammad b. 'Umar (d. 1144). *Al-Kashshaf 'an haqa'iq ghawamid al-tanzil.* Beirut: Dar al-Kitab al-'Arabi, 1947.

Index of Qur'an Passages

Index of Bible Passages

Old Testament

New Testament

Apocrypha

General Index